D0421536

Rethinking Instructional Supervision

New Prospects Series

General Editors: Professor Ivor Goodson, Faculty of
Education, University of Western
Ontario, Canada and
Professor Andy Hargreaves, Ontario
Institute for Studies in Education,
Canada.

1 Rethinking Instructional Supervision: Notes of its Language and Culture
Duncan Waite

New Prospects Series: 1

Rethinking Instructional Supervision:
Notes on Its Language and Culture

Duncan Waite

 The Falmer Press

(A member of the Taylor & Francis Group)
London • Washington, DC

UK   The Falmer Press, 4 John Street, London WC1N 2ET
USA   The Falmer Press, Taylor & Francis Inc., 1900 Frost Road, Suite 101, Bristol, PA 19007

© D. Waite 1995

First published in 1995

A catalogue record for this book is available from the British Library

Library of Congress Cataloging-in-Publication Data are available on request

ISBN 0 7507 0379 2 cased
ISBN 0 7507 0380 6 paper

Jacket design by Caroline Archer

Typeset in 10/12 pt Garamond by
Graphicraft Typesetters Ltd., Hong Kong.

Printed in Great Britain by Burgess Science Press, Basingstoke on paper which has a specified pH value on final paper manufacture of not less than 7.5 and is therefore 'acid free'.

Contents

Dedication

This book is dedicated to the loving memory of my grandfather, Lloyd M. 'Red' Bennett (c. 1900–1984), and to that of my uncle, Alan L. Bennett (c. 1926-1992), who both, and in their own ways, provided for me models, visions, and support for my life's journey.

Foreword

The field of supervision in education has a long history in the United States dating back more than one hundred years. Early attempts to closely monitor curriculum and instruction, even though geographic distances in rural areas made close control virtually impossible, and the influence of Frederick Taylor's industrial logic on educational administration during the early twentieth century, are often cited as evidence that supervision in education is inherently hierarchical and opposed to egalitarian values.

For some reason, the strong and clearly voiced dedication to principles of democracy, decentralization, and cooperative problem solving among pioneering supervision authors, such as Edward C. Elliott and James Fleming Hosic among others, is rarely acknowledged today. Also overlooked are publications of the National Education Association's Department of Supervisors and Directors of Instruction during the 1930s, which drew heavily on John Dewey's thinking. These works led to the view of supervision as a collaborative, problem-focused, democratic process, an idea popularized in a textbook by A. S. Barr, William H. Burton, and Leo J. Brueckner, which dominated educational supervision in the United States until the emergence of clinical supervision in the 1960s.

Clinical supervision represented a departure from the problem-focused, group strategies that had until then defined supervisory practice and theory. While retaining a focus on reflective thinking and problem solving, clinical supervision focused the supervisor's attention and efforts directly on individual classrooms as the targets and teachers as the agents of change.

Clinical supervision was invented and nurtured at Harvard University in the 1950s and 1960s by Morris Cogan, who considered it a way to develop professionally responsible teachers who were capable of analyzing their own performance, who were open to change and assistance from others, and who were, above all, self-directing. Many other authors, including Robert Goldhammer, Keith Acheson and Meredith Gall, Madeline Hunter, Carl Glickman, Noreen Garman, Kenneth Zeichner and Daniel Liston, and John Smyth, to name just a few, have since contributed their own interpretations to the concept and practice of clinical supervision.

This new book by Duncan Waite clearly falls within both the democratic and the clinical traditions in the literature of educational supervision. However, it departs significantly from most existing interpretations of those traditions by challenging the reader with substantive data, new terminology and concepts, and fresh theoretical perspectives drawn from a broad variety of disciplines, including sociology, anthropology, linguistics, and philosophy.

Duncan Waite develops an original approach, termed 'situationally contexted supervision', which appears to stretch democratic principles to their limits by adding issues of power, hegemony, and resistance to traditional supervisory concerns of involvement, cooperation, and problem solving. He uses detailed analysis of face-to-face interactions between teachers and supervisors to rethink supervision and supervisor-teacher relations, and then proposes a dialogic form of supervision that draws on ideas from postmodernism, communitarianism, and feminism.

Professor Waite attempts to link the multiple and various contexts of supervision within an organic whole that he believes is more suited and more sensitive to the rapidly changing contexts of modern social, economic, and political global realities. The result is a proposal for a new form of supervision where everything is open to question, where no assumption, behavior, ideology, or belief is above critique, and where every decision is always open to reconsideration. He urges supervisors and teachers to work together in a humane, caring, and egalitarian manner to create an institution that is flexible, supportive, and constantly renewing itself. Supervisors would become advocates of teachers in an ongoing quest for alternatives, instead of imposing their own beliefs or acting on behalf of the formally stated goals of the school.

While the reader may not always agree with the assertions or conclusions put forth in this book, Dr. Waite is eminently successful in accomplishing his own stated goal of problematizing issues related to supervision. Many times I found myself writing frantically in the margins of the manuscript, evidence that my own thinking and taken for granted assumptions were being challenged. Our field certainly needs books like this one, that dispute our convictions, stretch our imaginations, stimulate our thinking, and enrich our understandings of the complexity and subtle nuances of supervisory relationships in schools.

Professor Edward Pajak
The University of Georgia
September 1994

Acknowledgments

I gratefully acknowledge my indebtedness to a number of people who, through giving of their time and careful consideration, have improved the quality of the work contained in this volume. Joe Blase, Jim Deegan, Mark Faust, Jerry Gale, Peg Graham, Joan Kelly Hall, Penny Oldfather, Ed Pajak, Phillip Payne, and Harry Wolcott have all suggested improvements on past iterations of parts of this book. This book and I owe a great debt to those who have gone before, those giants on whose shoulders I've stood.

I also wish to sincerely thank all those people who have been my teachers and from whose knowledge, experience, nurturing and caring I have benefitted. Though the following list can only be partial, there are so many who have taught me and from whom I have learned so much. You know who you are, and I thank you. Those deserving of special mention for the roles they have played in my continuing education include Keith Acheson, Chet Bowers, Richard Chaney, Erma Inscore, Jan Jipson, Tom Ptacek, Rob Proudfoot, Judy Small, Jack Whalen, and Harry Wolcott. Rob Proudfoot saw something in me I didn't see myself and opened my eyes. Keith Acheson, my mentor and friend, modeled an open and inquisitive mind all the while I plied him with questions and bombarded him with arguments; while, with patience, he allowed me to spin my own philosophies of supervision. Harry Wolcott, ever growing himself, tended to my growth in so many ways. His humor, his easy way with people from all walks of life, his sheer intelligence, and his searing insight are but a few of the traits that make him, in my eyes, an inestimable mentor, friend, and colleague.

There are those who have encouraged me from more of a distance, but for that they are no less important. Ivor Goodson's humor, intelligence and energy have sustained me at one level and prodded me toward ever more accomplishments on another. He has caused doors to open for me that I didn't even know existed. Andy Hargreaves' critical insights, his valuing of my work, and his personal attention have contributed greatly to my growth as a scholar. Joe Kincheloe's enthusiasm, intelligence, and down-to-earth manner have combined to energize me. These three especially have become models for me, encouraging me to let my ideas lead where they might, to brave new intellectual horizons. Dell Hymes has always been there for me, always willing to offer suggestions, encouragement, and possibilities. Noreen Garman has encouraged me. I deeply appreciate her warmth and intellect. Jean Clandinin, as anyone who knows her is aware, is one of a kind. She has nurtured me at times, and I thank her.

Ginger Munday helped with the early stages of this book. Frances White has been of invaluable assistance throughout the process. I also want to thank the people at Falmer Press for the opportunities they have given me and for being both highly professional and amiable.

My immediate family has been my foundation, my joy and happiness, my *raison d'être*. Cecilia Santibáñez de Waite and her humor, her innate sense of life's essentials, and her interest and support have really made this whole thing possible. Tamara Waite Santibáñez has provided a *joie de vivre*, aside from her creativity, intelligence, and love. Hannah Waite Santibáñez has thrilled me endlessly, perplexed me, and made me laugh. Gabriel Allyn Waite Santibáñez has brought new joy and a renewed purpose to all of this.

To these people and all the others who have encouraged me, spiritually, emotionally and intellectually, thank you.

I also wish to thank the publishers and journals who have published my work, and who have permitted me to adapt it for this volume:

Sage Publications and *Urban Education* for the material in Chapter 1 (first published as WAITE, D. (1992) 'The instructional supervisor as a cultural guide', *Urban Education*, **26**(4), pp. 423–440).

The Association of Supervision and Curriculum Development and the *Journal of Curriculum and Supervision* for the material in Chapter 2 (first published as WAITE, D. (1992) 'Supervisors' talk: Making sense of conferences from an anthropological linguistic perspective', *Journal of Curriculum and Supervision*, **7**(4), pp. 349–371).

The American Educational Research Association and the *American Educational Research Journal* for material in Chapter 3 (first published as WAITE, D. (1993) 'Teachers in conference: A qualitative study of teacher-supervisor face-to-face interactions', *American Educational Research Journal*, **30**(4), pp. 675–702). Copyright 1993 by the American Educational Research Association. Adapted by permission of the publisher.

Hampton Press for material in Chapter 4 (first published as WAITE, D. (1994) 'Teacher resistance in a supervision conference', in D. CORSON (Ed.), *Discourse and Power in Educational Organizations* (pp. 71–86). Cresskill, NJ: Hampton Press).

Pergamon Press and *The International Journal of Teaching and Teacher Education* for material in Chapter 5 (first published as WAITE, D. (1992) 'Instructional supervision from a situational perspective', *Teaching & Teacher Education*, **8**(4), pp. 319–332).

RZO Incorporated, Index Music, and David Byrne for permission to use the lyrics from David Byrne's 'Make Believe Mambo'.

The Limits of Supervision and Beyond

This book is about different ways of seeing; different ways of seeing supervision, different ways for supervisors and those they work with to see themselves, and different ways for supervisors and other classroom observers to see classrooms. In an effort to expand thinking about supervision, this book takes a broad view of the field, its practitioners and their practices. There are many types of supervisors to be sure: university supervisors, central office supervisors of all types, local school-based supervisors – principals, assistant principals, media specialists and teacher-leaders – and many more who perform some supervisory tasks. This book is applicable to all of those and to others who are involved in instruction and instructional leadership, whether primarily school-based, university-based, central-office based, or based in a state department of education or a regional education service agency. In short, I do not want what is written here to be dismissed out-of-hand by a reader who might think the findings and implications of this book are only applicable to someone else. I invite anyone who works in/on instruction to read it and to make the proper applications, as they fit one's local situation.

One of the first premises on which this work is based is that in order to see where one is going, one must see from where one has come. The past is ever with us, on both personal and professional levels. This is true for the field of supervision.

In order for the reader to see where it is this book is going, it seems necessary to explain, to a certain degree, the personal/professional journey of its author specifically, and the field of supervision more generally.

This volume contains research on supervision informed by a variety of disciplines and their concomitant perspectives, primarily those of anthropology, linguistics, philosophy and sociology. This work has been influenced by such different fields as symbolic interactionism, ethnomethodology, ethnography and conversation analysis. This type of eclecticism presents advantages and disadvantages, but most of all it affords an entirely novel way of seeing, of examining a role, a social situation, an interaction, a culture. As such, this book represents a radical departure from other books on supervision. It is my wish that the reader may find much in these studies that is applicable to his or her practice, whether that practice is school-based, university-based, primarily pragmatic, theoretical, or some combination.

Years of research into supervision and into the beliefs and practices of supervisors have contributed to the evolution of the author's ideas about that practice and its future. Chapters 5 and 6 of this book, therefore, present alternatives to current supervisory practice, the last somewhat more theoretical and abstract than the first. As it is laid out, the book will take its reader through the history of supervision to the present, examining current supervisory practice in considerable depth, and suggesting alternative paths the individual supervisor and the field of supervision could take to extend supervision into the future, to make it a more robust, viable and relevant practice.

Since the author has so much invested in supervision and its study, it will come as no surprise that this book, though critical at times, overall can be seen as a defense of supervision. Another premise undergirding this work is that no practice, no ideology or belief, is sacrosanct, above critique. There is no practice that cannot benefit from well-intended criticism. This then is the thrust of this book. In developing that line of reasoning, I shall take a cue from The Mad Hatter in *Alice's Adventures in Wonderland:* begin at the beginning and when you reach the end, stop. But where to begin?

From Humble Beginnings to Monstrous Proportions

The beginnings of supervision, in the US at least, were really quite humble; administrators, principal–teachers, lead teachers and other instructional leaders were simply interested in bettering not just their own practice, but that of other teacher-colleagues as well. Community and school leaders were also interested in ensuring some level of competency in the personnel they employed. Due to the rural nature of the US in its early years, schools were widely dispersed over the countryside for the most part. Larger cities like New York, Boston, Philadelphia and others, developed much more quickly; their sheer numbers necessitated the development of some sort of hierarchy, some sort of organization. Unfortunately, instructional leaders, as is often the case even today, adopted and adapted that which was close to hand, taking their lead from the military and business. I say 'unfortunately' because many of the problems facing educational reform today can be laid at the feet of these now archaic organizational patterns and their vestiges.[1]

Still, during the early development of supervision, teachers and other instructional leaders were as interested in communicating with their colleagues, especially about innovations in pedagogy and best practices, as they were about standardization. Then, as is still the case today, teachers would often travel great distances to partake in teachers' meetings, often dedicating their Friday evenings and Saturdays to such study. These meetings were the humble beginning of what became the normal schools in the US. There is a venerable history of teachers seeking to improve their own practices, without any urging, prodding, policing or other coercion from administrators. In fact, in the early rural schools in the US there were no administrators at all; they came later when school size became an issue. As I said, in the larger cities, the need for administration was felt much earlier than in the hinterlands.

The ranks of administrators began to swell. As schools grew ever larger, the number of people employed by schools outside of the classroom grew until today, according to a report by the Organization for Economic Cooperation and Development (Centre for Educational Research and Innovation, 1993, pp. 99–100), there are more 'support personnel' employed by US schools than there are teachers![2] It may be that this trend has already reached its apex and is in decline; it is too early to tell. School reform, 'downsizing', decentralization, site-based decision making, and other similar programs seem destined to reduce the number of administrators at least, if not the other support staff such as bus drivers, cafeteria workers, and counselors. One central question resulting from the trend to decentralize, one which will be addressed later in this book, is 'Will supervision survive decentralization?'

Administrators are a breed apart from teachers (Hargreaves 1990). If they are not born that way, they quickly become so due to socialization pressures exerted on them by not only school organizations with their particular organizational patterns and cultures, but by teachers and others as well. Legion are the stories such as that told by a student of supervision who related that after assuming the role of Science Supervisor for her school district her next-door teaching colleague of 15 years refused to speak to her! Some of the difficulties encountered by my own supervision students in trying to carry out the alternative roles which I encourage them to assume are engendered by resistance on teachers' parts to any type of role flexibility.[3] Teachers, it seems, know a supervisor when they see one. They know how supervisors are supposed to act (Waite 1994b), or at least they proceed as though they do.

With the ever-increasing numbers of students served and the layering of hierarchical levels, administrators became more and more removed from the actual site of teaching and learning, the place 'where the rubber hits the road', to borrow a colorful and descriptive phrase from my own students. Not only did administrators become further removed in the physical and organizational sense, but, again owing to the increased pressures caused by sheer numbers, administrators' focus of concern and their role responsibilities eventually grew to such a point that many were solely concerned with the running and maintenance of schools, and laid aside loftier pursuits. Evidence of this trend is seen in research and op-ed pieces that deal with the principal or headteacher as instructional leader. Even those whose title explicitly includes 'supervisor' have had to struggle to resist being inundated by the sheer press of managerial duties occasioned by ever-increasing student populations.[4]

Role ambiguity – one of the causes of stress least amenable to treatment – and continual diminishment of supervisors' and others' attention to traditional supervisory tasks such as staff development has resulted from consolidation of several distinct roles and job responsibilities within a single position. In many school districts, and at all levels, the administrator or supervisor, whatever the term, is called on to perform more and more of the duties which were originally assigned to distinct positions. The result is that strictly supervisory tasks tend to get shelved or at best carried out only haphazardly, on a hit-or-miss basis. Another possible alternative is that such tasks devolve to 'lower' hierarchical positions within school organizations. This phenomenon may account for at least some of the popularity of teacher empowerment movements and recent efforts at decentralization. That is, those at the top find they can no longer carry out all their responsibilities due to the weight of enormous schools and their populations, so they delegate some of these responsibilities to subordinates. In one sense, this is a welcome change from high-handed, high-level bureaucratic management. However, it should be noted that often as the responsibilities are passed down, they are seldom accompanied by the requisite authority needed to see these tasks completely through. In the vernacular, if the school superintendent asked you to jump, you'd say 'how high?', but if someone further down the line asks the same, you'd probably think about it.

Part of the reason for this is to be found in the distinction between staff and line authority (Pajak 1989). Line authority captures the hierarchical, bureaucratic, chain-of-command style of leadership and authority. In other words, under this system superiors issue orders and subordinates must carry them out or be held accountable. Failure to carry out such commands or outright resistance is seen as insubordination, punishable by the loss of one's job. This is line authority: Any command, order, etc. issued by someone up the line carries considerable weight.

Supervisors, it is said, exercise staff authority (Pajak 1989), meaning that they have no direct authority *over* others with whom they work. Rather, their authority stems from other sources, such as expertise, knowledge and interpersonal skills.[5] It could be argued that these forms of authority are much less hegemonic than line authority (Dunlap and Goldman 1991).

Real life situations in today's schools are, of course, much more complex than the simple distinction between line and staff authority would have us believe, as will be demonstrated in the following chapters. Supervisors and administrators both enjoy and exercise constellations of authority. Indeed, it shall be shown in the pages to follow that authority and power are in fact interactional achievements, seldom embedded transcendentally in a position or person. It is within the margins, between the cracks so to speak, that much of school life, for both adults and children, gets played out. Such conditions provide the flexibility many people need to function with any sense of freedom. Hargreaves (1990: 315) writes of the 'back regions' of school life in such a way.[6]

Throughout much of the history of schooling, teachers have been caught in the middle, yet marginalized. They have been the target, the victim, if you will, of efforts at change, both well-meant and not so well-meant. This intent is exemplified in historical supervisory programs and processes such as administrative monitoring (Karier 1982; Bolin and Panaritis 1992), where administrators were out to cull the 'bad teachers' from the ranks. Unfortunately, traces of this attitude persist today. Such traces persist within the ranks and mindset of administrators and persist in the defensive posturing of teachers that results from such an adversarial process. Even today, no matter how competent the teacher, the rise in anxiety level is palpable when the administrator takes to the hall with her or his clipboard on the occasional evaluation round. Word quickly spreads among teachers, through notes and secret codes, that they had best be on guard. Unfortunately, many confuse or equate this process with supervision itself (Waite 1994b), such is the burden we as supervisors and supervision theorists must bear, the industrial model mindset. It is pervasive in teachers' minds and in the public's as well.

Indeed the industrial model mindset is so pervasive and entrenched that many in supervision have suggested jettisoning the term supervision in order to coin a word for the process we practice and in which we believe. Such a radical break with the past, with our roots, is not without complications of its own however. Generally, theorists have made peace with the fact that such history and connotations are part and parcel of what the field has become. Besides, many of us who write in the field have gotten certain mileage out of distinguishing ourselves from that Other. This is as it should be. Authors and thinkers as diverse as Anthony Giddens (1984) and M. Mikhail Bakhtin (1981a) realize that it is only in discourse with the Other that the Self is defined.

Still, it is unfortunate to my way of thinking that the field of supervision, drawn as it is from the predominant societal paradigm in the US and other northern European-influenced societies, has privileged the individual as actor and responsible agent (Liston and Zeichner 1990). I say it is unfortunate because, as has been the case in supervision as well as in the wider public's calls for reform, it has been the individual who has been singled out (so to speak) for treatment. Goodman (1988), Apple (1986) and others have reasoned why this is so, reasons that have to do primarily with the fact the majority of the teaching profession for much of the past has been female. This social fact, coupled with theories of power and economic interests (Smyth 1992), has made marionettes of teachers. Aside from the symbolic violence done to teachers as a result of such paradigms, targeting the individual is both ineffectual and misses the point entirely.

Support for this statement will be garnered from the studies to follow. However, having made such a provocative statement, I feel obliged to explain it a little more here.

Apple (1986) has written of the deskilling of teachers and Smyth (1992) has written of how global market forces affect teachers. These processes act to isolate and disempower teachers, to remove them from having a voice in how their work is conceived at the initial and most fundamental levels. Treating teachers solely as individual agents, making individual teachers responsible for their 'success' or 'failure' is Calvinistic – the individual is responsible for his or her own salvation. Aside from the argument which could be made that such conceptions are the result of Cartesianism, or a synthetic separation of the agent from all other systems (Bateson 1972), this view of the individual absolves larger systems – like schools, school systems, states, and federal governments and their policies – of the responsibility for the nurturing and growth of the individual. The attitude becomes, 'You take care of it. It's your problem.'

This very attitude is at least partially responsible (though there are, of course, other complicating factors) for the current and widespread (mis) conceptions concerning supervision. Holland *et al.* (1991) and others (Acheson, personal communication, April 11, 1992) have uncovered what appears to be the prevalent form of supervisory practice: that is, where a principal, or other authority, observes a teacher (and often only those who have given off signals of 'being in trouble'), and *tells* her or him what to fix and, sometimes, how to fix it. In this it's-your-problem-fix-it mode of operation, principals and others erroneously believe they have discharged their supervisory responsibilities completely by simply naming what, in their view, the problem is. No other suggestions are proffered, no other systems are put into place to assist the teacher who has been subjected to this bastardized form of supervision. It would not be too far amiss to label such supervisees as victims of the symbolic violence done by these erstwhile 'supervisors' and the beliefs and practices they employ. The damage does not stop with the individual teacher, however. Groups of teachers, their students, and the field of education as a whole, suffer under the misconception that supervision really equates with evaluation (Waite 1994b) and that the supervisor is 'out to get' the teacher. This popular misbelief hobbles supervision and has been the bane of supervision theorists for some years.

Aside for the symbolic violence done to the individual teacher through uninformed application of certain supervisory techniques, targeting the individual simply does not make good sense in the modern context. (This thesis will be elaborated in detail in Chapters 5 and 6.) Historically, and when operating as an arm of the administration, supervisors were often charged with seeing to the implementation of certain decisions made at a distance from the site of teaching and learning, that is, with curriculum implementation. These decisions, though often curricular in nature, had severe ramifications for life in classrooms and were, in this sense, political. Not only did these decisions by 'higher-ups' affect the micropolitical climate of classrooms, assignment to the supervisor of the responsibility to implement such decisions clearly and negatively affected the dynamic between supervisor and teacher. Again, in these cases, supervisors became 'snoopervisors' in teachers' eyes.

Today in many schools and school systems, teachers are being asked to come to the table to inform decisions affecting pedagogical, curricular and policy issues (Glickman 1993). Often in many schools there is a long history of suspicion to overcome before teachers feel unencumbered enough to engage freely in such discussions.

The last reason that targeting individual teachers is ineffectual (as will be discussed in Chapters 5 and 6) is that *teachers are only one variable* among many that affect school life and student learning. Attention must be paid, following this line of reasoning, to whole contexts of life in schools.

Following Apple (1986) and Smyth (1992), teachers have become disempowered, deskilled. What many fail to realize is that if one's colleagues (subordinates, or what have you) become disempowered, that selfsame process disempowers the supervisor. Here an analogy can be drawn upon to make the point.

Teachers is the US and elsewhere are under increasing pressure to 'teach to the test'. For the past several decades, cheap standardized tests have been used to measure the so-called achievement of students. As others have pointed out (Gardner 1983, 1991; Eisner 1991; Brandt 1993b), what becomes valued in schools in these situations is what can be measured, *not* what is most important, which may be difficult or impossible to measure. This unreasonable pressure on teachers to raise their students' test scores, being the only accepted measure of educational attainment, places severe restrictions on teachers' and students' time, restricts their curricular options, and restricts the range of pedagogical alternatives. Forces such as this increased pressure to raise test scores encourage many teachers to teach to the middle range of ability of students, and results in whole populations of students being neglected and/or having their learning styles ignored.

Within such contexts, what is the supervisor's job, if such ends are accepted as viable? The supervisor's role is not much different in such situations from the disempowered and embattled teacher, it is just performed in another arena and on another level. Often today supervisors are under increased pressure to deal with teachers as a mass, to spend much of their time shuffling paperwork; the tangible outcome and endeavor of the supervisors' jobs, in short, is to remain ensconced in their offices, away from the classroom and school where, it could be argued, they are needed the most. Sadly, I have seen cohort after cohort of my supervision students enter their coursework with idealistic expectations, only to become disillusioned with the mundane minutiae, the 'administrivia' of their new positions. The gap between the ideal and possible and the real, expected and valued is so great as to paralyze some promising leaders from acting upon their convictions. The rewards for acting on one's convictions in cases such as this are intrinsic, the pressures (negative reinforcements) are immediate and ever-present. Which would you choose? How would you cope?

Fortunately, to my way of thinking, there are those who struggle to put their convictions into practice. It is fortunate for the teachers and students who benefit from contact with such idealists, but, unfortunate, at times, for the supervisor herself or himself. Often living one's convictions becomes an act of defiance, or if done covertly, an act of resistance, and may bring a heavy psychic cost. Again however, to my way of thinking, it is fortunate that modern school organizations are not unified totalities, seamless and utterly oppressive. In such disunified school organizations well-meaning supervisors can work their magic, and teachers and students benefit. Still, it strikes me as tragic that such supervision, it is felt, needs to be done undercover. This is an indication that if it is not the case that our values are inverted, then at least the processes and policies currently in place run counter to the way things ought to be, to the way supervision ought to be practiced. (Alternatives to current supervisory practice, and rationales for them, will be presented in Chapters 5 and 6.)

In considering the disempowered teacher and supervisor, it is definitely *not* the case that teachers are waiting for some prince to ride up on a white horse to save them from their ineptitude! Rather, as I have attempted to show, teachers have long been concerned with the improvement of their instruction, often in spite of supervisors' efforts. One of the major themes of this book is that there are things supervisors and other administrators can do, because of their unique knowledge and position, to foster the conditions that can facilitate improvement (i.e. positive change) system-wide. What is at issue is whether those in such positions can and will move to become a part of efforts at improvement, or will they, that is supervisors and other administrators, become further removed from the instructional practices affecting schoolchildren and teachers?. Will supervisors and other administrators become further deskilled themselves and be seen as an alien, unwelcome presence in classrooms and hallways? Throughout this book I offer suggestions as to how well-meaning supervisors and administrators can function positively to remain a part of what I feel should be at the heart of schooling: positive teaching and learning experiences for those in schools!

For it remains the case that only when considering power and empowerment as a zero–sum game does the empowerment of the Other appear to disempower the Self. More recent conceptions of power, especially those informed by feminist critique (Mills 1992), belie this facile notion. Relational conceptions of power recognize 'power with' in addition to the traditional notions of 'power over' (Dunlap and Goldman 1991).

Blaming the teacher flies in the face of recent thinking in various disciplines of the social sciences. Giddens' (1984) theory of structuration and Fay's (1977, 1987) discussion of critical theory draw our attention to the fact that individual agents have great difficulty changing themselves. This is due to the fact that we seldom operate in isolation, apart from other forces – historical, social and otherwise. In fact, following a symbolic interactionist perspective, we continually construct social forms and structures through our interactions. Even so-called microprocess such as minute conversational processes have been shown to contribute to larger structures (Moerman 1988; Boden and Zimmerman 1991; Wilson 1991), the point being that contexts and outcomes are *jointly* constructed through interaction.

Blaming the teacher is falsely accusing an individual for something that may well be outside of his or her power to influence, let alone control. Disempowering the teacher, by treating her or him as an atomistic entity, alone responsible for all outcomes and processes in which she or he has a hand, also disempowers and deskills the supervisor. In such an atomistic perspective/paradigm the supervisor has quite a burden to bear.

In the area of adult development, or andragogy, certain scholars have recognized the need to expand our conceptions of what influences a person's growth throughout life (Dannefer and Perlmutter 1990). Dannefer and Perlmutter examined the processes influencing growth and development: ontogeny, habituation and cognitive generativity. Of these processes, they suggest that human ontogeny and habituation are the most fixed, with certain trajectories and expectancies. Cognitive generativity, on the other hand, remains fluid throughout an adult's life. Because of this relative flexibility, and depending on extra-individual factors such as the situations the individual operates in, an individual's capacity at cognitive generativity may peak early and plateau at a relatively low level or it may continue to climb throughout an individual's existence. The difference between individual levels of cognitive generativity, according to Dannefer and Perlmutter, depends on the situation. (See Chapter 5 for a more complete discussion of situations and situational supervision.) Cognitive generativity both contributes to and results from dialogic engagement with one's environment and with others' minds. It is the glory of human growth and development.

Overview

As was stated at the outset, this book is really about different ways of seeing supervision. The book is organized so as to lead its reader from a relatively more accessible, though new, conception of supervision through to ever more in-depth and esoteric discussions of supervisory practice, finally concluding in theoretical critiques of practice, each with recommendations for future work in the field. The book is organized into seven chapters. The first part of the book, Chapters 1 through 4, present alternative views, based on my research, of current supervisory practices. Chapters 5 and 6 each present a different theoretical critique of current practice and offer recommendations (for I hate to call them prescriptions) which I hope will serve to remedy the shortcomings I perceive in current practice – making supervision a more robust and viable alternative for teachers and supervisors alike.

Chapter 1 examines beliefs about supervision through an anthropological lens. It presents both various practitioners' and various theorists' views of supervision. These views about supervision hold cultural implications; indeed, it is suggested that there is a distinct culture of supervision, similar in certain regards to what authors have termed the cultures of teaching (Feiman-Nemser and Floden 1986), yet having distinct attributes.

Chapter 2 extends the motif of the first chapter in presenting research findings on supervision conferences, face-to-face interactions between supervisors and teachers, as interactional achievements. This chapter examines the supervisor's role in the conference, with implications for issues of power and control.

Chapter 3 takes the other side, examining those same conferences from teachers' perspectives. Three teacher conference roles are presented: the passive, the collaborative and the adversarial. These roles are examined with the theoretical frames of teacher socialization and school reform.

In Chapter 4, I expand the discussion of the adversarial teacher conference role, couching it in terms of teacher resistance. This strategy allows for critique of the literature on teacher resistance, and critique of supervision itself.

Chapter 5 begins the more theoretical portion of the book. In that chapter, I present a new approach to supervision, 'situationally-contexted supervision'. This approach is premised on an anthropological and interactionist view of classrooms and schools. From such a perspective, supervisors are deskilled to the extent that the teachers with whom they work are deskilled. The major thrust of this chapter is that supervisors need to supervise *contexts* rather than supervising *teachers*, as is the case with more conventional models of supervision.

Chapter 6 extends the theoretical work underlying the whole book. There I develop a theory of 'dialogic supervision', an approach intended to address the asymmetries of power relations inherent in conventional supervision. Dialogic supervision is grounded, to the extent that anything can be grounded, in the postmodern. The subtitle for that chapter is 're-embedding supervision within the contexts of change', and that really is the leitmotif for the whole book. As a believer in the purpose, process and power of supervision, this chapter, and the book as a whole, are really loving attempts to rehabilitate supervision.

I conclude by tying the work together and projecting supervision into the near future.

Notes

1 Hargreaves (1994) writes of the inflexibility of modern educational organizations when faced with pressures to change.
2 Of all the countries for which data were reported, the US is the *only* country with more non-teaching staff employed in the education sector of the economy than teaching staff.
3 See Burbules (1986) for a thorough discussion of inflexible role expectations and their effects. This issue will also be taken up in Chapters 3 and 4.
4 Sergiovanni (1991, 1992) writes about the many different ways schools could be managed.
5 Characteristics of authority as a form of authorship will be discussed in Chapter 6.
6 It is interesting to note that some administrators, especially those who operate within the efficiency paradigm, seek to do away with these 'backwaters'. Another perspective on this phenomenon is offered by Erving Goffman (1959) in his discussion of public and private, or backstage, performances.

Chapter 1

The Instructional Supervisor as a Cultural Guide and Other Not So Obvious Roles

Like teaching itself, instructional supervision lacks an agreed upon definition. The most common and least controversial definition is 'the improvement of instruction' (Weller 1971: 5).[1] However, since there is no agreed upon definition of 'instruction', this definition of supervision isn't of much help. Weller identified three functions of the supervisor: the counseling function, the teaching function and the training function (1971: 7–15). In this chapter, I suggest that an anthropologically-informed examination of supervisors and supervision would reveal other functions as well.

There is a need for such a qualitative understanding of supervision. This view was recently espoused by Pajak and Glickman (1989: 103) when they called for ethnographic study of supervision:

Ethnographic studies of teacher–supervisor interactions in actual school settings would be very enlightening . . . Both supervisory practice and subsequent research ought to be guided and tempered by perspectives that take personal meanings and social contexts into account.

Flinders (1991: 87) writes that 'the larger context of recent theoretical developments calls for new models of supervision firmly anchored in the concept of culture'. Additionally, he recommends 'extending the epistemology of culture into the practical realms that guide a supervisor's observations, discussions, and evaluations of classroom teaching' (p. 87). Though the primary thrust of Flinders's thesis is the classroom and its observation, he also extends his argument to cover teacher–supervisor interaction: 'This same framework . . . also promises to inform a second major aspect of the supervisor's work – providing teachers with the feedback that will lead to improved classroom teaching' (p. 103).

Thus there are those who feel that an ethnographic or anthropological perspective should aid in a re-examination of the assumptions and taken-for-granted nature of the practice of supervision. The advantages of an ethnographic view of supervision can well be imagined: such a view should encourage supervisors to examine their own practices in light of this qualitative understanding and this may result in more 'reflective practitioners'; such study may establish a definition of supervision and will almost certainly validate the numerous roles supervisors play in the professional lives of teachers, and there should be something in such a study which would inform change efforts targeting the practice of supervisors and their formal education.

What is the evidence that there are cultural aspects to supervision?[2] Basically, the evidence for a cultural dimension to supervision can be found reflected in actual practice and peppered throughout the literature.

Cultural References in the Supervision Literature

Some authors acknowledge the 'contexts of supervision' (Acheson and Gall 1987). Others have begun to the address the cultural aspects of classroom observation as an essential aspect of instructional supervision (Bowers and Flinders 1991; Flinders 1991). Sergiovanni (1985: 11–12) writes in 'Landscapes, Mindscapes, and Reflective Practice in Supervision' that

> the task of the supervisor is to make sense of messy situations by increasing understanding and discovering and communicating meaning . . . since supervisory messes are context bound and situationally determined . . .

Meanings and understandings are essential characteristics of culture, as is making sense (see for example Garfinkel 1967; McDermott and Church 1976).

Other authors examine the effects of colleges of education – with their preservice supervision components – and cooperating teachers on the socialization of student teachers (Tabachnick *et al.* 1979/80; Zeichner and Tabachnick 1981).[3] Lamenting the lack of a critical orientation among the supervisors they studied, Tabachnick *et al.* (1979/80: 22) note:

> Contrary to popular belief, the university and schools were not in competition with each other for the hearts and minds of students; instead they collaborated closely with one another to create a powerful conservative force for defending existing institutional arrangements from close scrutiny and challenge. The language of the university in seminars and supervisory conferences failed to penetrate the taken-for-granted world of the school and subtly encouraged acquiesence and conformity to existing school routines.

Zeichner *et al.* (1988: 351) discuss the '"traditional-craft" orientation' to the relationship between student teachers and their university supervisor and cooperating teacher. They find that:

The master–apprentice relationship is generally seen as the vehicle for transmitting *this cultural knowledge*. In this program both the cooperating teacher and the supervisor are construed as potential masters and the elementary student teacher as the student. (emphasis added)

Alfonso (1986) writes of school culture as an 'unseen supervisor' acting to restrain change efforts. Alfonso's treatment appears to be more concerned with the district supervisor than the university supervisor, though both are mentioned. His combination of these two, arguably distinct, roles creates some confusion and lessens the impact of his criticism. For, as I will argue, the university supervisor has a much greater impact on the student teacher's orientation to the cultures of teaching than the district supervisor may have in relation to that of the established teacher.

Alfonso (1986: 2) is critical of the role supervisors perform in schools: 'Evidence is sorely lacking that supervisors really make a difference'. The difference the author speaks of is that of changing 'the culture of the school' (p. 20). I wish to draw a distinction between my views and those of Alfonso. Alfonso assumes the supervisor's role to be that of change-agent within the organizational structure; in this chapter I argue that an essential role of the supervisor is that of guiding students in the process of becoming teachers by orienting them to school – and teacher culture. In fact, Alfonso argues that supervisors ought to take a more active role in socializing new teachers: 'The process through which new teachers are socialized is an area in which supervisors could have some influence, but in fact have very little' (1986: 23). I suggest that they already do as much, especially with student teachers and beginning teachers. Yet, as socialization differs from acculturation, Alfonso may be seen to be suggesting a weaker role for the supervisior, a more superficial and more bureaucratic function.[4] I, however, propose that supervisors act as cultural agents – involved in initiating new teachers to the local instantiation of teacher culture and working to change their worldviews at a more fundamental level.

Though the distinction between socialization and acculturation might, at first blush, seem trivial, much hinges on the distinction, both for the individual teacher and for the supervisor. For example, those who have worked in schools for awhile begin to notice a difference between levels of teacher commitment. There are those a principal-friend of mine refers to as the 'eight-to-three-type' of teacher, all packed and ready to leave when the bell rings. One of the central dilemmas facing supervisors is how to motivate such minimally-committed teachers to give more to their students and to the school community. This same issue – that between socialization and acculturation – is highlighted in the differences between those who see teaching as a calling and those who see it as a job. (More will be said about teacher socialization and the supervisor's role in it in Chapter 3.) It should be noted, however, that socialization and acculturation are *not* mutually exclusive processes. For example, a person's socialization may be an antecedent to his or her acculturation. In a sense, acculturation assumes successful socialization, but the reverse is not always the case, as discussed above. It may be that someone goes no further than socialization, refusing to be or unable to become acculturated.

Migra's (1976) 'The Transition from Theory into Practice: A Microethnography of Student Teaching as a Cultural Experience' bridges the gap between theory and practice in the examination of the paths student teachers take in becoming teachers. Though its focus seems to be the student teacher co-operating teacher relationship, it also offers a rare glimpse into the role played by the university supervisor.[5] Migra notes:

> Where the students sought immediate feedback and constructive criticism, the teachers were willing to give it with the condition that it be accepted on their terms. These terms were that the student not be defensive and the advice be followed. The difficulty stemmed from the fact that the cooperating teachers seldom communicated these terms of the relationship. The student teachers were left to guess this expected behavior. As a result, both participants in this communication gap sought out the university supervisor and expected her to mediate the situation. (1976: 77)

Hence the university supervisor's role was seen as a facilitator: 'Student teachers complained to the university supervisor that they didn't know what the cooperating teachers wanted' (p. 79). The university supervisor was oriented to viewing student teachers as professionals: 'Some students experienced difficulty because they were encouraged by the university supervisor to think of themselves as professionals, while the reality demanded that they "know their place"' (p. 91).

Other aspects of the university supervisor's role were made clear: 'The university supervisor played a liaison role acting as advisor to both students and teachers with regard to appropriateness of classroom activities and matters of sequence and timing' (Migra 1976: 97) and '[w]here the communication concerned professional growth in social, emotional, and technical areas, the primary contact was between the student teacher and the university supervisor.'

Migra (1976: 97) observed that it was the university supervisor and not the cooperating teacher who took the time and assumed the responsibility of dealing with the student teachers' 'questions, value conflicts, and needs'. She found that due to expectations and prior experiences this was what cooperating teachers and student teachers assumed the university supervisor's role entailed. She also noted that:

> It appears that the university supervisor assumed a facilitation role because neither cooperating teacher or student teacher clearly stated expectations or clarified value positions to the other. This seemed to be an expected part of the role of supervisor. The 'messenger' role of the supervisor was also part of role behavior expected by principal

and other staff members since the supervisor was designated 'respons-ible' for the student teachers. (1976: 98)

These, then, are a few of the pieces to be found in the literature which touch upon the role of the supervisor and the culture of supervision. What of practice?

Voices from the Field

Several of the previous works cited relied, at least partially, upon studies of supervisor–student teacher interaction. In augmenting these works in defense of my position, I wish to draw upon discussions I have held with four experi-enced supervisors charged with aiding intern teachers' transition from the university into teaching. Each of these supervisors holds both a university and a school district title.

Faye[6] – an old hand with over 15 years' experience in this particular pro-gram – describes her role in these terms:

I feel in my supervisory capacity I do a lot of 'mothering' to get started. I think that's what it would be called. In fact, I balk at the word 'supervisor'. Because it's like somebody's super and somebody else isn't. No, I'm not the ordinary supervisor . . . So it's really difficult for me to see myself as a supervisor; either as a mirror or as a superordinate kind of thing . . . I feel more comfortable with the word 'coordinator'.

So I guess I do 'mothering'. I do supply-giving. I do all of that band-aid stuff because I think it's the first step. If you don't have a crutch, you get one. So I do it and people call me 'mother hen' . . . Somebody said something about my mothering her [one of the teacher interns]. I do less than I did. I do less emotional support on her than I did because she's getting stronger. I know it's not where I want to be. It is what I do. It's my job, to help her keep functioning: if she needs more pats on the pooh-pooh to keep going, that she's doing a good job. And I'll give them to her until she can begin to see her own way. She won't need them anymore.

I feel like it's a kind of relationship kind of role – something like it is with the teacher and the kids – in that I would like to be their friend but it's not critical to their role in life that we be. I try.

They want to use us as a safety measure or as a protective device and I think they should be able to. I think they want to be able to say, 'Well, I can't do this because Faye says . . .' or, 'If I did that Faye would be really upset.' I think they want to be able to do that and if they need it, it's OK with me. If we're their best buddy I don't think they can use us in that way with their principals or with other teachers. They sometimes need it for their own defense.

Another supervisor with the program, Vern, talked about his interaction with some of his more 'ideal' intern teachers:

Rather than being [supervisor]/student, it became two colleagues – one of whom sat in the back of the classroom with that extra set of eyes and gave them feedback, which they could accept or reject.

Vern spoke of the problem of rapport and of negotiating rights to enter and observe an intern teacher's class:

I'd like to feel that I was trusted enough that I could just wander in and out. One of the things that taught me [an earlier, difficult relation-ship with an intern teacher] was the importance of establishing a working relationship and trust so if the teacher doesn't know you, you don't come in with your guns blazing right away. Instead you try to find good things and you establish a feeling of trust, even though that's never completely possible if you're a stranger.

Vern spoke of the qualities an ideal supervisor should possess:

I think that having a developmental sense of the candidate is impor-tant. I think just being willing to listen and to be there and be willing to make adjustments.

He also spoke of his style of observation:

I show up whenever I want to. I walk in at whatever part of the lesson. I sit down and I take what's called a 'modified verbatim'. I was trained in Madeline Hunter [Instructional Theory into Practice or ITIP] . . . I get key words and key phrases and key sentences down and key trigger-ideas that are those things that I'm thinking of talking about . . . At the beginning of the lesson it's kind of like listening . . . I have to get into the teacher so by just getting their words down – no matter what they're saying, the kids are saying – the first four or five minutes; all of that and not even making any judgment on that. That gets me loosened up to the class. It gets me really watching and focusing.

Vern talked more about his role:

Those are things that I'm paid to bring up, ethically and morally. I think that anything having an influence upon that person in the classroom should be brought up. Now, you have to approach some of those things appropriately.

When speaking of the teacher's need to fit the culture of the local school population, Vern asked:

How much do we make them adapt and how much do we adapt? It's a real Catch-22. Because if they don't adapt – even if there are a few of us around to believe in them – if they can't adapt enough, all those people here who pay the taxes to keep the school open, we don't have control over *their* adaptability, you know? And they're the ones who, in the long run, could sink the ship, so to speak.

Helen, another of the program's supervisors, was quite articulate in listing the responsibilities of a supervisor as she saw them:

And then the third thing is to have that knowledge of self and vision . . . and being able to help these 'kids' have a philosophy, a vision, and to translate that into classroom practice . . . You want them to teach one another; to be actively involved; to be reflective, prob- lem-solve. And that our responsibility . . . is to provide guidance. Not that we *do* the work for them, but that we provide guidance and help them. And so we, as you know, referred to them as 'our babies'. We call 'em 'our babies'. And what that means, basically, is that they are newborn entities and it's not *total* parenting but it is a whole aspect of parenting to these kids.

In reflecting upon her concerns for a new supervisor, Helen said:

Because she's had student teachers and graduate teaching assistants she might want to do too much for them rather than let them experi- ence failure, which is very important. And I like her willingness to help and go in and do things but she has to remember that these are individuals in charge of their classroom and that they are responsible. She is not to be the responsible person for them.

Kendra, the fourth supervisor, spoke of her role in helping her interns to 'keep a balance':

Helping them keep a balance; because I've learned with my years in life how very, very important that is and how it destroys my teaching if I don't keep a balance in my life. And I see them tipping the scales way, way off – to the point of focusing everything on the school, kids, problems, curriculum, report cards; and neglecting themselves and any significant people in their lives.

'Allowing them to fail' was a phrase Kendra used in speaking of the process of encouraging change in these adult learners:

> So they internalize it. It takes time. It has to be important to them. They have to see its value to them, personally, as a teacher. It has to fit into their value system, their philosophy. And there has to be an adult learner [the supervisor] that's strong enough to allow them to fail as they change.
>
> And the bottom line in being a [supervisor] with these full time professional teachers is: they will do what they choose to do because they are *not* student teachers. And, yes, you can give them assignments and you can make requirements but when you leave the room they will teach the way they want and they will write lesson plans the way they want to. So I help them figure out what is really effective for them. Because they want to be good teachers they're usually receptive to those kinds of ideas.

Kendra talked of her interns' growth:

> In other words, as they gain in expertise and knowledge and skill I find myself deferring to them and realizing that they have suddenly acquired some knowledge and skills and things that I don't know or that are extensions of things I know. Not that they didn't know things that I didn't know at the beginning but they become better teachers and I don't feel the need to point as many things out to them as I might have originally.

She spoke of the changes she made in her role in response to the yearly cycle of growth by her interns:

> I mean I'm obviously winding down this time of the year – taking as much pressure off of them as I possibly can. What they're going to change, they've changed already or they're not going to change it this year.

At another time, Kendra spoke of the uselessness of negative feedback and criticism in getting adult learners to grow or change:

> Well, I think one of the reasons is that research doesn't indicate that anybody's going to change with those kinds of comments being given to them. They will *not* make critical change. They might change for their supervisor, 'because my supervisor said it was the shits'. But once they're on their own without a supervisor, they're going right back – it isn't internalized. It isn't valued by them. Somehow, I think we all try to make it, to phrase it or to give them data or to overwhelm

them with the idea that, 'hey, this really wasn't very good and for the sake of the *kids*, [you] can do better. [You] need to do better.'

You give the person no room to move [with negative criticism]. You attack not just their teaching but them as people, as individuals, as professionals. You're hitting all the buttons when you come on like that, I think.

She also talked about the ambiguous nature of teaching and the incertitude of those interventions she might suggest: 'Nobody has any absolute answers.'

Both the literature and the field are ripe with evidence that, anthropologically speaking, one role supervisors perform – and acknowledge that they perform – is that of guiding the nascent teacher into the cultures of teaching and their realizations in their particular school.

Characteristics of the University Supervisor

What characteristics do university supervisors possess which make them ideal candidates for the role of guide in orienting their charges to teacher culture? Let us begin with a discussion of socialization. One assumption operating here is that socialization is an interactive process, a two-way street (Wentworth 1980), and that each actor affects the others. Zeichner and Tabachnick (1985), following Lacey (1977), identify three strategies novice teachers may employ in meeting the situational demands placed upon them: internalized adjustment, strategic compliance and strategic redefinition (pp. 9–10). In describing the complexity of the socialization process of student teachers and that of its study, they state:

> the induction of beginning teachers is highly context specific, related in each instance to unique interactions of persons (who possess varying levels of skills and capabilities) and school contexts (which differ in the constraints and opportunities for action they present to beginning teachers), it becomes necessary to study how specific beginning teachers are inducted into particular school contexts before attempting to formulate generalizations about the process of entry into the teaching role. (1985: 4)

For one to fulfill the role of guide, there also needs to be a 'follower', a student. Students or novice teachers have a say in who they will follow and who they will believe (though not necessarily in who is assigned them). Perhaps it's no more than supposition, but it would seem beginning teachers develop an affinity for those who support them in turn; those who were perceived to share some characteristics with the student or beginning teacher; and, quite possibly, those who seem accurately to interpret the world of the student and explicate the complexities of classrooms and schools. This is the meaning-making function of the guide and it manifests itself in the relation between the two people. It manifests itself in what the supervisor sees and says, in the language used in the conferences and what is communicated non-verbally.

University supervisors generally have been teachers – and often not too long ago.[7] As teachers, most of these supervisors became enculturated into both the general teacher culture (Feiman-Nemser and Floden 1986) and into some local variety. It may be advantageous for the student teacher if the supervisor has been a member in good standing in the district of the student teacher's current placement, or, if not, to have had experience and be recognized there. As Migra (1976) pointed out, it wasn't just the student teacher who was oriented to the university supervisor as a mediator or facilitator; cooperating teachers and principals were too.

Figuratively speaking, the university supervisor has a foot in each of the worlds of the student teacher: the school and the university. Though there are differences between university programs as to the frequency and duration of supervisor–teacher contact, the supervision models employed, and university teacher education curriculum, the university supervisor is usually familiar with the student teachers' courses and professors. The supervisor can facilitate communication between university and classroom. In fact, I would suggest that the usefulness of the supervisor as a guide depends, in part, on how successfully they are able to negotiate local teacher culture – where they are accepted as members by the cooperating teacher, the principal and the secretary. In this regard the intern teacher supervisor has a distinct advantage over the university supervisor. In my experience, unknown supervisors often need to establish their credentials for the cooperating teacher in the early face-to-face encounters.

In the case of the supervisors quoted above, there have been selection processes operating for them to come to be in the positions they hold; sometimes a certain mentor is mentioned, sometimes university coursework, or extensive district training through workshops, and so on. Also, because of the position they now hold, these supervisors have moved on to become something that is not quite a teacher. These supervisors, with their district appointments (one works in personnel), are committed to recruiting select interns for their district. I do not mean to suggest that the recruitment process is simple, however. Other factors are also in operation, such as the intern's decision, the principal's opinion of the new teacher, the community's acceptance and opinion of him or her (more relevant perhaps, the smaller the community), and district budget considerations. It is the building principal who makes the original hiring decision of this particular program's placements, and the principal who decides whether or not to make the position permanent. The supervisor acts to socialize the beginning teacher to *both* district *and* school norms and, through some subtle and some not-so-subtle interventions, to enculturate the new teacher. Ultimately, the supervisor has to make some decisions about who fits in and who doesn't.

This is at the crux of an important difference between the supervisor of interns and the supervisor of student teachers. The district – through its agent, the supervisor – is making an investment (by paying the supervisor's salary, etc.) in the intern teacher and demonstrating a high level of commitment; the university and its agent – usually a graduate student with no particular district affiliation at the time – doesn't make a like commitment, though doubtless it is true that some university professors supervise student teachers and there may be other district/university collaborations that are not specifically addressed here. It should be mentioned that some teachers-cum-graduate students functioning as supervisors are planning to return to the classroom and some plan not to. Still, it is generally true that people in whatever role or position have their primary and, perhaps, secondary affiliations and get some reinforcement for their beliefs when those in their charge show a willingness or interest to become members of their mentor's group, be that as a university professor, classroom teacher, or supervisor. Otherwise, why would someone even choose to mentor another?

Toward an Ethnography of Supervision: Supervisor Culture

I wish to join my voice to those of Pajak and Glickman (1989) in calling for a full-blown ethnography of supervision. Such an ethnography would reveal how supervisors go about doing what it is they do and would make explicit the meanings or understandings supervisors bring to their work. What might an ethnography of supervision reveal? As noted, supervisors generally have undergone enculturation as teachers (see Feiman-Nemser and Floden 1986) and may have evolved or been socialized beyond that into a 'supervisor culture'. The assumptions and worldview of a teacher then becomes part of the supervisor's baggage.

All participants in supervision hold some notion of what a supervisor is and does (Waite 1994b). These notions and their activation on the scene help to create a 'supervisor culture' that is both similar and dissimilar to teacher culture. The characteristics of any supervisor include a degree of adherence to the norms of supervisor culture.

What does supervisor culture contribute to the way supervisors think and operate? And – a related question – how can these norms, beliefs and actions be best brought to the level of awareness for either the supervisor or the student of supervision?

Like teachers, supervisors believe in individualization of instruction; quite common are the discussions of supervisors' desires to adapt to the needs and style of a new teacher. An idea that is related to individualization is that of 'autonomy', which in turn is related to the concept of professionalism.[8] Migra (1976) has shown how supervisors orient to the student teacher as a professional – a message often at odds with those received from cooperating teachers (or university professors). The supervisor's orientation towards the student teacher as a professional sets her or him apart from others with whom the budding teacher comes into contact. A student teacher may not become a bona fide member of a teacher culture in the eyes of its members until she or he has gained at least one year's experience, often more. During an intern's first year the metamorphosis is apparent soon after December. Supervisors may orient to the student teacher as a 'teacher' even earlier than the student herself or himself. The norms, the philosophy of many supervision models reinforce this.

Coupled with the definition of the student teacher as professional are norms that dictate how a supervisor is to interact with such a professional. Chief among these norms is that of non-interruption. The supervisor is aware of the statement they would be making if they were to interrupt a student teacher, intern, or teacher during the teacher's lesson and proceed to say or model 'this is how it should be done'. Supervisors point to this strategy's negative effect upon both student teachers and their pupils. One reason may be that supervisors realize the role that pupils play in the socialization/enculturation of new teachers (Blase 1986) and may seek to avoid any negative fallout from their actions, such as the undermining of the teacher.

Another norm of interaction between professionals influences the structure and content of feedback conferences. There is a preference for supervisors to avoid directives such as 'do this', (Pajak and Glickman 1989) in guiding teachers to become reflective. There may be a spill-over effect from the norms affecting reflective practice. This, coupled with the restraints introduced by notions of autonomy, may limit supervisors from being directive. Another rationale for supervisory avoidance of bald, affrontive remarks is to be found in the theoretical work of sociolinguistics concerning face threatening acts (FTAs) (e.g. Brown and Levinson 1978).[9] Conferences take on interesting dimensions when viewed cross-culturally. In cultures such as the Athapaskan of Alberta, Canada (Scollon and Scollon 1981) those who possess wisdom or knowledge are in the position of demonstrating or displaying that knowledge while the novice listens, watches and learns. The opposite is the case in North American society generally, and in teaching more specifically (Mehan 1979).

In supervision, it is the novice who displays and not the knowledgeable supervisor.[10] The supervisor arrives upon the scene and discusses the upcoming lesson with the student teacher or may simply assume a seat in the back of the room, depending upon the time available and the model of supervision in use. (See Vern's comments above about his technique.) Often a preconference is held to check that the student teacher has all the bases covered, but it also serves to orient the supervisor to the teacher's style and assumptions. The supervisor may choose to ask questions or make suggestions at this point in an attempt to lessen the possibility that something will go wrong – a protective role the supervisor assumes – or in an effort to assure the student teacher's fidelity to the view the university (or the supervisor, personally) has of teaching. This, again, is a meaning-making (i.e. cultural) activity in which the supervisor engages the student teacher.

The student teacher then may be asked to display again in answering the supervisor's question about which 'problem' or area the teacher would like feedback on or even which observational instrument would be most useful (this decision is often left to the supervisor). It should be noted that in managing these supervisory decisions, the supervisor and the student teacher act out their assumptions concerning the nature of supervision and the relationship between the participants (e.g. power-solidarity issues). (Chapters 2, 3, and 4 further the discussion of power and respective roles.)

The student teacher displays yet again in performing the teaching act, while the supervisor gathers whatever was agreed upon or what seems most relevant or problematic. In making these decisions, the supervisor acts out cultural assumptions concerning such things as the nature of teaching, the role of the teacher in interacting with students, what is permissible or desirable in 'managing' younger people, where this adult should be positioned in relation to the pupils, and so on.

In the 'post-conference' held after the teaching act, the student teacher is asked to display again in debriefing the lesson. At many institutions, students 'know the drill': 'What went well?' 'What you would you do differently?' These questions, as well as the conference itself, may take on ritualistic overtones (Garman 1990).

An ethnography of supervision may reveal that supervisors' warrants for what they do include:

1   concern for the student teacher;
2   concern for the pupils in the classroom;
3   the supervisor's or university's philosophical orientation; and
4   perceived time pressures – both in the observation and conference and in the length of the relationship.

Indeed, concern for the pupils in the classroom has been cited as 'the bottom line' and used as a warrant for violating the norms of supervisor–teacher interaction, for example, interrupting the lesson (Waite 1990/91). The time factor is often used as a warrant for violating the norms centered around professionalism when the supervisor feels a need to be direct.

An ethnography of supervision could benefit from an application of Hall's (1959) three levels of culture – the formal, the informal and the technical – in examining supervisor culture. Generally, the technical culture of teaching is the supervisor's domain. Such an ethnography of supervision would include attention being paid to the cultural aspects of teaching behavior such as 'time on task', method, strategy, planning, the pacing of the lesson, questioning, and the teacher's efforts to assess the student learning which resulted from the lesson. When the supervisor deviates from the technical and enters the informal or formal aspects of culture, an ethnography of supervision may reveal cultural aspects of the nation, the community and the school which have an impact upon how teaching is practiced and perceived. An ethnography of supervision may weave together Hall's three levels with the various contexts or geographical/political levels (global, national, regional and local) to show how they influence local practices. Such an undertaking is a tall order, requiring the investment of untold hours of work.[11]

Implications

If the general thrust of the ideas presented here is on target, then what are the implications for the education of supervisors? Abrell and Hanna (1978) caution supervisors against dealing with teachers as simple individual manifestations of the collective teacher culture. They warn that a teacher may possess knowledge of teacher culture sufficient enough to allow them to look and act like a teacher and yet be deficient in the technical skills required for the job. In fact, it has been suggested (Wolcott 1989) that teachers would be more successful in their jobs and be more favorably perceived by colleagues if they are well-versed in the informal rather than formal or technical aspects of teacher culture, a finding seemingly supported by Zeichner and Tabachnick (1985: 16) in their reporting of first-year teachers being able to ignore bureaucratic rules.

The same possibility exists for supervisors themselves. Granting the existence of a separate 'supervisor culture', one may have cultural knowledge of the formal and informal sufficient to act the part of a supervisor without possessing technical expertise. I imagine there are those in the position of supervisor who possess little or no expertise in any of these three levels of culture (Hall 1959).[12] It may be that the supervisor who operates more within the informal or formal may prove of more service to the beginning teacher than the more technically-oriented supervisor.

I would like to suggest that more educators become practitioners of the ethnographic study of their environment – which may aid in self-study also. With this I join a long line of others (Gearing and Hughes 1975; Hymes 1980; Kilbourn 1984). I'm not sure I would argue that all teachers receive the rigorous training or attack fieldwork with quite as much vigor as anthropologists have been known to do – though I certainly would not want to see the opportunity denied them (and with the schools filled with ethnographers, who's going to teach? And what?). The problem of 'nearsightedness' may yet remain, and people may still be prone to not see or else deny what was happening (Henry 1972). Actually, dyed-in-the-wool ethnographers probably wouldn't suit the needs of teachers, who are known for wanting immediate feedback. Is another set of eyes the only viable answer then? Ethnographic training, and its accompanying introspection, is essential to seeing beyond the simply technical level of teacher and school culture. Often, the instruments commonly in use for classroom observation are inadequate to reveal what is really going on in classrooms.

A supervisor who was trained in ethnography would be more apt to see the underlying cultural assumptions and resultant behaviors operating in a classroom or school. This ability to perceive cultural aspects of schooling may be accomplished simply through making greater use of the lessons from anthropology. I am not suggesting that ethnography is the only way to expand supervisors' awareness. I do believe, however, that I have shown how cultural aspects of thought and behavior deeply affect supervision. Nor has it been my intention to value a certain cultural knowledge over another. I believe all these aspects of supervision are important. I believe that they all should be openly acknowledged and valued.

To this end, the next chapter examines in detail interactions between supervisors and teachers. The same supervisors introduced in this chapter will be shown in face-to-face interactions with teachers. As will be explained shortly, an in-depth analytical procedure, conversation analysis, will be coupled with ethnographic techniques to reveal different views of these interactions, and the different analyses, interpretations and implications such different ways of seeing supervision permit.

Notes

1   Weller attributes this definition to Lucio and McNeil (1959: 26). He also wrote: 'Instructional supervision is a poorly defined and inadequately conceptualized process' (1971: 4).
2   The concept of culture employed in this chapter is that of a unified system of meaning people ascribe to their lives, both personal and professional. It should be noted that 'culture' is an heuristic employed by anthropologists and seldom contemplated or made explicit by the members themselves, hence its taken-for-granted nature. There is a definite distinction between so-called 'school culture' and 'school climate'. For a comprehensive discussion of 'the cultures of teaching' see the work of that same name by Feiman-Nemser and Floden (1986).
3   See Chapter 3 for a more complete discussion of beginning-teacher socialization and supervisors' effects on such socialization.
4   Socialization and enculturation (or acculturation) differ as to the degree of investment and taken-for-grantedness of the actor's beliefs and actions. Enculturation points to the phenomenon of internalization of shared beliefs. Socialization, on the other hand, tends to deal more with outward signs of compliance: Do the actor's actions fit the social norms of a locale? Whether the actor truly accepts a system of beliefs is not a primary concern for those interested in socialization.

Harry Wolcott (personal communication May 16, 1989) liked to give the example of his armed service career. In order to get along in the service, he had to act a certain way (socialization). Whether or not he truly believed in the philosophies and mindset of the military (acculturation) was open to question.
5   Presumably the supervisor of which she writes was Migra herself. Recently there have been a number of treatments of student teaching from an anthropological perspective (Head 1992; White 1989).
6   All names are pseudonyms.
7   Those supervisors quoted above would qualify as university supervisors because of their university affiliation – a role to which some status is attached, both by the supervisors themselves and by other district staff.
8   'Autonomy', as it is used in this context, is an elusive quality. Kilbourn (1982: 2) argues that the 'spirit of clinical supervision' lies in autonomy, evidence and

continuity. Yet how is it that one can be said to be autonomous when interacting with 30 vibrant human beings at one time? (cf. Lortie 1975: 100, 146–151; and Little 1990).

9 Chapter 2 includes a much more complete discussion of face threatening acts and their application to teacher–supervisor face-to-face interaction.

10 Levels of expertise and their ramifications become a bit more problematic when supervision is done for in-service teachers. Still, it is hoped (and claims for supervision are built on the fact) that the supervisor offers *something* to the teacher, if only 'another set of eyes'.

11 Hall wrote that these three levels of culture may operate simultaneously (1959: 72), so ferreting out the influences on any one area would be a considerable task. Also McDermott *et al.* (1978) suggest that an ethnographically-adequate description links local with global processes.

12 There is an easy relation here between Hall's (1959) levels of culture and Alfonso *et al.*'s (1984) supervisory skill mix of human, technical and managerial skills.

Chapter 2

Supervisors' Talk

Much, though certainly not all, of the work of supervisors is carried out in face-to-face interactions with teachers, administrators and others. The prevalent medium or channel for these encounters is talk. Supervisory conferences, especially pre- and post-observation conferences, have attracted the attention of researchers primarily because they are occasions for such face-to-face interaction with the ostensible purpose of improving instruction (Weller 1971: 4). How are supervisory conferences accomplished however, and what meaning do they hold for participants? To these questions, most supervision authors are mute.

However, advances in the fields of anthropological linguistics and sociolinguistics hold important implications for understanding supervisory practice. An anthropological linguistic examination of the supervisory conference as a unique type of talk not only yields its particular characteristics, but also aids in the understanding of the participants' orientations, and informs the theories and practice – the praxis – of supervision. One particular project of this book is to foster a revitalization of the practice and theory of supervision through a more profound understanding of its processes and practitioners' beliefs. Tangentially, such understandings should aid the practitioner who is so disposed in efforts at increased cooperation and collegiality. In short, such new understandings should facilitate reform.

Authors in the field of supervision have echoed Weller's (1971: 1) early call for research on the *processes* of supervision, yet there have been very few such studies. Research on supervisory conferences has relied heavily upon coding schemes and their predetermined categories (e.g. Weller 1971; Blumberg, 1980). Often these protocols are simply adaptations of classroom observation instruments not specifically designed for supervisory conferences (Zeichner and Liston 1985: 157). Other research on supervisory conferences has examined simulations involving actors in the role of supervisor (Pajak and Glickman 1989). More qualitatively-based research into supervisory conferences often has relied upon statistical aggregation of data (e.g. Zeichner and Liston 1985) or theoretical exegesis (e.g. Garman 1990; Smyth 1991b).

Other fields of inquiry have long since employed qualitative methodologies, yet it seems that the 'paradigm shift in education' (Guba 1991) toward more naturalistic study has only just begun to influence studies in supervision.[1] The disciplines of anthropology, sociology and linguistics have been in the forefront of research concerned with understanding the 'object of study' with regard to the 'subject's' own meaning system – a so-called 'emic' perspective (Pike 1954: 8). Advances in the fields of anthropological linguistics and socio-linguistics, for example, have contributed to our understanding of the nature of language and context. Such approaches are necessary to inform the discourse in supervision concerning its role and function in the lives of teachers *and* supervisors.

Some authors have already raised issues which could be explicated through qualitative study. Garman (1990: 211) has raised questions concerning the ritual nature of the conference and its value as an 'educative event'. Smyth (1991a), borrowing from Goldhammer (1969), has advanced a definition of clinical supervision as a collegial relation between *teachers*. Writing from a critical perspective based in the Australian experience, where the terms 'administrator' and 'supervisor' are synonymous, Smyth forcefully argues for clinical supervision as a form of critical inquiry into the nature of teachers' work. For him, this process is facilitated only in true collegial interaction, devoid of the power differential that often characterizes teacher–supervisor interaction. In another report, Smyth (1991b) cautioned that 'collegial' relations may serve technical and control functions at the same time that teachers become disenfranchised from curricular decisions. This is congruent with the work done by Hargreaves and Dawe (1990) on 'contrived collegiality'. Retallick reported on a project he initiated to facilitate 'enlightened self-knowledge for teachers in place of a hegemony of control' (Retallick 1990: 4) through supervisory structures that focused upon critical examination of 'distorted communication brought about by unequal power relationships' (p. 12).

These writings represent an important beginning. There still remain considerable gaps in our understanding, gaps that can be filled with more comprehensive, inductive studies of supervision, its contexts and its accomplishment. So why has so much of the research on conferences focused upon supervisor–teacher *verbal behavior* by employing coding schemes and categories, when other, more qualitative examinations of teacher–supervisor interaction hold such promise?

What seems to be at issue is the definition of 'conference'. If conferences are defined as discrete, unconnected events ordered by physical laws, then 'scientific' (i.e. positivistic) methods may be appropriate for their study. However, if conferences are seen to be nested within their contexts and understood to be human accomplishments, then it could be argued that only qualitative methods can make sense of them. Early on, Cogan (1973) suggested that 'all working contacts between the teacher and supervisor are "conference"' and proposed a 'contextual definition' (p. 196) of the conference, but later researchers and writers in supervision have abandoned this contextual definition for a narrower view of the conference as a discrete event, amenable to scientific analysis (e.g. Weller 1971).[2]

In this chapter I present descriptions and interpretations of processes supervisors employ for their part in conferences with teachers. (Later, in the next chapter, I will examine the processes teachers employ and some of the roles they assume in conferences with supervisors.) Here I will attempt to reconstruct a contextual definition of some supervision conferences, and suggest some implications for the future study and practice of supervision.

The following, then, is a report of an anthropological linguistic study of five supervisory conferences. My research combined observation, interview and 'hermeneutic dialectic negotiation' (Guba and Lincoln 1989: 151) with conversation analysis – an analytical technique with roots in symbolic interactionism and ethnomethodology and focused on talk-in-interaction (Shutz 1962, 1964; Garfinkel 1967; Goffman 1967).

Research Context and Participants

The supervisors of this study, some of whom were introduced in the previous chapter, and the teachers with whom they worked were participants in a graduate program for beginning teachers sponsored by a college of education in the northwestern United States. The program was modeled after the Harvard master of arts in teaching summer school program (Goldhammer 1969; see Cogan 1973; Garman 1990).

Teachers admitted to the program attended summer courses on the university campus. They then left for their assigned districts, where they had probationary contracts for that year. For two weeks before the start of their public school classes, these teachers met daily with their district supervisor to receive instruction designed to help them with the start of classes.

The understanding between the university and the participating districts was that the supervisors would make weekly visits to the teachers' classrooms and also conduct weekly seminars for them, generally held at their central office after school. The visits were to be formative. The supervisors were prohibited by contractual obligations, program policy and other, self-imposed restraints from formally evaluating their teachers for district administrators. One supervisor, Faye, said she actively resisted the requests of principals to 'stack them up like cordwood'.

Though the supervisors, as their school district's liaison with the university, had originally identified those candidates who were to be interviewed for these positions, building principals made the hiring decisions affecting placement. At the end of the year the building principal decided whether to offer the teacher a regular contract.

Supervisors

The three supervisors discussed here – Faye, Vern, and Kendra – all held central office appointments and each was charged with supervising five or six beginning teachers.

Faye, whose district was a mill town, was a full time central office administrator; supervision was an additional responsibility. Her early experience had been as an elementary teacher. She had been with this program for 15 years and her district was peppered with teachers she had supervised. She was two years from retirement.

Vern held a half time appointment as a program supervisor and a half time appointment as a personnel officer. His district included the international headquarters of many high tech firms and was a 'bedroom community' of the state's largest metropolitan area. His classroom experience was in high school English, and this was his second year with the program. He considered himself to be collegial in his working relationships with teachers.

Kendra, whose district was in the same area as a major research university with a large teachers college, was released from the classroom to supervise full time with this program. She had an office at the university and one in the district central offices. She had taught in an alternative elementary school. Her teachers referred to her as 'supportive'.

Teachers

Bea, one of Faye's supervisees, was in her early to mid-40s. She was 'local' – from the area of her new teaching assignment – and had done her student teaching there. She taught fifth grade. Her entry into the program was problematic because of irregularities with her basic skills tests. Still, at least one principal in her district had lobbied heavily for her inclusion in the program.

Ed was in his second year of teaching, having transferred from a more rural district further south to Vern's district. Ed also taught fifth grade. He and Doug were two of Vern's charges and both were considered 'affirmative action hires' – Ed was Chinese-Hawaiian and Doug was Vietnamese. Doug taught in a first-grade classroom and was the only teacher in this program who did not have full responsibility for his own classroom; he was placed in another teacher's classroom because of peculiarities with his certification and, similar to a student teacher's experience, was expected to assume greater responsibility as the year progressed.

Kari worked with Kendra in the university district. She was a younger teacher, in her mid to late 20s. Kendra related to me that Kari had been hired by her principal to reinvigorate a staff whose modal age was near 50. She taught language arts in a middle school.

Fieldwork

As assistant director for the program, I had established a professional relationship with the program participants. In an effort to understand what supervisors did when they were 'doing supervision', I asked to be allowed to interview

Figure 2.1: Transcript notation

–	A dash is used to signal a slight pause, generally of less than 0.2 seconds.
(0.0)	Parentheses show longer pauses, timed in tenths of a second.
^	Caret shows rising intonation.
˅	Subscripted caret shows falling intonation.
° °	Superscripted 'o's enclose passages which are quieter than the surrounding talk.
⌐ ⌐	Brackets enclose simultaneous talk, marking onset and resolution.
ital	Words italicized are given stress by the speaker.
( )	Parentheses show transcriber's doubt, or inaudible passages.
(( ))	Double parentheses show occurrences in the setting that are not part of the talk.
> <	Arrows are used to enclose passages spoken at a much quicker rate than surrounding talk.
=	Latches show where one speaker's turn begins immediately after the preceding speaker's with no pause.
:	Colons show elongated sounds; generally each colon represents a beat.
CAPS	Capitals show talk that is louder than surrounding talk.
·h	shows an audible in-breath.
h	shows an audible exhalation.

Note: This protocol was derived from the work initially done by Gail Jefferson and reported in Schenkein (1978).

them and follow them as they interacted with their teachers. I conducted at least three 'career history interviews' (Agar 1986: 64) with each of the supervisors, centered on their professional life histories and their definitions of supervision. These interviews took place at the supervisors' convenience, generally in their offices or while they went about fulfilling their professional responsibilities, and lasted an hour to an hour-and-a-half each.

I accompanied each supervisor on at least one classroom observation. After the observation I conducted a 'debriefing interview' with each supervisor of an hour-and-a-half to two hours long. These observations and interviews took place in May and June, near the end of the school year. I recorded five supervisory conferences in all: one pre- and one post-observation conference with Kari, the middle school teacher (occurring between periods), and post-observation conferences with the elementary school teachers Bea, Ed and Doug. The conferences lasted from five to 28 minutes. Four of the conferences took place in the teacher's classroom, and the fifth, Doug's was held on folding chairs in a storage room. I transcribed the conference tapes using a conversation analysis transcript notation protocol (see Figure 2.1).

Analysis

The term 'analysis' when applied to a qualitative study is somewhat misleading, implying, among other things, a discrete phase of a research project. I prefer the term 'understanding', or the plural, 'understandings', which speaks to the holistic, tentative and ongoing process of making sense of what the researcher has seen and heard. Understanding has long been a goal of qualitative researchers (Wax 1971; Wolcott 1990: 146) and it is a less restrictive term than 'analysis' in that it allows for other knowledge, such as that gained through subsequent reading(s), to inform a particular study. This process is similar to what Guba and Lincoln (1989: 89–90) describe as a 'constructivist', or 'hermeneutic' research process and what Bakhtin termed 'dialogue' or 'dialogization' (Bakhtin 1981a: 283) – internalized or externalized discourse among competing definitions of the same phenomenon. The constructivist paradigm admits to a dialectical tacking back and forth between 'emic' and 'etic' conceptions (Guba and Lincoln 1989: 84) or 'experience-near' and 'experience-distant' conceptions, respectively (Geertz 1983: 57).

My understandings of supervision and supervisory conferences actually started with my experience as a graduate assistant charged with supervising student teachers. As I reflected upon that role, I was inclined to examine my face-to-face interactions with those teachers. Concern for my role and responsibilities drew me into classes on clinical supervision with Keith Acheson, co-author of *Techniques in the Clinical Supervision of Teachers* (Acheson and Gall 1992).

Upon entering the field to begin this study, I found I had as much unlearning to do as I did learning. My teachers, the supervisors mentioned, were gentle and patient, yet insistent that I understand them and their world. 'Analysis' truly began upon entering the field. My understandings were continually checked with my informants and against the wealth of literature I was able to uncover that dealt with both supervision and supervisory conferences.

Common Conference Processes

Unboundedness

Unlike previous researchers of supervisory conferences (e.g. Blumberg 1970, 1980; Kyte 1971; Weller 1971; Holloway 1982), I found conferences to be 'unbounded'. By this, I mean that the conferences were differentially related to the numerous contexts within which they occurred, a phenomenon Cicourel (1992) terms interpenetration of contexts. There is ample evidence from both the ethnographic material and the conversation transcripts of the interrelationship of conference and context.

This notion of context is reinforced by the literature of anthropological linguistics (Cook-Gumperz and Gumperz 1976) and sociolinguistics (Cicourel 1974; Mehan 1979; Briggs 1986). The anthropological perspective considers contexts to be 'interpretative frames that are *constructed* by the participants in the course of discourse' (Briggs 1986: 12). The sociological perspective is of contexts as phenomenological constructs created jointly by participants that are 'continually renegotiated in the course of the interaction' (Briggs 1986: 25). Such considerations of context eschew macro–micro distinctions for their artificiality, and are more comprehensive than simple listings of the physical attributes of a setting or of the participants themselves.

As stated, every conference but one took place in the teacher's classroom, generally with students present. Doug's conference, however, was convened in a storage area adjacent to the music room with strains of 'My Favorite Things', as practiced by an elementary school strings class, wafting in and out of the conference. The transcripts show repeatedly that participants were aware of the contexts in which they found themselves, often made reference to them, and had recourse to employ the contexts in accomplishing their 'moves', that is, in realizing their particular turns at talk.[3] As an example, the middle school teacher, Kari, terminated both her pre- and post-observation conferences by addressing her remarks to students in the room. Vern and Ed modulated the volume of their voices when speaking of sensitive matters or stopped conferencing altogether while Ed disciplined students during their conference, which was held in the front of Ed's fifth-grade classroom as the students did seatwork. In so doing, these two were able to establish and reinforce their shared perceptions of each other as educators, a process known as 'identity work' – 'the behavior a person generates in an attempt to make sense of and to feel good about an ongoing situation' (McDermott and Church 1976: 122). (Chapter 3 will examine teachers' roles in these conferences in more detail.)

Another example of the unboundedness of conferences comes from the conference in which the teacher, Bea, mentioned her class outside:

Transcript Fragment 2.1

145		((Bea goes to window))
146	*Bea:*	=I'm jus – *concerned* that *my kids* are out
147		⌄*there* ((at recess)) with no *supervi*₁*sion*
148	*Faye:*	OH::¹
149		*well* you'd *better* get out^*the*₁*re,* ^*then.*
150	*Bea:*	^ *no*¹ he's
151		*still* out ⌄there – *that's* good (1.2) >just
152		let me ⌄*check* and make ⌄*sure*< – ^O⌄K=

Notice the negotiation evident here. At this point in the conference, the teacher got up – actually 'leaving' the conference momentarily – to go to the window. This occurrence followed two other 'interruptions': an electronic bell (probably ignored on any conscious level), and that of another teacher who stopped by to borrow a stopwatch. Later in the same conference the teacher monitoring Bea's class knocked on the door to confer with her. At this point, Bea again 'left' the conference to negotiate another 'three or four minutes' with the teacher (actually the conference lasted *much* longer).

This teacher never again mentioned her group outside, but the supervisor, Faye, did. Near the end of this face-to-face encounter, and after she had attempted to take her leave by employing other leave-taking strategies, Faye brought up the group outside (lines 759–760 and 762):

Transcript Fragment 2.2

```
754  Faye:  ((to observer)) well Dun˄can – do you wanna
755         ˄go: – or are you gonna ˄stay. Here I am –
756         walkin' outta here and ^he's stayin' ˄here
757         ((laughs)) and he's – watching me –
758  Bea:   ((to observer)) yeah, thank you ((laughs))
759  Faye:  leave. It's because – I'm thinking you need
760         to be out on that play˄ground.
761  Bea:   I'm going ˄out – I'm gonna take=
762  Faye:  =I SEE YOU looking out there – so –
763         ⌊frequent    ly
764  Bea:   I'm gonna t-⌋
```

This transcript fragment shows that the group outside – part of the larger, physical context – held continuing conversational relevance for the participants throughout the conference. Again, contexts influenced all the conferences, though perhaps never as explicitly as in the preceding example.

Conference Phases

Another common characteristic of the conferences I observed was what I refer to as 'phases'. In these conference transcripts I noted three phases:

1   the supervisor report phase;
2   the teacher response phase; and
3   a programmatic phase.

I do not mean to imply that phases are discrete. Participants move in and out of phases with relative ease. Phases are dynamic. For the present analysis, whenever both participants exhibit the behaviors indicative of a particular orientation to 'what is happening now', they are in a particular phase. When in a particular phase certain characteristics hold for all conferences.

Scheflen (1973: 65) employed the term 'phase' in writing of the hierarchical organization of non-verbal behavior:

When two or more people come together they engage in a common activity . . . These activities form a context for the relations, which become phases in the sequences of the activity. Each phase is a context for the particular kinds of communicative behavior which each participant contributes.

The term 'phase' is applied in this sense.

The (analyst's) attributions of phases were assigned according to these criteria: who initiated topics; who succeeded in any overlap or competition for the floor, and who conceded; which participant, the supervisor or the teacher, had the most and the longest turns at talk; and which participant's turns were simply 'acknowledgment tokens', such as 'um hum', etc. (Goodwin and Heritage 1990: 288).[4]

Due to the nature of participants' turns at the floor, topic initiation, turn size, and the result of occasional competition for the floor, 'ownership' of each of these phases has been ascribed to one of the participants or the other. The first phase is the *supervisor report phase*. Here the supervisor initiates topics and has the longest turns at the floor. The supervisor usually escalates in response to any (perceived) competition for the floor and the teacher usually concedes in such instances. The teacher's turns are generally and simply acknowledgments such as 'um hum' or 'uh huh'. 'Acknowledgment tokens' such as these are seen as implying the speaker's orientation to other's talk as not yet done:

> the projection of an acknowledgment token (such as 'mm hm') projects (but does not require) the continuation of another speaker's talk. Simultaneously it usually displays an analysis of the other speaker's prior talk as being incomplete so far. (Goodwin and Heritage, 1990: 288)

Teachers' extensive use of acknowledgment tokens during this phase demonstrates their orientation to and even acceptance of the supervisor's dominance of the supervisor's report phase.

Though teachers have longer turns and the supervisor assumes an acknowledging posture during the *teacher response phase*, it *is* a response to supervisor initiated topics. In this sense, the supervisor's control extends across even this phase. A further rationale for assigning ownership of this phase to the teacher is that when simultaneous talk occurs during this phase, it is usually the supervisor who drops out. As teachers generally have and can keep the floor during this phase, they may advance their own agenda as well as their rationale for observed teaching behaviors.

In the third phase, the *programmatic phase,* ownership is ascribed to the teacher. While the size of turns and their distribution are relatively equal for supervisor and teacher, it is generally the teacher who initiates topics in this phase. Three of the four teachers in this study brought up programmatic concerns during their conferences. Kari did not. Ed's programmatic concerns were situated at the beginning of his conference.

In the first phase, the supervisor report phase, the supervisor took the floor to report on what he or she had observed in the lesson. Both supervisor and teacher seemed oriented to this reporting as the role and responsibility of the supervisor and as being the primary, ostensible purpose for a conference. That is why, of all three phases, the supervisor report phase came at the beginning of the conference and the teacher took an acknowledging posture. Literature in the field of instructional supervision supports this interpretation (Hunter 1980; Retallick 1990: 22).

This reporting was usually done chronologically – beginning with the first bit of data the supervisor had written, and continuing until either the end of the data was reached or other topics were introduced and exhausted.[5] If other topics were introduced, the supervisor often initiated a return to the reporting function at a later time.

Strong support for my assertion that the participants were oriented to the opening of the post-conference as a time for the supervisor's report is given in the conference between Kendra and Kari, where the supervisor opened with (lines 1–2):

Transcript Fragment 2.3

```
1   Kendra:   I just took ˄down ^all kinds of ^stuff
2             ˄here ((excited voice)) (0.3) u: ⌈:m
3   Kari:                                       OK]
4   Kendra:   I first I ˄started doing a little
5             break˄ down of ti:me – for ˄you.
6   Kari:     °um ^hum°
```

Note that the teacher's assent (lines 3 and 6) demonstrates an orientation to the fact that the supervisor should begin with just such a report. The supervisor implied that she had collected data *for* the teacher (line 5).

During this portion of the conference, supervisors reported upon classroom occurrences from their particular points of view. One supervisor, Vern, saw a gender issue develop. Another, Kendra, saw a management issue with a boy who was acting out. Faye saw the teacher not focus the group or clarify the intent of her questions.

Supervisors had the floor for most of this phase and they initiated most of the topics. Some of these topics were only loosely associated with the data. Vern's discussion of the gender-equity issue as it relates to science and math education is an example of this. In the course of the discussion, he mentioned his trip to Harvard, works by the author Carol Gilligan, cultural constraints and norms that operate against inclusion of girls in science lessons, an anecdote about a female teaching colleague who crumpled up and threw away the 'consumables' from her science curriculum, and more, all not directly related to the supervisor's 'observation'.

During the report phase, teachers' turns at talk were filled with acknowledgment tokens such as 'uh huh', and 'um'. Acknowledgment tokens, while technically turns at talk, are definitely *not* attempts to take and hold the floor. As suggested above, acknowledgment tokens can be used to encourage the other – the supervisor in this case – to continue speaking. Teachers seldom interrupted and hardly ever initiated discussion of a new topic during the supervisor report phase.

Supervisors also employed various strategies to retain the floor, *especially* during the supervisor report phase. Raised voice, increased speed, overlapping, repetition, and elongation of utterances or use of 'floor holders' such as 'um' were used by supervisors, alone or in combination, to retain the floor during this phase. Transcript Fragment 2.4 is an example of the supervisor's use of raised voice in overlap to keep the floor – an interruption (note line 157):

Transcript Fragment 2.4

```
153   Faye:   =the – intent of this question – is:
154           (0.8) if: – you wer:e=
155   Bea:    =oh, I forgot to take
156           ₁my (                    )
157   Faye:   IF – YOU WERE ⌃TAKING⌋ – °a pen⌃cil – at
158           the end° see what you're after ^here: –
159           IS: – THEM to th:ink
```

Once this supervisor was certain she had indeed retained the floor, once she was 'in the clear' after a slight pause (denoted by a dash), she lowered her voice.

Some supervisors quickly employed these strategies at the slightest hint that the teacher may have been making a bid for the floor, for instance, when the teacher may have 'misplaced' an acknowledgment token in mid-turn instead of at the 'appropriate' juncture. Transcript Fragment 2.5 is such an example. Lines 456 and 458 demonstrate how the supervisor, Vern, increased his speed to retain the floor; line 460 demonstrates how he signalled his intention to continue speaking with an inhalation (·h), and continued over Doug's acknowledgment.

Transcript Fragment 2.5

```
449   Vern:   go back ·h and (finally- ) th- you know – you
450           – did it again< and you got Tim to go back
451           to his DESK. THERE'S A KID WHO WAS BEING
452           RESISTANT but you: – WERE PERSISTENT. – OK
453           ? ·h THAT WAS GOOD – you did not choose
454           to ig^nore ⌃that, because – >you know<
455           sometimes it's easiest to ignore it when
456           they don' ₁t do it >sometimes
457   Doug:   um hum⌋
458   Vern:   they QUIT< (0.5) but they don't- in- – >ya
459           know< th- he might have quit – misbehaving
460           ₍ ·h but he do esn't ignore
461   Doug:   um hum  ⌋
462   Vern:   ^it. ·h and – the moment he ignores one of a
463           com⌃mand, when you make a com⌃mand at that –
464           strength and that commitment – ·h other kids
465           are wa:tching. (0.7)
```

Supervisors worked at retaining control of 'their' conference phase. Some worked harder than others. Perhaps the amount of work needed to be done by supervisors depended on how much the teacher shared the supervisor's orientation as to the function of the conference and their respective roles in it. This may explain the contentious nature of the conference between Faye and Bea, why Bea constantly 'interrupted' the conference, and why – according to Faye – she was prone to 'arguing'.[6] This explanation is bolstered by Herbert Blumer's (1972: 73) discussion of the importance of gesture for symbolic interactionism. He wrote:

> When the gesture has the same meaning for both, the two parties understand each other . . . [Gesture] signifies what the person to whom it is directed is to do; it signifies what the person who is making the gesture plans to do; and it signifies the joint action that is to arise by the articulation of the acts of both . . . If there is confusion or mis-understanding along any one of those three lines of meaning, communication is ineffective, interaction is impeded, and the formation of joint action is blocked.

An equally persuasive interpretation of the contentious nature of this conference is offered by consideration of the concept of resistance. Following this line of reasoning, because of the control Faye exerted over Bea and the conference, the only option Bea had to assert herself was in 'breaking the frame' (Briggs 1986: 56) of the conference. Comparison between an interview and a supervisory conference is problematic; however, certain analytical leverage is gained in considering Briggs's discussion of the social roles in interviews:

> The typical interview situation grants the interviewer principal rights to topical selection by virtue of her or his provision of the questions. He or she further determines whether a response counts as an answer by choosing whether or not to reiterate the question during his or her next turn . . . In sum, the interviewer maintains a great deal of control over the interaction; the respondent's principal means of subverting this power lies in breaking the frame of the interview. (1986: 56)

Further, Briggs stated that 'when the system is working properly, the participants accept the roles assigned to them by the structure of the interview' (1986: 56).

The other conference phases seemed to belong to the teacher. In the teacher response phase, the teachers' turns at talk were large and the supervisors usually took the acknowledging posture, punctuating the teachers' turns with 'um hum's, etc. Though I have written that this phase belongs to the teacher, one must remember that, though the teachers' turn sizes were relatively unrestricted, the teachers' choice of topic was heavily restricted, that is,

in this phase the teachers' turns were restricted to responding to the topics –
such as teaching behaviors – originally identified by the supervisor.[7]

The programmatic phase may be particular to these conferences and this
program, though I suspect that other supervisory conferences have similar,
non-observation related elements that may be termed 'rapport building'. For
example, in counseling interviews Erickson (1975) and his associates (Erickson
and Shultz 1981) found that 'the institutional objectivity of the gatekeeping
situation is easily overridden by extra-institutional factors' (Scollon 1981a: 4),
such as co-membership in groups or organizations outside the immediate
context. Scollon continues:

> These personal factors . . . have the power to override the purely in-
> stitutional considerations to such an extent that they may be thought
> of as *the primary determinants* of life chances in institutional
> gatekeeping encounters. (emphasis added)

In the programmatic phase, teachers and supervisors discussed class assignments, upcoming mock job interviews and future career opportunities. My
warrant for assigning 'ownership' of the programmatic phase to the teacher is
that, though the turns at talk were relatively equally distributed in both turn
size and turn order, it was generally the teacher who initiated the topics during
this phase.

Questions

Another feature of supervisory conferences is the participants' use of questions. Generally, the conferences began with a supervisor question.

Questions can perform several tasks but they almost always require some
response. The question–answer dyad has been labeled 'an adjacency pair' by
Sacks *et al.* (1978: 28). According to these authors a specific 'first-pair part'
makes relevant a particular 'second-pair part' (e.g. a greeting makes a return
greeting relevant). Moreover, people orient to the lack of the second-pair part.
If a question is asked, the lack of an answer becomes apparent. More complex
questions may require an account as a response.

These teachers seemed oriented to providing an answer in the form of an
account to the initial supervisor question. Generally, these global accounts
were constructed so as to comprise a debriefing of the lesson. One such initial
supervisor question is shown here:

Transcript Fragment 2.6
| 1 | *Vern*: | (How did you) feel about the various parts |
| 2 | | of the lesson? |

These early questions call for global, not specifically detailed, accounts.
This may be why these teachers took only one to three turns at the beginning

of a post-conference before topic control reverted to the supervisor. The rules or routines governing the question–answer dyad, or 'adjacency pair' (Sacks *et al.* 1978), above illustrate how this can occur. Schematically, if the conference proceeds Q (Supervisor) – A (Teacher), the next turn 'belongs' to the supervisor, who, as noted, has a free, or unencumbered, turn, unlike the teacher. Even in more complex question–answer exchanges, for instance those involving embedded question–answer adjacency pairs (where, before or in order to answer the original question, the teacher asks a question himself or herself for clarification, etc.) even in these exchanges the free, unencumbered turn returns to the supervisor. Schematically: Q (Supervisor) – Q (Teacher) – A (Supervisor) – A (Teacher). For example:

Supervisor: How did you feel about the lesson?
Teacher: Which part of the lesson?
Supervisor: I mean, did you accomplish your objective?
Teacher: I feel like I did.
Supervisor: (free to change topics, introduce new topic, seek additional information, and so on.)[8]

In the post-conferences of this data set, the supervisor got the floor back after the teacher responded to the initial, global supervisor question. The supervisor then elaborated on the teacher's response, clarified the question, called for a further account, or actually provided a candidate, or alternate, and equally acceptable response to the question before continuing with the supervisor report phase.

Specific Conference Processes

Mitigation of Criticisms and Suggestions

These three supervisors often lessened the force of their criticisms and suggestions. While Pajak and Seyfarth (1983) wrote of this as 'inauthentic supervisory behavior', I will not render such a judgment here. Rather, I simply wish to describe this interactional phenomenon and offer an explanation of how and why this may occur in the face-to-face interaction between supervisor and teacher.

I found supervisors lessened, or mitigated, the force of their criticisms or suggestions in at least two distinct ways: through the use of 'I' statements; and through the use of modal auxiliaries, such as 'might', 'could', 'would', and so on. These verbal strategies were often used in combination.

'I' Statements

In the example below, the supervisor began her suggestion with 'you', then switched to an 'I' statement in mid-turn (line 2):

Transcript Fragment 2.7
33 *Faye:* ·h and *th-* – *the* in*tent* of *this* ques⌄*tion*
34   (0.5) is – to *de*⌄*al:* (0.7) *sometimes* you th-
35   it *helps* me to word *'em* into another °(kind
36   of) question°

The use of 'I' statements may show respect for the professional autonomy of teachers while allowing them to benefit from the classroom experience of the supervisor – if the teachers so choose. It remains up to the professional judgment of teachers whether to accept the suggestion. They may conclude that a particular suggestion is not best for this group at this time, or that it does not fit their teaching style. In other words, teachers are left with the option of thinking 'yes, *you* may; but I am not you'.

Another explanation for these 'I' statements is that supervisors may use this strategy to emphasize their solidarity with the teacher. Brown and Gilman (1972) have written of this as the usage of 'pronouns of power and solidarity'.[9] Courtney Cazden (1976: 88) also discussed the pronouns of power and solidarity in school language, and their effect: 'There is accumulating evidence that power relationships exert a constraining effect on the language of the less powerful person.'

Brown and Gilman (1972) wrote that a shift in pronominal usage – for example from the formal V (for *ústed*) to the informal T (for *tú*) in Latin-based languages like French, Italian and Spanish – signified a shift in the relationship for the speaker. A shift from the formal to the informal indicates that the speaker wishes to emphasize solidarity and de-emphasize any power differential between the speaker and listener. Following this line of reasoning, in adopting the 'I' perspective supervisors would be making the most radical pronominal shift possible and, in a sense, be taking the teacher's voice. In effect, the supervisor is saying, 'I'm just like you.'

Modal Auxiliaries
Modal auxiliaries (such as 'might've', 'could've' or 'would've') sometimes were employed by supervisors when criticizing or suggesting alternatives to teachers (line 172 below):

Transcript Fragment 2.8
170 *Vern:* to: g₍o on ·h °one *thing*
171 *Ed:*   um hum |
172 *Vern:* you *might've* – *wanted* to uh- be *do*^*ing*
173   ⌄*there*° – is *Brent did* ^*not give* ⌄*you* the
174   *cor*^*rect* ⌄*re*⌄*spons:e* – if you ^re⌄call – *he*
175   – ·h was c- he gave a *con:*⌄*fuse*₍*d* resp ond
176 *Ed:*   *different*|
177   respon₍se

bit later in the same conference (lines 196–201):

Transcript Fragment 2.9
```
196   Vern:   °one of the ˰things you ˆmight wanna've
197           ˰done° – >when you were doing ˰that ˆac˰tive
198           ˰parˆticipa˰tion piece< was to have ·h –
199           ˰mo:ved arou:nd – and ˆlis˰tened to – ˰what
200           they ˰were talkˆing a˰bout ·h 'cause you
201           ˆwould've ˰heard it ˰ra:nge >every˰thing<
202           from these ˰two – >°over here< who didn't
203           ˰know so they ˰were – >ˆthey were< –
204           >polite< but they were si˰lent –
205           ˆlis˰tenˆing to° ˄these ˰two over ˰here – he
206           po- he ˰proˆbab˰ly ˰knew
207   Ed:     uh huh=
```

This strategy also may allow the teacher some professional autonomy in decision making. Notice the difference in force between the possible ways to state the same suggestion or criticism, between 'you should have' and the less forceful 'you might have' or 'you could have'.

As stated, these strategies also were used in combination (lines 32, 35 and 38):

Transcript Fragment 2.10
```
28   Vern:   uh::m, things and I think we practiced
29           this one because one ((chuckle in voice))
30           of the things ·hh that I was going to ·h
31           mention – in watching that was – wa:s
32           (0.6) I: – might've – because they had
33           been on the carpet before=
34   Doug:   =um hum=
35   Vern:   =when ·hh I might've – felt a need for
36           physical change. ·h and at – THAT point
37           in time your only option for physical
38           change– would've been to have 'em – re-
39           – go back to their desks, and then ·hh
40           have 'em in their individual seats –
41           while- – you gave instructions.
```

A functional explanation for these strategies is found in Brown and Levinson's discussion of 'face threatening acts' (Brown and Levinson 1978: 65). Face threatening acts (FTAs) are speech acts which may entail a loss of face for participants in a conversation. For the listener (the teacher in this case), these FTAs can be orders, requests, suggestions, advice, reminders, threats, warnings, dares, expressions of disapproval, contempt or ridicule, complaints or reprimands, accusations, insults, contradictions or disagreements, and/or challenges.

Brown and Levinson (1978) outline some strategies of how one might go about performing an FTA. One such strategy, that of performing the FTA with 'redressive action' and employing 'positive politeness' (pp. 74–75), seems to explain one supervisor's strategy in conference. During our debrief, Faye commented to me that the lesson we had just witnessed was 'the poorest role-play of any of them'. Still, in conference with the teacher, she said this:

Transcript Fragment 2.11

625	*Faye*:	But – uh (0.5) *it* would be g:*ood* – for *her*
626		to be *able* to see ˏ*your:s* – because *she*
627		would *say* – oh – >I *shoulda* done *that*< or –
628		*yep* – *that* worked *really* ˏ*well* and *it* would
629		probab₁ly be ^*good* – for ˏ*you* to be *able* to
630	*Bea*:	ye^ah]
631	*Faye*:	see ˏ*hers*. if ₁IF she's *willing* to
632	*Bea*:	°um° *I'D* ^LI KE – to do ˏ*that*]
633	*Faye*:	ex ˏ*change*.
634	*Bea*:	°yeah° ^O ˏK – *we* can *talk* about
635		i₁t-
636	*Faye*:	AL]RIGH*T*=

This supervisor had videotaped all her teachers' role-play lessons and suggested that Bea view that of another (lines 628–629, 631). Notice that she implied that the other teacher could learn something from watching the videotape of this lesson (lines 625–8). The supervisor's strategy seemed to be to help Bea to grow through watching the other's videotape. Still, Faye felt she needed to give attention to Bea's 'face' in making the suggestion. Notice how enthusiastically the teacher responded to her suggestion (line 636) – it gave her a readily acceptable plan of action, an 'out'.

The Role of Data in Supervisors' Conference Strategies

In a comprehensive review of the literature, Holland (1989) discussed the implicit assumptions surrounding supervisory conferences. One aspect of her treatment dealt with assumptions concerning the role of observational data in conferences and another related to the degree of the supervisor's preparation for the ensuing conference. The views cited by Holland included Hunter's (1980) prescription for highly structured conferences, based upon the observational records and Sergiovanni's and Starratt's (1988) opinion that the supervisor should prepare with tentative objectives and processes 'but in a manner that does not program the course of the conference too much' (p. 360). Holland noted that this last view seemed to reflect Cogan's (1973: 197) original position that the supervisor should not completely preplan the course of the conference because it could not be predicted what concerns the teacher would bring. In my role as an ethnographer of supervision, I was interested to see how 'data' were dealt with in the conferences I witnessed.

Faye entered her conference in a highly structured manner by employing a checksheet. This was something she thought necessary owing to her perception of the teacher, Bea, as highly 'distractable'. Faye's comments to me were informative:

> As soon as I mention a change or a situation, she starts what I call 'arguing', where she'll say, 'But this is what I thought da-da-da-da-da-da'. By the time she goes through this long explanation of why she did what she did about something, we lose the whole intent and purpose. I do best in my conference with her when I have a guide, like a checksheet, because it guides our discussion. Otherwise, time is gone and you haven't gone anyplace with the discussion.

Throughout this conference, Faye worked to keep Bea focused through her use of the checksheet as an observation instrument and by referring to it in the dialogue.

Vern and Kendra, the other supervisors, employed different observation techniques and conference processes. Vern talked about his conference strategy with Ed:

> [The focus] unfolds somewhat naturally. I never had intended in that science class to see the boy/girl thing going on but it gave me a chance to talk about an issue that's very near and dear to my soul – girls in terms of science instruction. In a post-conference I try to talk about just some of what I would call 'basic teaching act' things that were good – Ed's use of some vocabulary words. And Ed's perceptive. Rather than just say, 'Oh, thank you', he said, 'But can it be too confusing?' So I used the teaching part: If it's a new concept, then to do what he did might muddy the waters, it's a bird walk. My goal was not to strategize about the girls today. My goal was two-fold. Initially, when I first picked that up, my mind was going, 'Oh, this is how it is and this is how it will unfold.' As I said, though, Ed called on about 60 per cent girls. So at that point, I realized that when he questions kids he does a good job of breaking it down boy/girl. That took care of one of my concerns. The second issue was how does he get the girls to be more involved in those situations and discussions. You know, bringing up Carol Gilligan's work out of Harvard was an intellectual way of dealing with it, something he might come to eventually. I talked about the cooperative learning things. My goal today was at the awareness level; it wasn't mastery of a new concept.[10]

However, in his conference with Doug, his other teacher, Vern saw the focus as being different:

I wanted to talk with Doug about – I want to use the word more 'global' issues, but that's not the word. I wanted to talk to him about essential classroom management issues and I didn't have to quote him lines. He himself was aware of how many times he had to say to the students, 'Sit down', and those sorts of things.

With him, I retaught the lesson. I did a 'reteach the lesson', and with that – except to generally refer to what he was doing – I don't need to say 'Doug, you said that, then you said this.' I assume that's in his mind. I didn't do any counting in his, you know. One time I did show him the notes. It was because I had drawn a very quick diagram of what the seating arrangement in the class looked like to me.

I took verbatim for the most part, or 'modified verbatim' as I call it.

Vern compared his observation and conference of Ed with those of Doug:

It was the same style of notes [in both observations], but for what I wanted to talk with Doug about, I didn't feel the need to refer to them as much. Ed also tends to sit down. I have the sense he likes the notes there and he likes me pointing things out to him. Doug has not given me that sense of need. I think Doug is more formal by nature.[11] Our conference tends to be more formal – our body language and things. I'm sitting there across from him. With Ed, I'm always at the table next to him and we both lean on the table. With Doug, there tends to be a whole different approach going on.

Vern found Ed to be a satisfactory teacher on a number of counts. He calls on the appropriate number of girls in science, and 'Ed's perceptive', he asks questions in conference that raise the level of the discussion. Other considerations may have contributed to Vern's different conference styles, however. He had expressed concerns to me about Doug's English language proficiency, prompted by parental complaints – evidence that Doug was not being accepted by the community of parents as qualified to teach their children. There are definite cultural overtones here. Vern may have felt prohibited from discussing these issues with Doug, and instead may have felt it more acceptable to fault Doug's teaching on the more technical aspects of the job.

Another translation from 'data' to conference came in the interaction between Kendra and Kari. At one point in their conference Kendra began to list the positive behaviors she thought Kari had displayed in the lesson. She had listed these on her data sheet – a single sheet of 'NCR' paper that automatically produces three copies, one of which I kept. What was listed there as 'appropriate reinforcement given to student responses' became lines 161–5 and 167:

Transcript Fragment 2.12

```
160   Kendra:   u:m (1.3) °I commented on: u:m (0.3) y-
161             your- re^laxed ^man^ner° (0.7) (ap) propriate
162             rein^force^ment – you were giving (0.4)
163             rea:lly appropriate reinforcement to ^some
164             >you were saying< that's interes^ting or I
165             hadn't – thought about that before:
166   Kari:     °uh huh°
167   Kendra:   good idea:
168   Kari:     °uh hum:°=
169   Kendra:   =you were doing a lot of ^that.=
```

This change from the written to the verbal comment shows changes made in response to the interactional demands of the conference, that is, the context. Kendra didn't mention all of the positive points she had on her list at that time, although she brought up another nearer the end of the conference. In that instance, the written phrase 'good questions' became lines 235–8:

Transcript Fragment 2.13

```
234   Kendra:   anyways I ^was- I ^was – >^pleased< and
235             ^your – level of – ^question^ing (0.4) was
236             ^ex^cel^lent – some- ther- 'as: there 'as
237             some ^big ^thin^kin' goin' on in
238             ^he₁re ^to ^day
239   Kari:     um ^um]      um ^hum
```

Also note the supervisor's positive global evaluation in line 234 above.

This supervisor departed from her data in other ways. Though she had listed the time (in hours and minutes) along one side of her data sheet, she referred to them in vague terms (e.g. 'about', 'there was one point') or in clearly erroneous terms (line 147):

Transcript Fragment 2.14

```
143   Kendra:   and- y- look how ^long the discus^sion
144             ^went- now this is ^my₁:   ^clock
145   Kari:                               this is a lo:]ng
146             ti^m₁e:
147   Kendra:       ^nine th]ir^ty no n- I me:an (0.2)
148             they did ^well – cl₁ear    up to: –
149   Kari:                      yeah]
150   Kendra:   ten fif^teen
```

Kendra erroneously mentioned the starting time as 9:30 (line 147), when according to the data sheet the discussion began at 9:41. Notice how in this transcript fragment (lines 145–8), Kendra – as supervisor – quickly sought to repair Kari's misunderstanding of her previous remark. Apparently, Kari took Kendra's 'look how long the discussion went' as an implied criticism and demonstrated her agreement (lines 145 and 146). Kendra seemed anxious that she not be left with that mistaken impression; though erroneous and vague (at least on this point), Kendra was supportive.

Only *after* Kendra had shared her list of positive lesson points with Kari did she turn the floor over to her with a question calling for a global evaluation:

Transcript Fragment 2.15
185   Kendra: ^any^way (0.3) u:h – OVER^*ALL* DID IT ˏ*GO*
186   THE *WAY* YOU *WANTED* IT ^ *TO*?

Conference Focus

Insight into conference processes is gained through consideration of Ron Scollon's (1981b) notion of 'focus' in talk. Scollon writes of a continuum of focus, dependent on the 'amount of negotiation possible among the participants about the nature of the situation' (p. 17). For Scollon, focus has three variables that limit negotiation among participants: time restrictions, the number of participants and the medium of communication. I include 'agenda' as a variant of the medium of communication. Agenda as an aspect of focus has to do with the supervisors' concerns, how they intend to approach the conference (their amount of planning, organization or structure) and what they hope to accomplish in the conference.

Since these conferences were dyadic, that variable is constant. The time restrictions on these conferences differed, as did the media of communication, when thought of as the supervisors' agenda. Faye entered her conference with Bea with a strong agenda. She intended to keep Bea focused and on task through her use of a checksheet. This conference was under a moderate time restriction, but Bea eased that by negotiating more time with the teacher monitoring her class on the playground. Kendra had assumed that she and Kari were to have had a whole planning period for their conference, it was not until students began coming into the classroom that Kendra realized that this assumption was mistaken. Also, Kendra's agenda was relatively weak because it was so near the end of the school year and she already knew Kari would be returning the next year.

The differential effects of agenda are illuminated through comparison of Vern's two conferences. Vern had accepted Ed and vice versa. They had each contributed to a mutually constructed perception of themselves as competent educators. Their conference reinforced this. Lacking a strong agenda, and with a relatively weak time restriction because the students were there in front of them doing seatwork, their conference tended to be more of a discussion among co-equals and more rambling, less focused. However, Vern had already sensed that Doug was not going to be accepted by significant others in his situation and had developed 'global' concerns – 'essential classroom management issues', he had said. His agenda was stronger in his conference with Doug and he exerted much more control.

Summary and Discussion

I have demonstrated some of the processes supervisors use to exert control over conference direction and over teachers while in conference. Supervisors did this in several ways:

1   control of the floor during the supervisor report phase;
2   topic selection during this phase, and its continued relevance during the teacher response phase;
3   supervisor questions; and
4   supervisor ownership of and presentation of data.

Supervisor initiation of the conference, the chronological presentation of the data, and the complementary introduction of topics have ramifications for what gets discussed and who introduces topics, that is, who 'controls' the conference. Because of the usual linear progression of conference topics, teachers seldom have an opportunity to introduce topics of *their* concern. One can easily imagine a scenario whereby the conference time runs out before the teacher gets a free turn at the floor, one that isn't a response to supervisor-initiated topics. This chronological discussion of data may, then, be impositional on the teacher's time and may very well limit what gets discussed; it may, in fact, severely limit teacher reflection.

I have also presented several moderating influences on supervisor control. These included:

1   supervisors themselves mitigating their suggestions or criticisms through the use of 'I' statements[12] and modal auxiliaries;
2   supervisors attending to the teacher's 'face' needs; and
3   conference contexts, including conference focuses, when seen as being interpersonally constructed and negotiated throughout the conference.

The influence these phenomena have on teacher reflection and growth is still unresolved at this point.

One implication of this study is readily apparent. 'Collegial' relations between supervisor and teacher are highly problematic, though perhaps not impossible. Supervisors who take the lead in the presentation and analysis of observational data severely limit the teacher's potential for participation, reflection and growth. This is a reflection of the technical control other authors have discussed (Retallick 1986; St Maurice 1987). This interpretation seems to lend support both to Smyth's (1991a) position that a power differential is endemic to supervisor–teacher relations and to Retallick's (1990) view that such differences are reproduced in conference discourse. Though it would seem that there is a propensity for such unbalanced power relationships, that such is often the case, I suggest that it *does not have to be so*; it is much more complicated than these authors suggest. I have shown that teachers have resources with which they may counteract a supervisor's hegemony. (These points will be discussed at length in Chapters 3 and 4.) Supervisors themselves do not always baldly exert control in face-to-face encounters with teachers; the interactions of Kendra with Kari, and Vern with Ed support this contention. Variables other than power also affect the processes and outcomes of supervisory conferences.

Glickman (1990) has written of supervisory behaviors as being non-directive, collaborative, directive-informational or directive-control. What is clear from this study is that the most uncommon of these behaviors is the non-directive supervisory behavior, possibly because is the most difficult to practice – even given the best of supervisor intentions. It also seems difficult to achieve a truly collaborative conference or relationship. Complications arise from the structures of 'normal' conferences and the behaviors that result from the participants' role perceptions and expectations. In order to effect a change in conferences and thereby teacher participation and reflection, it would be necessary for practitioners of supervision to be aware of these phenomena so that they might counteract their negative effects. Supervisors interested in accentuating their own non-directive or collaborative behaviors would do well to practice them in supervision classes and in the field. This would be facilitated if professors of supervision encouraged extended practice of these behaviors and reflection on them in class, even before their students meet their first teacher face to face. This alone would necessitate professors reconstructing their own roles and values concerning the relation of 'intellectual knowledge' and 'practical knowledge'.

Though I have discussed how data were used in conference, I have not addressed what role data *should* play. What are the alternatives? To this question, I have no ready answer. I would like to suggest that answers to this and related questions may be sought in the orientations of the participants to supervision, especially that of the supervisor. How supervisors conceive of their role will determine to what extent they perceive themselves to be arms of the organization or, when organizational and individual goals are incongruent, to what extent they are concerned with fostering, or empowering, individual teachers' growth apart from, or in opposition to, organizational goals. Agenda and data play a strong role here. Supervisors would do well to consider these questions seriously.

For both supervision practitioners and theorists these questions could be addressed through further qualitative, constructivist research, research in which supervisors and teachers take part. Such efforts would imbue the contexts of supervision with norms that favor learning on the part of all the schools' participants – students, teachers, supervisors and quite possibly administrators. It would resurrect supervision as it was envisioned by Cogan and Goldhammer, and likely resolve the criticisms of current practice as voiced by authors such as Garman, Retallick, Smyth and myself.

As has been shown in this chapter, and perhaps confirming uninformed assumptions, supervisors influence the trajectory of supervisory conferences. As will be shown in the next two chapters, however, this is only half the story. The next two chapters detail how it is that teachers come to influence (i.e. to exert control on) conferences also.

Notes

1 Notable departures from the received paradigm include Garman (1990), Holland (1990), and McCoombe (1984).
2 I imagine that such a view makes conference research much more manageable.
3 Please refer to the Appendix for complete conference transcripts. I employ the original line numbers in the transcript fragments I extract for discussion and illustration. This should allow the interested reader the opportunity to refer to the complete transcript and thereby gain more of the context and overall sense of the trajectory of the conference.
4 Further discussion of conference phases is found in Waite (1990/91).
5 From my observations I have come to believe that this chronological reporting of the data is a result of the type of observation instrument used and the data gathered. When supervisors used a techinque such as script-taping (Hunter 1983) or selective verbatim (Acheson and Gall 1992), in fact *any* instrument that collected data in such a linear fashion as a time line, the conference usually proceeded linearly as well. Such linear reporting may serve to disenfranchise a teacher, as will be shown shortly.
6 This conference between Faye and Bea is fully examined in Chapter 4, where the interpretation given is that it is an exemplar of teacher resistance.
7 Ramifications of supervisory control of topics – even though conferences are co-constructed – and the stifling of teachers' voices is discussed in Chapter 6, and represented schematically in Figure 6.1.
8 This is one reason I advise my supervision students to try not to begin with a question – especially one calling for a global assessment – as an opening gambit, because it really just delays the eventual. Ron and Susane Scollon (1986) encourage one to give information, if at all possible, in place of asking questions, because questions do a lot more interactional work than just obtaining information. Questions establish relationships – some power-laden – and can carry implied (or inferred) criticism, and so on. Besides, if a supervisor pauses adequately and appropriately after giving his or her information, the teacher can respond to the information if she or he wants, in a way she or he wants, and is much less encumbered than when the teacher answers a question.
9 Here I must beg the reader's indulgence, as there is no similar phenomenon in English other than that presented to make my case. Older dialect forms of English, of course, employed 'thou' and 'thee' to make such distinctions.
10 The alert reader will have noticed that Vern had been heavily trained in the Madeline Hunter model of teaching and supervision, hence such terms as 'bird walk', and his explicit attempt to praise Ed for those things he felt he had done well.

11   Recall that Doug was a relatively recent Vietnamese immigrant and Ed was a Chinese-Hawaiian, that is, a second or third generation US citizen.

12   Fairclough (1989: 15) wrote that the 'use of "we" can be manipulative; it can claim a spurious solidarity, for instance when a politician uses it to convince people that she is "one of them"'. Though this is a distinct possibility, and one of which supervisors should be aware, my interpretation of this corpus did not support such a conclusion and I would be irresponsible if I were to allege that these supervisors were so motivated.

Chapter 3

Teachers in Conference

The previous chapters have hinted at the voluminous nature of the literature of instructional supervision. What those chapters did not show, however, is how most, if not all, of this literature is theoretical, prescriptive, or both. Other than the occasional doctoral dissertation, supervision has not had the benefit of much inductive, empirical research of its lived, phenomenological processes. What little research done to date on the interactive processes of supervision, particularly the supervisory conference, has relied upon a priori coding schemes and categories (e.g. Weller 1971; Blumberg 1980). Often such protocols are simply adaptations of classroom observation instruments, not specifically designed for supervisory conferences (Zeichner and Liston 1985: 157). Other research on interactive supervisory conference processes examines either actors' simulations (e.g. Pajak and Glickman 1989) or commercially-produced training videos (e.g. Rivers 1989).

Weller's (1971) early call for research on the processes of supervision has been echoed by others (Zeichner and Liston 1985; Holland, 1989; Pajak and Glickman 1989). Zeichner and Liston state, for example:

> Given the ascribed importance of supervisory conferences to the processes of formal teacher education, one finds it ironic that so little attention has been given to understanding the quality of what transpires during these encounters . . . [T]he amount of resources which are typically allocated to the conduct of supervision . . . necessitates a closer examination of the use of these resources. (1985: 171)

Holland (1989) and Pajak and Glickman (1989) are quite specific in defining the needs for inquiry in the field of supervision. Holland calls for 'qualitative methods such as discourse analysis to explore the interpretive aspects of the supervisory conference', suggesting that such methods could provide 'a new understanding of a dimension of conferencing often cited in the theoretical literature but as yet not researched in any thorough, systematic way' (1989: 378). In light of their research using simulated supervisory conferences, Pajak and Glickman (1989: 103) conclude that '[e]thnographic studies of teacher–supervisor interactions in actual school settings would be very enlightening'.

Although such attention to supervision and supervisory conferences has shown a noticeable increase (e.g. Smyth 1984, 1991b; Holland 1990; Retallick

1990; Waite 1990/1991, 1992b, 1992c) efforts aimed at understanding supervision and supervisory conferences have given little attention to the role *teachers* play in the process. Notable exceptions include the work of Zeichner and Liston (1985), Zeichner and Tabachnick (1985) and McCoombe's (1984) teacher's view of clinical supervision. However, while these studies contribute to our overall understanding of supervision, it is my contention that these studies are lacking in certain important aspects. Zeichner and Liston's study aggregates teachers' data for statistical analysis and, by definition, cannot portray any one case in depth. The work of Zeichner and Tabachnick presents a more 'macro',[1] or coarse-grained, understanding of teachers' attitudes, strategies, perceptions and their relative change or stability over time, neglecting the 'micro', fine-grained interactional particulars of how those processes come about or are instantiated. The same can be said of McCoombe's study, where his subjective recollections generally gloss the more 'micro', or interactive, processes required for a close examination of supervisor–teacher interaction.

As implied above, 'coarse-grained' or 'macro', studies and analyses represent only half the picture. Therefore rather than seeking to replace 'coarse-grained' research, the studies reported in this volume, and studies like them in the 'fine-grained' mode, complement such research (Erickson 1992). Close examination of the *interactive processes* between teacher and supervisor ought to yield a fuller understanding of supervision and teachers' roles in the process. Studies of this type ought to inform our understanding, design and implementation of programs of supervision, mentoring and peer coaching. Such projects are especially timely in this, the era of educational reform. An understanding of how supervision is interactionally achieved should empower those involved to change what they feel needs to be changed and keep that which is worth keeping in the supervision of teachers. As the literature of teacher socialization is replete with studies of first-year teachers (e.g. Edgar and Warren 1969; Hoy and Rees 1977; Lacey 1977; Zeichner and Tabachnick 1985; Etheridge 1989), perhaps it is not too much to expect that studies of the type reported here might also inform our notions of that critical phase in teachers' work lives. Though generalization is always problematic from studies such as these, there is reason to believe that the reader may find that much of what is discussed here has relevance for his or her practice and situation (Firestone 1993).

The discussion in this chapter draws on data from a larger study (Waite 1990/1991) that investigated how participants in the supervisory process, teachers *and* supervisors, view and enact supervision. The participants in this study include those same three supervisors introduced in Chapter 2, and those same beginning teachers.

Fieldwork

To understand what it means to 'do supervision' – and to understand each participant's part in and perception of the process – I held three interviews with each supervisor and shadowed them as they interacted with teachers. Informal ethnographic interviews (Agar 1980) were held with the teachers involved. Only the interviews with Ed were taperecorded and transcribed, the others were recorded in fieldnote form.

The observation techniques I used ranged from non-participant observation (while in the schools) to participant observation (while in university environs). I accompanied each supervisor on at least one classroom visit and met with the teachers at their schools, in their district seminars and/or during the monthly, day-long total university program seminars, which were often held at the participating schools.

In total, five teacher–supervisor conferences were recorded, transcribed and analyzed. These conferences are the same that informed the analysis in the preceding chapter (and which can be found in their entirety in the Appendix). Conference tapes were transcribed using a conversation analysis transcript notation protocol (see Figure 2.1), excerpts of which will provide the basis of the discussion to follow. The observations and the interviews (both formal and informal) will be treated as secondary material – meant to explicate understanding of the conference talk. The transcription process, and the close examination of the conversational processes it captured and later revealed, added a dimension to my understanding of supervisory conferences which would have been unavailable through casual observation, interviewing and reflection.

General Conference Characteristics

I distinguish three types of teachers' roles that occurred in supervisory conferences: passive, collaborative and adversarial.[2] By this, I do not wish to be taken to mean that teachers steadfastly held to a particular role exclusively throughout their conference. In fact, most of the teachers studied exhibited characteristics of each of these roles at various times during conferences. 'Role', in the sense I use it here, is a more holistic representation, a gestalt, meant to characterize the *general* nature of the teacher's behaviors in the conference when taken as a whole.

Previous researchers of teacher socialization (Lacey 1977; Zeichner and Tabachnick 1985) have identified the teacher social strategies of internalized adjustment, strategic compliance and strategic redefinition. Zeichner and Tabachnick made a distinction between successful and unsuccessful strategic redefinition strategies. The teacher conference roles identified in the present study are roughly equivalent to those cited above, but with some minor qualifications.

Generally speaking, the social strategy of internalized adjustment corresponds with the passive teacher conference role. As will be shown in the following discussion, the passive conference role correlates with a relatively strong supervisory agenda, and with the teacher enacting this role offering little or no resistance. Rather, he or she accepts both the supervisor's authority and suggestions, attempting to align his or her teaching with the supervisor's beliefs.

The collaborative teacher conference role, as envisioned here, includes both the strategies of strategic compliance *and* that of *successful* strategic redefinition. As will be shown, the collaborative conference role correlates with a much weaker supervisory agenda and allows the teachers enacting this conference role more determination in deciding to which of the supervisor's interpretations and suggestions they respond and how they do so. If the teacher only appears to accept the supervisor and her or his suggestions this qualifies as Lacey's (1977) strategic compliance. If the teacher is actually able to effect changes in the situation or the supervisor's understanding of the situation this qualifies as strategic redefinition in Lacey's terms or successful strategic redefinition in Zeichner and Tabachnick's (1985).

The social strategy of unsuccessful strategic redefinition parallels the adversarial teacher conference role. When both teacher and supervisor bring strong agendas to the conference and the teacher does not capitulate, the teacher may enact the adversarial conference role as described below in detail. (This particular 'role' will be treated to an alternative interpretation in Chapter 4 and examined there as a form of teacher resistance.)

In order to understand teachers' roles as conference participants one must have an understanding of the structure of the typical conference, that is, a conference's participant structures (Phillips 1972). One form of such participant structures, though perhaps not the only one, is the conference phase. Chapter 2 includes a thorough discussion of three conference phases: the supervisor's report phase, the teacher's response phase and the programmatic phase. Conference participants interactionally construct these important contexts of/for their interaction, and being interactionally constructed, the conference phases reflexively influence participants' actions.

Teachers and Their Conference Roles

Doug, Enacting a Passive Conference Role

Generally, Doug's role was that of a passive participant in his conferences with Vern. This conference role would be consistent with Lacey's (1977) teacher social strategy of internalized adjustment, where the teacher accepts the authority figure's definition of the situation. Doug tended to accept what his supervisor said during the report phase with acknowledgment but without much other comment. This was true even when the supervisor criticized his teaching in either a direct or an indirect manner. The teacher's remarks from the following conference segment are evidence of this behavior (lines 150, 155, 157, 162, 169 and 180):

Transcript Fragment 3.1

142	Vern:	·h *um – but – once* ^again – if you were
143		*going* to *have* them *up there*, you *might've* –
144		>*taken* a more< *proactive role* in *seating*
145		them. (0.8) *I* don't *know* if y- a *boy* ^*girl*
146		*boy* ^*girl pat*^*tern'* II be *better*, or the
147		*ones* who you *know* are going to interact
148		^*here* – ·h *you* do *that*. It's like a *seating*
149		ˏchart=
150	Doug:	=um hum um ₗhum yeah
151	Vern:	you knˡow? *AN:D* – u:m – u:m
152		(1.0) *I*^: *did it* with *ninth graders* – *so* the
153		*likelihood* that you'd *have* to do *it* with
154		*first graders* – *would* be *great*.
155	Doug:	um hum
156	Vern:	OK?
157	Doug:	yeah – *that* would be a *good* ^*idea* hhh
158	Vern:	*WHAT* – *WHATCHU NEE*^*::D* is to ˏ*expand* the
159		*repertoire* – of *skills* – *that you* can ^*use* –
160		to – *ensure classroom management.* And
161		ₗwhatchu *h*₎ *ad* going on: – *up* ^*front* – was
162	Doug:	um hum
163	Vern:	less than *productive* classroom *management* –
164		because there *were* – a *number* of *times* –
165		>*you had* to go< – *T:im* (0.8) >you know< –
166		*Zack.* – um: m-m-m >you know< *what*^*ever* the
167		*names* ˏ*were* :: – or wha- *whatever* u- w-
168		yoₗu *ha d* to go o::n with
169	Doug:	um: ˡ
170	Vern:	*that* – a few *times* ·h *so that* w- would *be* of
171		*something* – you *really* need *to* focus *on.* h
172		the *second thing* – *that* – I would *mention*
173		*here* is is (3.0) °*and in* an art *lesson* – I
174		might *add* there- – there *isn't* – an *easy way*
175		of *doing* this, ·h – b:ut it's *something* for
176		you to *think* about.° (0.8) U::M (2.3) THE
177		*OL::D* >we've *talked* about *this* bef:ore< the
178		^*ol::d* (0.7) *never* give *more* than *three*
179		directions to k- *anybody* at *one time*=
180	Doug:	=um hum=

This was the teacher's behavior exhibited during the supervisor's report phase. Even when the ownership of a conference phase shifted to the teacher – during the teacher response phase or the programmatic phase, for instance – Doug remained passive. He did respond to the issues or topics raised by Vern, but never in a collaborative or adversarial manner (compare this teacher's behavior with those to follow).

The following fragment is taken from the beginning of this teacher's first response phase. Note Doug's responses in Transcript Fragment 3.2 at lines 592 and 594. Vern, the supervisor, took the floor from Doug (lines 588–91) with raised voice and by talking through Doug's simultaneous utterances, in effect, competing with Doug for the floor and employing the two escalation techniques noted above. The combination of these floor-gaining techniques along with the differential supervisor status or power are too much for Doug in this instance. Vern then uses his control of the floor to issue a negative evaluation of Doug's teaching and provides alternatives for how the teacher might have taught the lesson. This brings that particular teacher response phase to a close. Doug lapses back into an acknowledging mode, conceding the floor to the supervisor who initiates another supervisor report phase. The teacher then punctuates the supervisor's comments with 'uh huh's.

Transcript Fragment 3.2

564		(1.7)
565	*Doug:*	₁uh I see *i*₁ *t* as s-s- *yeah*, we've been *using*
566	*Vern:*	other-
567	*Doug:*	them (0.6) some *kind* of *a- – left* it *off*
568		right *now* but *we've* been *using* the a-
569		*beanstalk* – about *Jack* and the *b*₁*eanstalk*
570	*Vern:*	OH, OK¹ I
571		*didn't –* I *didn't* see ₁that
572	*Doug:*	and *th*¹*ey –* are *there*
573		for the (0.3) *behavior.=*
574	*Vern:*	=uh huh
575	*Doug:*	and *it's* ^been – been ˄*working:* (0.6) ˄*kind*
576		of ^*well* – I think *it's* the *last – week –*
577		*some* of them *had –* for *those who –* climb up
578		the *air* on the *castle –* ₁*they* ( )
579	*Vern:*	OH – I *DID –* I¹ did
580		*notice* that *last* time I was ˄*in,=*
581	*Doug:*	=uh huh yeah so *they* a- – *they – they* had
582		*lunch* with *me.* Also so *I – they* have *some –*
583		^*cou*˄*pons – trading* for – *thing* and fo::r –
584		*good* things an- ·h ₁*and* they work *well,* but
585	*Vern:*	an- ¹
586	*Doug:*	*today* I didn't use *it* much
587		ye₁ah right *not* a s *much* as I-
588	*Vern:*	hh yeah I ^*see*¹ SO – *THERE*
589		WAS ^*A* ·h *THERE* ₁WAS A ^*TRI CKT* – you *had* in
590	*Doug:*	I thought ¹
591	*Vern:*	your ˄*bag –* that you *didn't* pull *ou:t.*

592 *Doug*: ₁uh huh
593 *Vern*:   *Maybe* ¹ you *could've* – at *times*.
594 *Doug*: uh huh

Particularly relevant to the issue under discussion are lines 588 and 589, 591 and 593 of Transcript Fragment 3.2. These data illustrate how the supervisor, Vern, reworked Doug's assertion that he had been using behavior management techniques to good effect ('it's been working kind of well', lines 575 and 576, 'and they work well', line 584). Vern reinterpreted the teacher's remarks. He stressed that Doug did have 'tricks' at his disposal, that he didn't use them, but that he could have. Note how forcefully Vern asserted his interpretation – shown by raised voice (lines 588 and 589). A rationale for attributing passivity to this teacher's conference behavior comes from a synthesis of the ethnographic and conversational data (see below). One of the outcomes of this conference was that the supervisor was able to define this teacher as a novice, and the teacher did not refute that notion successfully; the supervisor's definition became the accepted definition.

In his conference with Doug, Vern worked to establish his definition of the situation. He continually compared Doug with his supervising teacher, Lynne, and insisted that Doug needed more behavior management 'tricks' in his repertoire.

Transcript Fragment 3.3

435 *Vern*: so *THAT*'s (0.6) >*you* know *where* you're gonna
436   go< (0.4) >*one* of the *things* I just
437   *mentioned* to< *Lynne*: – is to *WORK* with *you* –
438   on *expanding* that *bag* of *refinement* and
439   *organizational* t- (0.7) tr:*icks*: – or
440   *tech*ₐ*niques*, ·h u-um you *used to*ₐ*day*, a

Or later:

Transcript Fragment 3.4

533 *Vern*: *everybody* has their: *tricks*, they're
534   ₐcalled behavior *modi*₁*fi*^*cation* ^*tri cks* –
535 *Doug*:   um hum um hum¹
536 *Vern*: and mister *O'Riley's* ₐnot ^real ^*big* ^on
537   ^*them* but – you know if if – *that's* ^what's
538   gonna ^*work* – in *those* situations, *that* ^ *is*:
539   – to *help* you *expand* that *bag* of *tricks*.
540 *Doug*: um hum
541 *Vern*: *Lynne* has a *very* small *bag* of *tricks* she
542   *uses* 'cause *she* doesn't *need* to *use* ^many.
543   ·h *Newer* teachers – *have* to have a *bigger*
544   *bag* of *tricks*, – and *unfortunately* they
545   *often* don't *have* ₐit – and *Lynne's* the *one*
546   that ^*has* ₐ*it* but you *never* see ₐ*it*.

```
547   Doug:   um hum ⌐um hum
548   Vern:              >becaus ⌐e she doesn't have to pull
549           it out< ·h but the uh- >newer teachers don't
550           have it but they're the ones who need it
551           because y- you're still< (0.5) trying to
552           (0.5) play around and get that right match:
553           for ˰you,
554   Doug:   °um hum°=
555   Vern:   =with the − kids − so that it mo:ves − as
556           smoothly and as quickly as it does, − as it
557           would when °you're a seventh or tenth year
558           teacher°=
559   Doug:   =uh huh − yeah (1.2) °um°
560   Vern:   I was out on-n one of my lecture: − ty- s- s-
561           things, (seems we) haven't done so much of a
562           discussion. Di- I- − you- are there
563           anything?
564           (1.7)
```

The above portion of the conference transcript reveals a number of moves relevant to the present discussion. Here the supervisor explained what he felt to be a difference in the management needs of beginning and experienced teachers. He implied that Doug was such a teacher (lines 549–53) and therefore in need of an expanded 'bag of tricks' – that is, that those he did have and demonstrated were inadequate. Illustrative of this move is the pronominal shift Vern employs, from talk about newer teachers, 'they', to Doug, 'you' (lines 550–1).

This conference transcript portion ends with Vern's meta-linguistic analysis of the tenor of the conference, and a question that served to close the supervisor report phase and begin the teacher response phase. Doug then responded to Vern's assertions by mentioning those 'behavior management tricks' he had, in fact, used and his estimation of their success. A teacher response phase, where Doug responded to Vern's assertions and evaluations, was interjected between the end of the previous segment (Transcript Fragment 3.2) and the beginning of the following:

Transcript Fragment 3.5
```
595   Vern:   you did towards the en::d − once − ˰quiet
596           them ˰dow:n, and say: − >you know< −
597           something >you looked at the clock< you
598           ^looked impatient, I mean you ^looked −
599           frustrated, and then ·h >you know< you said
600           − a − made some comment that we weren't- −
601           you weren't going to mo- ^go ^anyplace 'til
602           they had don::e this, so- I don't know how
```

603		you *put it* but ·h *but* >you know< and *then*
604		that *quiet*⌐ed 'em for a *second.* ·h AND
605	*Doug:*	°um hum°⌐
606	*Vern:*	YOU ALSO *dismissed* 'em *back*- – by ^*rows*
607		again, (0.2) *to-day* – >you know< you w-were
608		*working* on *things* like m-m- *smoother*
609		^ *move-ment* °from one *place* to *another*
610		so ⌐: *those* were so *me*°
611	*Doug:*	um hum um hum⌐
612		(1.8)
613	*Doug:*	yeah – *basically* they – ^they ^*do* – tend to
614		*responds-* uh – *respond* to *me* – *more* (0.9)
615		°kind of uh – *immediately* an-°
616	*Vern:*	um hum
617	*Doug:*	*more* effectively than *before* – °*because* of
618		uh they just *before* sometime *just*- – *they*
619		*just keep-*° – *kept talking* an-
620	*Vern:*	yeah
621	*Doug:*	°while I was-° – ·h *but now* when they're
622		*asked* for their *attention* (t- it the-) – um-
623		*most* of *them* will give *it* right – just
624		like *that.* (0.7) So *I* can see *that* – or I
625		can *pro:ve* that. *I'm still* working on *it.*
626		hhh ((laughs)) You *see* it *again.* I don't
627		know ^*how* -*well* – I try to s:*ee* how *well*
628		they can – *hear me* – *back* there (0.3) just
629		because *they-* – *they* chose *not* to *respond* or
630		*because* they didn't *hear me* – °very well –
631		(most impor⌐tant to my-)°
632	*Vern:*	*now you're*⌐ *talking* about back
633		*where?*
634	*Doug:*	I mean *whenever* I say (0.5) in *their:* – *at*
635		their *chair* – at their *seat* or (0.8)
636	*Vern:*	·h ⌐THEY COULD- ^*TH: EY* CAN HEAR -YOU.
637	*Doug:*	on the (counter) ⌐
638		(0.5)
639	*Vern:*	°⌐yeah° ·h *I* don't *think* – *hearing's:*
640	*Doug:*	yeah ⌐
641		that hh – yeah
642	*Vern:*	an *issue. Unless* there's- – would (*it*) be *a*
643		*lot* of *other* -*noise* around=
644	*Doug:*	=um hum

The lengths of the various turns at the floor throughout the exchange cited (Transcript Fragments 3.2 and 3.5) are also indicative of the roles enacted by teacher and supervisor, and their relations. The teacher's turns were considerably longer at the beginning, until the supervisor made his assertion/evaluation. What may be seen as an attempt at praising the teacher begins at line 595 and continues through line 610. The teacher resumed his acknowledging posture for these supervisor turns at the floor. Basically, the supervisor's evaluation stands as stated to this point.

What follows is a pause of 1.8 seconds (line 612), which marked the boundary of the previous supervisor report. Doug resumed his response, again attempting to build the case for the effectiveness of his classroom management strategies. He stated this relatively forcefully at lines 624 and 625 with 'so I can see that or I can prove that'.

However, Vern, the supervisor, retrieved and asked a question for clarification about something Doug had made passing mention of – whether the children couldn't hear him or simply chose not to respond. By posing a question in eliciting the clarification (lines 632 and 633), Vern effectively shifted the topic to the students' ability to hear. He chose what to retrieve from the prior teacher turn, and posing it as a question made an answer situationally relevant (Sacks *et al.* 1978). Responding in this way, the supervisor did not address again the issue of the effectiveness of the teacher's classroom management. Doug's passivity, in this instance, allowed the supervisor's definition of him as a novice in need of an expanded repertoire of behavior management 'tricks' to stand.

Even in the programmatic phase, the second phase to which I have ascribed teacher ownership, Doug remained passive. (The boundary marking the end of the previous phase and the beginning of the programmatic phase is Doug's 'uh huh, good', Transcript Fragment 3.6, line 693, followed by Vern's 'so', line 692, preceding a 2.7 second pause.) It is notable that in the beginning of this phase Doug actually turned the floor over to Vern, the supervisor, with a question (line 695), to which Vern responded with programmatic information; other 'safe' topics were brought up and discussed, including that night's mock interviews for Vern's group of teachers and Doug's summer graduate registration.

Transcript Fragment 3.6

680	*Vern:*	=₁*obviously* ·h *and so:* – *when* you *have* a:
681	*Doug:*	that's true¹
682	*Vern:*	series of ^*instruc*₋*tions*, if you – >*break* it
683		in *pieces*< then you *have active*
684		participation in *between those* pieces, –
685		*there's* two ^*ways* of getting *kids* actively
686		*in*VOL₁*VED* >*one*'s to< ·h *be* – *fore*
687	*Doug:*	uh huh
688	*Vern:*	((sound of paper rustling)) *all* discussion,
689		*turn* to your *neigh*₋*bor share* with your
690		*neigh*₋*bor*, – *say* it in *unison*. ·h >*That* type

```
691              of thing.< The other is that –
692              manipula₍tive part        °so°
693   Doug:                   uh huh gˡood      uh huh
694              (2.7)
695   Doug      ^O₌K – is the₍re anyth ing? (0.9)
696   Vern:                   °okay?° ⌐            I ^don't
697              think ₌SO. I- I ·h I know that – um – ^I:
698              just having a: – little bit of a discussion
699              the other ₌day: – with He₌len: – and Lyn₌ne:
700              – an::d – ₌Molly – an:d ^KE:N – all met
701              (0.3) and I think what they – ta:lked about
702              and arranged was fer: – between now and the
703              – end o' the ^year: – and – I – think – that
704              >Lynne probably< shared with you (0.2) what-
705              – they're going to do is – >she's coming in
706              NOW< to teach the LOGO part,
707   Doug:     uh huh
```

Doug's passive conference role behavior may be due, in large part, to his biography. The fact that he had only recently immigrated to the US from Vietnam meant that he was still adjusting to American culture and language, as should be obvious from a close reading of the transcripts. Bourdieu's (1986: 243) concept of cultural capital effectively explains Doug's predicament, especially the form of such capital which Bourdieu believes exists in the embodied state:

> The accumulation of cultural capital in the embodied state . . . which, insofar as it implies a labor of inculcation and assimilation, costs time, time which must be invested personally by the investor (1986: 244).

Doug was at a loss as to how to advance his interests assertively. Compared with the other teachers discussed in this report, Doug had fewer culturally-appropriate conversational strategies by which he may have made his case – constellations of which Hymes (1972: xxxvi) refers to as communicative competence. Also, Doug was an immigrant, in Bauman's (1988/89) terms, 'a stranger', and as such had little capital upon which to draw in this situation, be it economic, social or cultural capital. As Bauman points out, there are few repercussions for sanctioning a stranger. He or she has fewer resources upon which to draw in his or her defense. Doug could not appeal to higher-ups nor assert any other pressure on his supervisor. When Vern started to hear parents' complaints about Doug's appropriateness as a model for their first graders, this, coupled with his concerns as a personnel officer about the costs and benefits of working with Doug intensively for at least another year before his skills were acceptable led to the decision not to renew Doug's contract. The cultural capital Doug did have was not prized in this situation; it was not prized by his first-grade students (he didn't have the 'appropriate' behavior modification tricks to get them to respond to him), nor by his supervising teacher, nor by his students' parents, and, finally, his cultural capital was not valued by his supervisor. He was let go.

The irony here is that Doug was more than willing to incorporate Vern's suggestions. He simply could not progress far enough fast enough to suit the supervisor and his constituents. This raises serious questions for supervision.

Kari and Ed, Enacting Collaborative Conference Roles

Both Kari and Ed were highly collaborative in their conferences with their respective supervisors, Kendra and Vern. At the beginning of her post-observation conference, Kari demonstrated acceptance of Kendra's role (note lines 3 and 6) during the supervisor's report phase:

Transcript Fragment 3.7
```
1  Kendra:  I just took ˄down ˄all kinds of stuff ˄here
2           ((excited voice))    (0.3) u:ɾ:m
3  Kari:                               okˡay
4  Kendra:  I first I started doing a little break˄down
5           of ti:me – for ˄you.
6  Kari:    °um ˄hum°
```

In line 1 above, Kendra reports that she has taken 'all kinds' of data and Kari demonstrates her positive orientation to that fact (line 3), implying she accepts it as Kendra's role to report upon the lesson. Also, after Kendra reports how she had gathered the data (line 4 and 5), Kari's use of an acknowledgment token in her next turn may be seen as meant to encourage Kendra to continue. The fact that Kari assented to how Kendra enacted her role suggests that, for these two, their conference roles and role expectations of the other were unproblematic.

An example of the extraordinary collaboration exhibited between Kari and Kendra followed (note lines 26 and 27):

Transcript Fragment 3.8
```
11          (3.4)
12  Kendra:  then – when you got into your ˄dis˄cussion
13           (0.5) I started ˄counting the – different –
14           stu˄dents >look at ˄this:< (1.0) five >ten
15           fifteen twenty< twenty five – twenty se˄ven
16           – you called on – twₗenty    s even (0.2)
17  Kari:                          >˄good<ˡ
18  Kendra:  different kids
19  Kari:    just about – ˄every˄body
```

```
20   Kendra:   that's ˏjust ^about ˏevery^body >except for
21             the ˏones that wouldn't 'ave ₁respon ded
22   Kari:                             >great<ˡ
23   Kendra:   ˏanyway I mean< ·hh you took a ^little
24             str.etch – break (0.8) um (0.4) HOW DIDCHU
25             FEEL about the – discus˄sion – ^af˄ter –
26             the (0.2) ₁stretch ^break
27   Kari:                   stretch ^breakˡ
28             (1.2)
```

Here Kari supplied the proper term to end Kendra's turn (note that the voicing
is exactly the same). This shows Kari's orientation to the construction of the
turn and its trajectory, and results from her active listening. Though Kendra
had mentioned the term 'stretch break' previously (line 24), the fact that Kari
can supply the same term, at the same time, and in exactly the same intonation
demonstrates both a remarkable collaboration and, quite possibly, a shared
orientation to the stretch break as a trouble spot in the lesson.

Kari also demonstrated that she shared an orientation with her supervisor
on each other's observation and conference rights, responsibilities and roles at
other times in their conferences (Waite 1990/1991). Note, however, that it was
Kari who terminated both their pre-observation and post-observation conferences. She did this by addressing her remarks to students entering the classroom, terminating her teacher's response phase:

Transcript Fragment 3.9 (from pre-observation conference)

```
38             (0.8)
39   Kari:     and so these are just some some uh ^these
40             are my ^brain˄storm^ing
41             ques₁˄tions that  ₁I've-
42   Kendra:            sure ˡ   s ure ˡ
43   Kari:     ^hey: WELCOME TO CLASS – BUDDY ((to student
44             entering)) (2.1) ((breathy, quiet laugh))
```

and

Transcript Fragment 3.10 (from post-observation conference)

```
222  Kari:     um hum
223  Kendra:   >it was like< just ^be˄cause there're only
224            ˏeight ^days of school ˏleft:
225  Kari:     ˏum ^hum
226  Kendra:   I still expect you to ₁lis^ten    ˏan-
227  Kari:                       oh ^yeahˡ            ^oh
228            ^yeah WE'RE PUS₁HING TH IS ^STORY TO THE
229  Kendra:                    attend    ˡ
```

230 *Kari*:   *LA:S₁:T: ^ WE:DNES:↗DAY:*
231 *Kendra*:   >YOU'RE GONNA GET< *THIS* WEDNES|DAY?
232 *Kari*:   ((laughs))
233   ((student in background: Oh ↗No))
234 *Kendra*:   anyways . . . ((the conference soon ends))

Neither of Kari's conferences had a programmatic phase. Such an absence may be due to the time constraints occasioned by holding her conferences between the classes of her middle school schedule, because she saw no need for a programmatic discussion, or because students exerted more influence on her in this situation than her supervisor did.

The same remarkable degree of collaboration shown between Kari and Kendra was evident with Ed and his supervisor, Vern (who was also Doug's supervisor). Evidence of such collaboration comes from near the end of their conference transcript, when Ed and Vern have included me in their talk and have begun recounting Ed's early days with the program:

Transcript Fragment 3.11

1065 *Vern*: and – and you *do:* – I mean *you* – *really*
1066   (0.2) I *remember* when you *first* came in *last*
1067   ↗*August*, last *fall* – or (when it stopped)
1068   *everything* – you know – it – was just-
1069   s₁hh shh
1070 *Ed*:   just *i*¹*t* ((laughs))
1071 *Vern*: and *we* would – *then* say – *mellow* – ^*OUT* –
1072   ↗Ed.
1073 *Ed*:   hhhh but I'm *still* like *that* – but not
1074   ₁as::
1075 *Vern*:   yeah¹
1076   (1.8)

This conference took place at the front of the classroom, while the fifth-grade students did seatwork. Note lines 1069 and 1070 above. Vern and Ed together collaborated in voicing the phrase 'just shit' – a phrase either would have been prohibited from voicing individually in such a setting. There was also much humor evident in both this conference and that between Kari and Kendra.

Other evidence of Ed's highly collaborative role enactment is reflected in the tactics he employed in providing candidate terms for the supervisor's talk – a repair strategy (see McHoul 1990, for discussion of repair and its place in classroom talk). This demonstrated a high degree of competence in attending behavior, or what Ed referred to as 'active listening' when speaking of a strategy he employed with his class. Writing of such phenomena, Goodwin and Heritage (1990: 294), relate how conversation analysis has revealed how:

recipients ['hearers'] can demonstrate their understanding of speakers' actions by participating in them with facial displays, head movements, intonation and even substantial comments of their own that overlap the continuing development of speakers' utterances. Speakers can then modify their emerging talk to take into account these listener displays . . . the placement of overlap can demonstrate precision tracking of the emerging course of an utterance.

At times, the terms Ed proposed were more technically correct than the supervisor's (as shown in the following segment of the supervisor's report phase, Transcript Fragment 3.12, line 613):

Transcript Fragment 3.12

603	*Vern:*	=er- uh- well *she – she* has *done* a lot of
604		*research* ˄on (0.2) *girls* – and uh w- e- and
605		– um partic- more ˄*teen*˄*age* ˄*girls* ·hh and
606		it's >particularly in the areas< of *math* and
607		*science* and *why* – they *fall* – *be*˄*hind*:
608		(0.2) in *math* and *science* ·hh and what uh-
609		two >two reasons< – *one* – *math* and- *science*
610		are generally ˄done in what you might *call*
611		for (0.6) >*quick* summary *purpose*< – *l::inear*
612		*way*₍:s
613	*Ed:*	>linear m⌐odalitie₍s<
614	*Vern:*	*modal⌐i-ties* and *boy:s*
615		– tend to *learn:* *-that* – *way* – *better* by the
616		time *they* – you know – *they* always *claim*
617		that ·h that boys're right *brained* – to – to
618		*left* brain. They're *right* brain when they're
619		*supposed* to be learning *reading* and- that's
620		why *they* fall *be*˄*hind*, because it's a *left*
621		brain *activity* ₍the *ba sic learning* process
622	*Ed:*	u h huh ⌐

The collaborative nature of the conference is highlighted by the fact that the supervisor accepted and incorporated the repair in his own talk (line 614).

Ed often employed this strategy to gain the floor (note line 238):

Transcript Fragment 3.13

231	*Vern:*	=and they're ˄*ad*˄*ded* – there's ˄*con*˄*fu*˄*sion* –
232		'cause *he* ˄*ga*˄ve *this* ˄*re*˄*spon*˄*se* – >but
233		there're< ˄*re*˄*spon*˄*ses* over ˄*here* – ˄so ˄*now*
234		·h >˄*ra*˄ther than just< *hav*˄ing – ˄*one*
235		˄*cor*˄rect *re*˄*spon*˄*se* – they ha˄ve ˄*to* sort
236		˄*out* the ˄ *incor*˄*rect* – °*from* the

237		*cor‸rec₁tº*
238	*Ed:*	>t‍ⁱ he *cor‸rect<* ·hh >and in< *st‸ill:*
239		∧mak‸ing *sure* that the ‸*lear‸ner* – ‸feels
240		that *they've* >‸con^tribu‸ted<
241		an₁d *not*
242	*Vern:*	(>you accept‍ⁱ him<) ºyeahº it's- ₁hh

This floor-gaining strategy is much less competitive than others that could be used (e.g. escalation by raised voice). It projects cooperation and collaboration in production of the talk. The flow of talk between these two also was characterized by rapid turn changes that were often achieved through *latching* (see Figure 2.1). Latching requires that listeners attend to the talk and project the completion of turns or other possible turn-transition points (Sacks *et al.* 1978; Goodwin and Heritage 1990) and time their own talk accordingly.

Both Kari and Ed displayed the communicative competence necessary to participate collaboratively in their conferences. They were able to advance their own positions without appearing to violate any norms of propriety. They neither confronted nor undermined their supervisor and his or her position. Granted, the supervisors in both cases viewed these two teachers as unproblematic. Both Kari and Ed were offered contracts for the following year.

Bea, Enacting an Adversarial Conference Role

Faye, Bea's supervisor, had shared with me her negative opinion of Bea as a teacher before I witnessed her teaching and their subsequent conference. This negative opinion and Bea's probable knowledge of it may have greatly influenced the nature of their conference. Bea used none of the tactics I have shown to be characteristic of either the passive or collaborative teacher conference roles.

Bea's conference was ripe with competition for the floor (note lines 71 and 78, from a supervisor's report phase of the conference):

Transcript Fragment 3.14

71	*Faye:*	*because* – ‸*no:* – I don't *see* this kinda
72		‸*scene.* – in the *real* ‸world. – *That* kinda
73		stuff ^*ne:‸ver:* happens – and *so* – *then* you
74		*write* – *no* – *right there* (0.4) AND *you* would
75		*expect* them ^*not* to *be* able to *finish* – the
76		‸*rest* – *because* – they've *never* seen any
77		₁such *thing* HAP ^*PEN* ₁in the *real*
78	*Bea:*	O-OK so th-‍ⁱ I see: ‍ⁱ
79	*Faye:*	‸*world.* – ‸O‸K *so* then – *what* are the
80		^*fee‸lings* of the *play‸ers?* – you should've
81		‸*ha:d* – *two:* – *feelings* (0.3) the ^*tea‸cher:*
82		– an:d – the – *stu‸dent.*

Or note lines 574 and 575, 578–581 below (taken from a transition between a supervisor's report phase and a teacher's response phase of the conference):

Transcript Fragment 3.15

573	*Bea:*	umkay
574	*Faye:*	i ₍s-
575	*Bea:*	>A¹ND YOU *KNOW* WHEN I ^*READ*< – ˏTHE – *the*
576		pacˏket thatchu *gave* us – *on* role *play*ˏ*ing,*
577		it was *con*ˏ*fu*^*sing* because *I* didn't –
578	*Faye:*	*it's* so *detail*₍*ed* that you- you'd go >^*on*
579	*Bea:*	ye¹ah:
580	*Faye:*	and ^*on* and ^*o*₍*n*<
581	*Bea:*	ye¹ah=

Seldom was Bea successful in her bids for the floor. Although the transcript fragment above (line 575) does show one such successful interruption, note that many different tactics were involved in its accomplishment. Both increased speed, as shown by the arrows, and raised voice, as shown by the capital letters, were used in combination to accomplish what could be construed as an interruption. Even then, a slight pause suggests that Bea stopped to check whether she had actually gained the floor before she proceeded.

In most other instances of simultaneous talk in this conference (and there were many) it was Faye who escalated and retained the floor. This strategy of the supervisor's was probably due, in part, to her opinion that whenever she mentioned a problem, Bea started 'arguing'. She felt she needed to work at keeping this teacher on task, something she did throughout the conference.

Experiencing little success in getting the floor to voice her opinions or concerns, Bea employed other tactics for her part in 'managing' her conference. Two of the tactics she used were having recourse to the (physical) context within which the conference occurred, and invoking tenets of teacher culture in her defense.

The external physical environment often became a conversationally relevant part of the conference for Bea and Faye. There was an electronic bell that sounded, a teacher who came by to borrow a stopwatch, and another teacher who knocked at her outside classroom door causing Bea to leave the conference to answer the knock. Bea, herself, made mention of her class outside at recess and her concern that they might not have the proper supervision.

Transcript Fragment 3.16

145		((Bea goes to window))
146	*Bea:*	=I'm jus- *concerned* that *my kids* are out
147		ˏ*there* ((at recess)) with no *supervi*₍*sion*
148	*Faye:*	OH::¹
149		*well* you'd *better* get out^*the*₍*re,* ˏ*then.*

```
150   Bea:                                        ^no¹        he's
151            still out ˅there – that's good (1.2) >just
152            let me ˅check and make ˅sure< – ^O˅K=
153   Faye:   =the – intent of this question – is: (0.8)
154            if: – you wer:e=
155   Bea:    =oh, I forgot to take
156            ₁my (                    )
157   Faye:   IF – YOU WERE ˅TAKING¹ – °a pen˅cil – at the
158            end° see what you're after ^here: – IS: –
159            THEM to th:ink
160   Bea:    UM HU:M=
```

Bea 'left' the conference momentarily. When she came back, Faye worked to retrieve another previous conference topic and to hold Bea to it (line 157). Bea did not mention this group again during the conference. It is interesting to speculate why she chose to mention her group just when she did.

Perhaps Bea had become uncomfortable with the trajectory of the conference. Just prior to Bea's mention of the group outside, Faye apologized for actually interrupting Bea's lesson and addressing her class. Such interruptions are particularly forceful violations of the norms of professional interaction between supervisor and teacher (Goldhammer 1969: 89; Waite 1990/1991, 1992c). Having committed such a violation, Faye apologized profusely (note lines 132–4 and 136, and Bea's reaction at lines 135 and 137).

Transcript Fragment 3.17

```
125   Bea:    =yeah – it does=
126   Faye:   =FIRST – PREDICT WHAt's gonna happen as a
127            result of this ˅scene – now when Dorothy did
128            ^hers, she predicted (0.2) another way, like
129            you did – and so that was the next ˅sc:ene.
130            – Well that kinda gotchu into ^trou˅ble –
131            when they – predicted – that they were gonna
132            punch ˅ou:t – and – I – could not (0.6)
133            °lis˅ten° – I tried to stay out of it, but I
134            ₁could NOT leave ˅it        ₁I could n ot
135   Bea:    OH I'M GLAD – you d¹id tha t's fine     ¹
136   Faye:   lea₁ve – that          because it – e:^volved so
137   Bea:          °that's fine°¹
138   Faye:   – naturally – that – >it got ˅worse<
139   Bea:    um hum um ₁hum               um ₁hum
140   Faye:                >th¹at it ^es˅calated< once¹
141            you use an ^escala˅tion: – whether it
142            involves t- I mean they were just ^thrilled
143            – because here's a scene they hadn't seen
144            ˅before=
```

```
145            ((Bea goes to window))
146    Bea:    =I'm jus- concerned that my kids are out
147            ˄there ((at recess)) with no supervi₁sion
148    Faye:                               OH::¹
149            well you'd better get out^the₁re,   ˄then.
150    Bea:                                ^no¹        he's
151            still out ˄there – that's good (1.2)
```

Bea tried unsuccessfully to close down the topic (lines 135 and 137) and, having failed in those attempts, 'left' the conference, mentioning the class outside. When she returned, she was rewarded. Faye retrieved another lesson-related topic for discussion rather than the topic of her interruption.

In a discussion of participants' roles in interviews, a face-to-face encounter not unlike supervisory conferences, Briggs (1986: 56) speaks of moves like Bea's as 'breaking the frame of the interview'. He states that this is 'the respondent's principal means of subverting' (p. 56) the interviewer's (or supervisor's) power or 'communicative hegemony' (p. 90). Bea's move may then be seen as a teacher resistance strategy.[3]

At another time, when Faye was probing Bea as to why she refused to include a particular boy, Cody, in her role-play lesson, Bea drew upon a tenet of teacher culture for her defense. Briefly stated, that tenet may read: The teacher knows the students best. In discussing the cultures of teaching, Feiman-Nemser and Floden (1986) mention the cellular organization of schools, the norms of non-interference, and those of individualism. They write, 'Some teachers resent the fact that the person responsible for judging their competence observes them infrequently and knows less than they do about what is going on in their room' (p. 517).

Bea's response to Faye's (implied) criticism for not including Cody in the role play took this form:

Transcript Fragment 3.18

```
336    Bea:    and the reason – I didn't call on him ˄today
337            is just because he's been totally off the
338            ˄wall: and so (0.6) ha:ving him up there –
339            participating >would've been a very bad<
340            ˄choice:. because – he would have – just
341            been (0.4) more obnoxious – than he was by
342            sitting back there – stac^king: – ˄books
343            around and doing the things that he's- ^IN
344            ˄FACT – he's been so bad throughout the
345            whole schoo:l – that – somebody said – if
346            Faye's coming to watch – to day you don't
347            wanna be sabotaged by Cody – >send him outta
348            the ˄room – and I didn't – do that
349    Faye:   do – uh – yet – but – some^ti:mes – his –
```

```
350              thorough – involvement in it
351              (0.9)
352   Bea:       well we tr⌐ied      ⌐al ⌐ready
353   Faye:                  cut⌐ ou ts⌐          the behavior. –
354              But you're saying that wouldn't work f⌐or
355   Bea:                                              it⌐
356   Faye:      ⌐(    )
357   Bea:       di dn't w-⌐ it hasn't worked so ⌐far: –
358              today – >an I'd< – 'cause I was really going
359              to ^use: ⌐him.
```

Note how Bea brought others to her aid (lines 345–8 and again at line 352). She stated that another teacher had suggested a ploy – removing Cody from the room during the observation – that she had refused to implement. She used the inclusive 'we' (line 352). Though she said 'we tried already', she never stated what it was that 'they' had tried; surely, it wasn't the boy's thorough involvement in the lesson. Bea asserted that her intention had been to use him in the lesson (lines 358 and 359) and implied that she would have, except for his behavior.

Faye retreated and acknowledged the teacher's belief (line 354) that it 'wouldn't work'. Still Faye pursued the topic. Bea then brought up another student, a girl, who also had wanted to participate in the role-play and whom Bea had not included; again she gave an account of the student's abhorrent behavior as her rationale. Faye continued probing and pursuing this notion of including the 'target kids'. Bea admitted she had been afraid to attempt it and, after this admission, Faye encouraged Bea to consider this strategy in the future (Transcript Fragment 3.19). Bea readily accepted this resolution.

Transcript Fragment 3.19
```
438   Faye:      can – pre⌐dic⌐t            ⌐so
439   Bea:                    I⌐ wish I ha⌐dn't – been – so –
440              afraid to do ⌐that – I wish I hadn't had
441   Faye:      we:ll – it isn't like this is gonna to go
442              a⌐way – you can try it again
443              so⌐meTIME   hhh
444   Bea:          oh   ye⌐s   >oh the thing is -s that<
445              they wa- – the kids an- and the kids – I
446              think they do wa^nna try it again, >I got
447              the feeling< they'd like to do: – try it
448              ^again,
```

They closed out that sensitive topic and the conference moved on.

Faye's agenda for the conference had been to keep Bea focused, something she achieved by working to control the turns at talk and the topics. Bea, though, influenced the flow of the conference through her introduction of contextual considerations (e.g. the class outside and her responsibility to them); through the activation of cultural norms; and by invoking the power of the opinions of the other (unseen) teachers, her colleagues. Bea's enactment of an adversarial conference role through exploitation of the conversational rights accruing to her during both the teacher response phase and the programmatic phase (not here reported) literally caused Faye to back off and, in a sense, forced her out of the room. Much to Faye's chagrin, Bea's contract was renewed, but on a continuing probationary basis.

Summary and Discussion

Analysis of the conferences here presented concerned at least three distinctive teacher roles in supervision conferences: the passive, the collaborative and the adversarial. The teacher who enacted a passive conference role, Doug, mainly acknowledged the supervisor's remarks, encouraging the supervisor to speak more. Due to his passivity, he was unable or unwilling to counter forcefully the supervisor's direct and indirect criticisms. The teachers who enacted the collaborative conference role, Kari and Ed, did so by timing and phrasing their utterances so as not to appear confrontational. This requires a high level of active listening and communicative competence. Still, these two teachers successfully advanced their agendas. The teacher who enacted an adversarial conference role, Bea, did so through marked competition for the floor and actions that demonstrated her reluctance to accept either what her supervisor, Faye, had to say or her role as her evaluator. She 'broke the frame of the conference' and enlisted tenets of teacher culture and other, absent, teachers in her defense.

In Doug's case, Bourdieu's (1986) notion of cultural capital was mentioned as a way to make sense of the processes and outcomes of both the conference and his tenure with his district. Kari's and Ed's supervisors did not view their teaching as problematic; they retained their jobs. There may have been a reflexive relationship between their conference behaviors and the supervisors' estimation of their teaching. Since their teaching was viewed as not problematic, their conferences might tend to be so; or, as their conferences went smoothly, the supervisors might have been more favorably disposed toward their teaching. The notion of cultural capital may also explain these teachers' success, for in both cases they possessed something their districts wanted. Kari was recruited by her principal in spite of, or because of, her alternative views and lifestyle, as he wanted to reinvigorate an aging teaching staff. Ed was recruited by Vern partially as an affirmative action hire due to his ethnicity and gender (male primary teachers were affirmative action hires in that district). These social facts, however, should not detract from the competencies these two demonstrated.

Bea's case was more problematic for both the supervisor and this researcher. How was it that, given her supervisor's poor estimation of her teaching and social skills, she was able to retain her position?

Bea was a local. I suspect that this fact outweighed other considerations. As I have intimated elsewhere (Waite 1989, in press and Chapter 4, this volume), Bea had negotiated two of Hall's (1959) three levels of (teacher) culture successfully – the informal and the formal, if not the technical. Perhaps the cultural capital she did possess – being a local – was what was the most valued by her district.[4]

This study points to the importance of the recruitment and placement of beginning teachers. There are implications here for mentor programs, as well as for supervision and teacher socialization. The human consequences of poor choices in teacher recruitment and placement are too severe for administrators, principals or supervisors, to unthinkingly fill teaching slots in the old 'sink or swim' mode. Bea's and Doug's cases underscore this point – Bea's case, in that program faculty succumbed to political pressure and admitted her when all available indicators suggested otherwise; Doug's case, as one where a change in any of several variables may have led to a more successful conclusion. Both these cases beg that local educational leaders search their hearts and souls for answers to questions concerning local values, priorities and commitment of support.

Conclusion

This research contributes to our understanding of teacher socialization and supervision. It corroborates previous research, especially in the area of teacher socialization, highlighting the interactive processes of such socialization (Lacey 1977; Zeichner and Tabachnick 1985; Etheridge 1989). Where previous claims rested upon 'coarse-grained' research, this study examines how such interactive processes actually take place moment-to-moment and face-to-face.

In taking a qualitative, some might say micro-ethnographic, perspective, the present research deepens our understanding of the phenomena of supervision and supervisory conferences. Such efforts are especially important today in the current era of educational reform. Today practitioners and theorists alike have been given license to re-examine traditional roles and relationships. The present study informs those decisions.

Supervision can no longer be viewed as a one-way phenomenon, an imposition of supervisory control on a docile teacher. Though other issues of control, such as the hegemony of supervisory *systems*, may need further examination before being settled, the present discussion of supervisor–teacher face-to-face interactions has shown that both parties have resources on which they may draw – neither is defenseless and both are responsible for the environment, the context, they co-construct.

Although supervisors enjoy a privileged position in conferences with teachers – they generate the 'data'; they initiate the conference and introduce topics for discussion; they determine what counts as a sufficient teacher response and may redirect when the teacher's account is deemed insufficient – teachers' resources are not to be underestimated. This study has identified a few of those teacher resources. Teachers influence the trajectory of all conferences, but only the collaborative teacher conference role allows teachers to co-construct, with supervisors, a positive image of Self and Other.

For the teacher, the collaborative supervisory conference seems to be the most felicitous of the three types discussed (Ovando 1993). True collaboration, however, is hampered especially by fixed and negative supervisory agendas (Waite 1992b, see also Chapter 2, this volume). In fact, it may be that any strong supervisor (or teacher) agenda restricts the degree of negotiation possible between teacher and supervisor, and complicates collaboration (Fullan 1992; Hargreaves and Dawe 1990). Also, concretized roles and role expectations negatively influence negotiation and collaboration (Burbules 1986; Waite, in press). Blindly holding either oneself or another to a certain role restricts the resources and approaches that can be brought to bear on educational problems.

Supervisors ought to heed as warning signs those indicators which suggest that their conferences are other than collaborative. If supervision and supervisors are to play a role in restructured schools and systems, they had best divest themselves of the vestiges of the 'snoopervisor' image. This involves work and education. Supervisors need to prove themselves capable of such collaborative effort.[5]

To be robust and viable within the context of school reform, supervisors, and indeed supervision itself, must simultaneously navigate two courses of self-renewal: the personal or individual, and the systemic. On the personal level, supervisors must model those skills, attitudes and knowledge that they prize in empowered teachers: reflection, collaboration, risk taking, an ethic of caring and the ability to enable the learning and growth of self and others.

Supervisors wishing to exhibit more collaborative behaviors must seriously examine their agenda and motivations before engaging with a teacher in a conference. Further, they may wish to record, analyze and reflect upon their conference behaviors. In conference, they may give the floor to the teacher and his or her concerns by allowing the teacher to begin the conference, by pausing more often and longer, by using more acknowledgment tokens, and by modeling some of the behaviors exhibited by the more collaborative teachers discussed in this research: active listening and incorporating what the other speaker says in one's own talk. Such behaviors signal acceptance. In brief, such attitudes and behaviors would approximate Benhabib's (1992: 8) 'model of a moral conversation in which the capacity to reverse perspectives, that is, the willingness to reason from the others' point of view, and the sensitivity to hear their voice is paramount'.

Other collaborative supervisory behaviors are offered in Scollon and Scollon's (1986) *Responsive Communication: Patterns for Making Sense.* Use of the Scollons' 'patterns' increases both personal and organizational responsiveness. Applied to supervision they suggest, for example, that supervisors should:

- 'study the whole situation and leave alone anything that is outside your power to control' (p. 10);
- 'confine your actions to your local place in the system. Study listening there first' (p. 11);
- 'foster loose organizational structures and *favor local responsiveness over institutional objectives*' (p. 12, emphasis added);
- 'emphasize the other person's autonomy and freedom of action. Offer alternatives' (p. 33);
- find neutral turf (p. 39);
- 'speak last' (p. 40);
- 'pause' (p. 41);
- 'wait . . . watch others for signs that you have interrupted them. Apologize and let them continue' (p. 42);
- 'slow down' (p. 43);
- 'hedge . . . emphasize the conditionality of everything you say' (p. 44);
- 'relax in your organizational position. Do not be afraid to let your humanity show through' (p. 48); and
- 'be vulnerable . . . practice stepping out of your professional role' (p. 52; this last communicates trust to others).

Just as it has been shown that teachers have previously unrecognized power to influence supervision conferences, so too do supervisors have the power to influence the *systems* of supervision. Just as Eisner (1991: 11) suggests that teachers mediate the curriculum, supervisors likewise mediate school organizations. The provision of organizational 'flex' for teachers and a willingness to take risks on their behalf demonstrate supervisors' ethic of caring, among other things. Indeed, supervisors and their interventions may be more palatable to teachers if they focus their efforts on supervising *contexts* rather than supervising teaching *behaviors* (a point developed in Chapter 5). To do so may require that supervisors and teachers become co-researchers of their situations.

Supervision conferences are embedded within multiple contexts; teaching and learning are also. In order to practice collaboration, supervisors need to recognize that teachers are one, and only one, variable among all those that have an impact on learning. Supervisors must quit blaming teachers, and should simultaneously examine the 'micro' and 'macro' contexts and processes influencing teaching and learning. What I am proposing is that supervisors involve teachers in action research projects focused upon improving learning and students' lived experiences – a process similar to organization development. Supervisors may choose to renegotiate professional roles – theirs and teachers' – to accommodate such research and action. In this way, supervisors, with teachers, could provide the leadership needed for the radical restructuring of schools.

Notes

1 The terms 'micro' and 'macro' are problematic because they foster a naive and inaccurate dichotomy – hence the use of 'scare quotes'. However, following convention, they will be used because, even in spite of their problematic nature, they economically convey what more accurately might be termed 'fine-grained' and 'coarse-grained' focuses and analysis.

2 These terms are simply heuristic devices. The term 'collaborative' could tend to be misleading in this regard. All conversations, as concerted action, are collaborations. Grice (1975: 45) wrote of a 'cooperative principle' as an underlying orientation of participants in conversations. However, as stated, the term 'collaborative' here refers to the general nature of the interaction, the gestalt, and emphasizes the active collaboration of the teacher, as will be shown.

   There is an easy association between the terminology I use to describe these teachers and that used by Glickman (1990) to distinguish supervisory behaviors: non-directive, collaborative and directive. It would be interesting to compare styles of teachers and supervisors in this regard.

3 Chapter 4 is devoted to an explication of Bea's resistance strategies.

4 Bea continued to work for this district until her husband was transferred in 1991. She completed her master's degree two years behind her cohort. Faye retired the year after fieldwork for this study was completed. She is now traveling with her husband.

5 Some suggestions as to how supervisors may foster collaborative relationships and environments are presented in Chapters 5 and 6.

Chapter 4

Problematizing Supervision and Teacher Resistance

In this chapter I deconstruct and then reinflect the concept of teacher resistance in order to re-establish it as a polysemic term (i.e. in order to re-establish its multiple meanings) and to unsettle popular misconceptions of supervision.[1] Recently, the term *teacher resistance* has been appropriated by some who define it as *only* that which is collective *and* progressive (e.g. Giroux 1981, 1983; McLaren 1985; Walker 1985; Kanpol 1988, 1991).[2] Such appropriation runs the risk of placing the observer or reader in an Archimedean position of judging what does and what does not qualify as resistance. In another context Quigley (1992: 306) cautioned that such issues cannot 'be settled by references to vague or ultimate principles whereby we establish yet another hierarchical power arrangement'. Quoting Ryan (1982), Quigley reminds us that '[t]he tendency to posit transcendent principles, whether for resistance or power structures, establishes . . . "a point of authority (an agency), a hierarchical command structure, and a police force"' (p. 295). Rather, as is the project of this chapter, Quigley (p. 301, fn. 44) admonishes us to 'make provisional choices . . . act knowing that the action is not a move toward an answer, a settling of the question, but just the reverse, an unsettling of power'.

If successful, the research and discussion presented here will unsettle notions of teacher resistance and the presumed hegemony of supervisors as well.

Teachers' Representation in the Literature of Supervision

Teachers have long been marginalized by the mainstream literature of instructional supervision, just as teachers' roles in supervision have been trivialized and objectified.[3] Its literature rationalizes supervision as being growth inducing for teachers, defining itself as 'the improvement of instruction' (e.g. Weller 1971). Seldom is this notion problematized. Rather, within the mainstream literature of supervision, teachers are subject to objectification, rationalization and commodification.[4] This lamentable state of affairs is reflected in the rhetoric of even some of the most liberal-minded educators, as it is voiced in public and political spheres in calls for reform, where teachers are perceived to be the only culpable party.[5]

Of course, supervision as a field of study cannot be separated from the larger historical-political milieu in which it operates (Bolin and Panaritis 1992). Through the years, researchers and theorists have examined supervision through their particular methodological and ideological lenses. Recently, critical theorists have begun to examine supervision (Smyth 1985, 1991b; St Maurice 1987) while concurrently critical theory itself is being refined.[6] The application of critical theory to the study and development of supervision is felicitous given that a prime motivation of critical theory is its educative agenda (Fay 1987). However, as Fay asserts, critical theorists have not dealt adequately with the ontological presuppositions to notions of resistance. Moreover, theorists generally and critical theorists specifically have been shown to neglect the lived, phenomenological world of teachers (Bowers 1982).

This chapter is premised on the belief that the study of teachers and their lived experiences – as evidenced in the moment-by-moment unfolding of a teacher–supervisor conference – will enhance understanding of supervision, especially teachers' roles in the process. What follows is an examination of a particularly problematic teacher–supervisor conference, with attention given to the phenomena of teacher resistance.

Methodology and Perspective

The conference reported here was taken from that same corpus of data which formed the basis of the discussion in Chapters 2 and 3 of this volume (see the Appendix). These data form the basis for the analysis of a teacher–supervisor conference. Use of a single case may trouble some readers. However, an appropriate response to the skeptical what-can-we-learn-from-just-one-of-any-thing-question is Wolcott's (1988: 16) pithy reply: 'All we can!' Friedrich (1989: 299) makes the argument for studying the individual, at whatever level of analysis:

> Individuals at these and yet other levels of analysis should be included because they give critical margins of understanding, insight and intuition into 'how political economy works' and how it is lived out in real life . . . margins that elude the rigidly sociocentric or socioeconomic modes of research. When the biographical and autobiographical dimensions are not dealt with, the study of language . . . and of political economy . . . tends to remain somehow unreal, and hence vulnerable to the charge of objectification and even of structuralist fetishization and alienation . . . [T]o exclude the unique individual as a matter of methodological principle is disturbingly analogous to the suppression of dissent in a totalitarian society. Also, ideologies, like poems, are always originally generated and contributed to by individuals.

I chose this particular case – that between Faye and Bea – because it so clearly illustrates one type of teacher resistance.

The Context and the Actors

The Program

The program that frames this study is the same program discussed in Chapters 2 and 3. It was modeled after the Harvard Master of Arts in Teaching summer school program (Goldhammer 1969; Cogan 1973; Garman 1990). It was a collaborative university–school program designed to offer beginning teachers field support and graduate courses culminating in a masters degree.

The program's teachers were under the direction of a school district supervisor – a 'clinical professor', in the program's terminology. These supervisors acted as liaisons between the university and their local district. These clinical professors (supervisors) were responsible for grading their teachers' graduate course work.

The Actors

The supervisor-protagonist of this chapter, Faye, was two years short of retirement at the time of this study. She had been with her district, Milltown, for more than 20 years. She began her career as an elementary school teacher and had been a clinical professor with this program for 15 years. In that role, she was expected to provide some of her beginning teachers' graduate course work and their instructional support in the field. (These beginning teachers were also appointed an on-site mentor.) Supervisory support consisted, as it did for all program supervisors and teachers, of classroom observations and feedback.

Bea, the teacher-protagonist of this report, was one of Faye's six beginning teachers that year. Bea was a 'non-traditional student'. She was the oldest of her cohort, pursuing a career as a teacher after having raised a family. She came from Milltown and had done her student teaching there, when she had caught the attention of a local principal.

The Immediate Historical Context

The observation and conference reported here occurred in the late spring/ early summer, a week before the end of public school classes. Bea was carrying an 'incomplete' in her graduate courses from the previous term. Faye had the habit of structuring her seminars around certain teaching and observation techniques. Her students, the beginning teachers in this district, were to complete the observations and practice the teaching methods as assignments. The most recent teaching technique Faye had taught the group was that of role-play, and that was the lesson of Bea's which Faye and I were to observe. Bea arranged the observation at her convenience – having called and left a message at Faye's office changing the agreed-upon observation time to one later in the day.

The Lesson

Faye brought a video camera to record the lesson. Before the lesson actually began, Faye addressed Bea's fifth-grade class. Mentioning the camera, she reminded them that they had all seen cameras before and implored them to not act any differently than usual:

> *Faye:* How many of you have seen a classroom on TV? None of you have watched a classroom on TV where some kid looked at the camera as you do. And you people are pretty good about letting me videotape without making a face into the camera. It's going to be really helpful and you'll be really proud of your tape afterwards when you get a chance to look at it. You'll get a chance to see yourself on tape if everybody is doing what they're supposed to be doing and not watching (me). So I know it's really hard when there's somebody in here videotaping, while you're supposed to be paying attention . . . pay attention, and just give me a glance, but don't do anything that's going to show up on the (tape). All right? Thanks, I'm sure you'll do just fine.

Bea began the lesson.

> *Bea:* [taking the floor from Faye] Okay, thanks for paying so much attention, you did a good job and I appreciate it too. Okay, well, what we're going to do today is, I think it's going to be really fun, because this is new for me, too. As you know, we did it, we've never done it before, so it's going to be fun to see how it turns out . . . Well, it's going to be a different kind of lesson, it's not the normal lesson. (fieldnotes, 6 June 1989)

Bea then posed the problem that the class was going to be dealing with in the role-play, a hypothetical case of thievery. Well into the lesson some students suggested 'punching out' the make-believe culprit. Faye interrupted the lesson, stating that she thought some of the resolutions offered by students were inappropriate:

> *Faye:* [to class] (it was) like the teacher was going to punch back, the teacher was angry. And you know what I heard happen out in the crowd? Somebody said, 'Hit 'em, hit 'em!'
> *Student:* Chris!

Faye:	I heard things like that. And I felt sad because I thought if people begin to use violence, what I saw happening was it got worse. When [student] punched the teacher, the teacher was angry back and was likely to do something back, and then pretty soon the audience was saying, 'Hit 'em!' And I saw things getting worse in that scene.
Bea:	Good. Anybody have any thoughts on that? Anybody have any thoughts on that?
Student:	Can we go to lunch? [general laughter]
Student:	Nice thought!
Student:	Mrs Quincy! Mrs Quincy!
Bea:	OK, I need quiet. Yes, Cody, you had your hand up.
Cody:	Um, Chris, Chris wasn't saying have Garret hit him back, it was . . .
Faye:	It was about using that as a way of solving problems. Doesn't sound like a very safe place to be to me! I'd be frightened if I were in a place where people were punching. (fieldnotes, 6 June 1989)

The lesson ended soon thereafter. When the students left for recess, Faye, Bea and I sat at a table in the back of the room, me off to one side, and the conference began.

The Conference

Faye worked from a checklist, something she felt she needed to do because she felt Bea was prone to 'arguing' (fieldnotes, 6 June 1989). The checklist was entitled 'Guide for Evaluating Your Performance: Role-Playing and Interactive Teaching' and consisted of 11 questions. Only yes answers were scored, the highest possible score being 11. Faye had scored Bea's lesson as a 5.5.

In the conference, Faye asked Bea questions from the checklist and Bea responded. Aside from topic initiation, Faye exerted her control in other ways (see Chapter 2). One such technique manifested itself in competition for the floor, or turns-at-talk. For example, when both spoke simultaneously (in overlap), it was most often Faye who retained the floor and Bea who dropped out. This is not meant to imply, as the present discussion will bear out, that such supervisor control is total and unified. It is not.

Teacher Resistance Tactics

The following transcript segments represent sites of contestation and demonstrate the resistance tactics Bea employed.

Breaking the Frame of the Conference

Briggs' (1986) sociolinguistic reappraisal of the interview as a communicative event led him to the conclusion that 'the respondent's principal means of subverting power lies in breaking the frame of the interview' (p. 56). As communicative events, interviews are not too dissimilar from supervision conferences. If a supervisor controls the topics, asks the questions, and even determines the relevancy and adequacy of a teacher's response, little more is left to a teacher if he or she chooses to resist than to refuse to play by the rules.

As Faye was addressing the questions from her checklist she and Bea were discussing what the result for the students would be of the scene portrayed in the role-play. Faye brought up her own intervention in the lesson and apologized (Transcript Fragment 4.1, lines 132–134, 136, 138):

Transcript Fragment 4.1

126	*Faye*:	=*FIRST – PREDICT* WHAt's gonna *happen* as a
127		*result* of this ˬ*scene* – now when *Dorothy* did
128		^ *hers*, she *predicted* (0.2) *another way*, like
129		you *did* – and so *that* was the next ˬ*sc:ene.*
130		– *well* that *kinda* gotchu into ^ *trou* ˬ *ble* –
131		when they – *predicted* – that *they* were gonna
132		*punch* ˬ*ou:t* – *and* – I – *could not* (0.6)
133		°*lis* ˬ *ten*° – I *tried* to stay *out* of *it*, but I
134		₁could NOT leave ˬ*it* ₁I could *n ot*
135	*Bea*:	*OH* I'M *GLAD* – you *d*¹*id* tha *t's fine* ¹
136	*Faye*:	*lea*₁*ve* – *that* because *it* – *e:*^*volved* so
137	*Bea*:	°*that's fine*°¹
138	*Faye*:	– *naturally* – *that* – >*it* got ˬ*worse*<
139	*Bea*:	um hum um ₁hum um ₁hum
140	*Faye*:	>*th*¹*at* it ^ *es* ˬ *calated*< once¹
141		you *use* an ^ *escala* ˬ *tion:* – whether it
142		*involves* t- I mean *they* were just ʌ*thrilled*
143		– *because* here's a *scene* they hadn't *seen*
144		ˬ*before*=
145		((Bea goes to window))
146	*Bea*:	=I'm jus- *concerned* that *my kids* are out
147		ˬ*there* ((at recess)) with no *supervi*₁*sion*
148	*Faye*:	*OH::*¹
149		*well* you'd *better* get out^*the*₁*re*, ˬ*then.*
150	*Bea*:	^*no*¹ *he's*
151		*still* out ˬ*there* – *that's* good (1.2) >just
152		let me ˬ*check* and make ˬ*sure*< – ^O ˬ K=
153	*Faye*:	=*the* – *intent* of *this question* – *is*: (0.8)
154		*if*: – *you* wer:e=
155	*Bea*:	=oh, I *forgot* to take

```
156              ₁my (                    )
157   Faye:  IF – YOU WERE ⌄TAKING¹ – °a pen⌄cil – at the
158          end° see what you're after ^here: – IS: –
159          THEM to th:ink
160   Bea:   UM HU:M=
```

Bea's protestations (line 135) can be seen as an attempt to close discussion of this topic. An interruption by a supervisor is a strong violation of the norms of professional conduct. It may even be construed as a negative evaluation of the teacher's performance, her ability to conduct this type of lesson and to manage the class. During our debrief, Faye said, 'I try not to ever interrupt a lesson, but that one [of Bea's] . . .' (fieldnotes, 6 June 1989). Even after Bea's protestations, Faye continued on this topic – possibly wishing to justify her interruption.

This discussion made Bea uncomfortable (notice the repeated overlaps, line 135, in raised voice). She then broke the frame of the conference, getting up and 'leaving' the conference to go to the window. When she returned, the topic changed. Faye retrieved the discussion of the scene and the intent of the teacher's question during the role play (line 153). Bea attempted a radical topic shift, to break the frame of the conference again (lines 155 and 156). Faye held her to the task by not allowing her to finish.

Bea initiated another radical topic shift much later in the conference (Transcript Fragment 4.2, line 330).

Transcript Fragment 4.2
```
310   Faye:  U::h – did they genera⌄lize >whatda you
311          ^think?< do you think your kids left here
312          with – a (1.0) °way: – of dealing with that
313          prob⌄lem?°
314   Bea:   °no – I don't ^think they ⌄did° – because I
315          th- I don't think they were in tune: with
316          what was goi- I don- th- I ^didn't feel
317          comfor⌄table.
318          (0.4)
319   Faye:  I think it's °right,° and I think you're
320          right – I think it was right here=
321   Bea:   =yeah=
322   Faye:  =I think we °got off right there°
323   Bea:   um hum
324   Faye:  and they needed – uh – EI^ther – explanation
325          °at the beginning,°
326   Bea:   um 'kay
327   Faye:  it's: – realistic to tell ⌄'em (0.4) that
328          you're gonna play something you've ⌄seen
329          (0.6) you've seen ₁kids
```

```
330  Bea:                          >SEE¹ I didn't know
331         whether- a- because see – the boy that was
332         in the very back:< (0.9) Cody? – um – he –
333         he is. I mean I have a huge ba:g – he's – he
334         has done ⌐that. A⌐lot
335  Faye:                    um hˡum
```

Here (lines 330–4) Bea begins talking about Cody and the number of times he has taken things from a bag she keeps. Bea has taken the floor in overlap, using raised voice and increased speed – two escalation tactics which gain her the floor. This constitutes an interruption (as compared with other occurrences of overlap that do not so constitute an interruption). Faye's acknowledgment token, the 'um hum' of line 335, projects Faye's orientation to Bea's continuing, in essence, Faye concedes to Bea.[7] Bea continued (Transcript Fragment 4.3).

Activation of a Counter-Discourse

According to Terdiman (1985: 39–40):

> dominant forms of discourse have achieved unprecedented degrees of penetration and an astonishingly sophisticated capacity to enforce their control of the forms of social communication and social practice . . . But at the same time, in intimate connection with the power of such an apparatus, discourses of resistance ceaselessly interrupt what would otherwise be the seamless serenity of the dominant, its obliviousness to any contestation. For every level at which the discourse of power determines dominant forms of speech and thinking, counter-dominant strains challenge and subvert the appearance of inevitability which is ideology's primary mechanism for sustaining its own self-reproduction.

Though supervisory discourses may have a decided advantage, especially in dyadic encounters, no discourse is so totalizing, so unified, as to be immune from some forms of counter-discourse.[8]

One point of contestation in this conference was Faye's questioning of why the student, Cody, was not included in the role-play. She argued that his inclusion may have mitigated his disruptive behavior. In response, Bea invoked the teacher collective as part of her rationale (Transcript Fragment 4.3, lines 344–8, especially the 'we' of line 352):[9]

Transcript Fragment 4.3
```
336  Bea:   and the reason – I didn't call on him ⌐today
337         is just because he's been totally off the
```

338		⌃*wall*: and so (0.6) *ha:ving him* up *there* –
339		*participating* >*would've been* a *very* bad<
340		⌃*choice*:. *Because* – *he* would *have* – *just*
341		*been* (0.4) *more obnoxious* – than he *was* by
342		*sitting* back *there* – stac⌃king: – ⌃*books*
343		*around* and doing the *things* that he's- ⌃IN
344		⌃*FACT* – *he's* been *so bad* throughout the
345		whole *schoo:l* – *that* – some*b*ody *said* – if
346		*Faye's* coming to *watch* – to*day* you *don't*
347		wanna be *sabotaged* by *Cody* – >*send* him *outta*
348		the ⌃*room* – and *I* didn't – *do that*
349	*Faye*:	*do* – uh – yet – but – *some*⌃*ti:mes* – his –
350		*thorough* – *involvement* in *it*
351		(0.9)
352	*Bea*:	*well* we *tr₍ied* ₍al ⌃*ready*
353	*Faye*:	*cut*₎ ou ts₎ the *behavior.* –
354		*But you're* saying *that* wouldn't *work* f₍or
355	*Bea*:	*it*₎
356	*Faye*:	₍( )
357	*Bea*:	Di dn't w-₎ *it* hasn't *worked* so ⌃*far:* –
358		*today* – >an I'd< – 'cause *I* was *really* going
359		to ⌃*use:* ⌃*him*.

Invoking the collective and activating its counter-discourse put Bea and her rationale beyond Faye's reach. In essence, this counter-discourse legitimizes the teacher as *the* authority on classroom occurrences.[10] The tension and negotiation between discourses is evident, even within Bea herself, in her 'and I didn't do that' (line 348).[11] The power of this counter-discourse is revealed in Faye's acknowledgment of Bea's negative estimation of the boy's status as a potentially worthy participant (line 354).

Once activated, Bea defended herself, her choices and her actions using these counter-discourses. To parry Faye's insistence on Cody's inclusion, Bea used phrases such as (see Appendix): 'I'd already given him many chances, he hit a kid in the head' (lines 377–9); '[he's just] totally off the wall' (line 381); and 'not today, because he would have made a circus, a three-ring circus out of it up there today' (lines 388–91). These are all opinions based upon the boy's actions 'throughout the whole school' and before Faye's arrival. The authority of the teacher and her decisions are now effectively beyond Faye's interrogation.

The Fine Line between Resistance and Oppression

Ellsworth (1989: 322) reminds us that 'any group – any position – can move into the oppressor role'. Likewise, Burbules (1986: 103) writes of a 'relational conception of power', whereby, 'in the power relation itself each party might gain a particular gratification from the negotiated balance between compliance and resistance'. Seeing power relations as a web, Burbules believes, reveals that 'relations of power are to some extent reciprocal . . . [in that] a person in power over another in one respect may be relatively powerless in other respects' (p. 104). Similarly, Terdiman (1985: 65–66) writes of the counter-discourse which 'situates its struggle somehow and somewhere within the conflicted cultural field . . . [and] functions by a kind of violence'.

Such complex notions of power, compliance and resistance aid in understanding this particular teacher's actions. Bea can at one time be oppressed by her supervisor, while at another time she can resist the supervisor's attempts at discursive hegemony, and at other times she herself may oppress her supervisor. There is no inconsistency here if power and its opposition are relational processes, rather than fixed, static positions.

Just how might Bea oppress her supervisor, Faye? Faye and Bea colluded in the co-construction of this conference.[12] One important aspect of such construction is the production and interpretation of contextualization cues (Gumperz 1992). Contextualization cues signal participants' orientations to 'what is happening now' and 'who we are' in the process. Through her activation of the counter-discourses of teacher culture, Bea has signaled her orientation toward who Faye is, how Bea expects the supervisor to behave, and what Bea thinks her own role is. When rigidly fixed, such role expectations 'constrain the alternatives the agents see as possible' and 'constitute a template or pattern which the relationship will tend to follow' (Burbules 1986: 97). Role expectations that are neither shared nor negotiable are potentially hegemonic.

Bea, alluding to unseen teachers, socially constructs Faye's role as that of *stranger* within their school community and within Bea's classroom. The stranger 'may be forced to go or, at least, forcing him (*sic*) to go may be contemplated without violating the order of things' (Bauman 1988/89: 9). In addition to the tactics cited above, Bea pressed her attack on Faye's position through manipulation of her rights as a conference participant, especially those rights that accrue to the teacher during the last phase of the conference.

In general, supervision conferences have three phases (Waite 1992a; also see Chapters 2 and 3, this volume): the supervisor report phase, the teacher response phase and the programmatic phase. Due to consideration of local conversational issues – resolution of overlap (who drops out, who succeeds in competition for the floor), who employs acknowledgment tokens most often during a particular phase, and who initiates topics – teachers were found to be able to dominate the programmatic phase quite easily.

The programmatic phase of this conference began after Faye completed her last supervisor report. Faye had offered Bea a candidate future action as a remedy for the shortcomings Faye saw in the lesson. Bea agreed to pursue the suggestion (Transcript Fragment 4.4, lines 632, 634–5). The boundary between phases comes with Faye's 'ALL RIGHT', said at line 636. This was Faye's first attempt to close the conference. However, Bea hurriedly began another turn (latching her turn immediately to Faye's prior turn, with no pause and with rapid voicing). Refusing to accept the closure, Bea began the programmatic phase of this conference. She initiated discussion of her class assignments, hoping to resolve her incomplete credits.

Transcript Fragment 4.4

625	*Faye*:	But – uh (0.5) *it* would be g:*ood* – for *her*
626		to be *able* to see ˏ*your:s* – because *she*
627		would *say* – oh – >I *shoulda* done *that*< or –
628		*yep* – *that* worked *really* ˏ*well* and *it* would
629		probabˌly be ^*good* – for ˏ*you* to be *able* to
630	*Bea*:	ye^ah¹
631	*Faye*:	see ˏ*hers*. If ₍*IF* she's *willing* to
632	*Bea*:	°um° *I'D* ^*LI KE* – to do ˏ*that*¹
633	*Faye*:	ex ˏ*change*.
634	*Bea*:	°yeah° ^O ˏK – *we* can *talk* about
635		iˌt-
636	*Faye*:	*ALL*¹ *RIGHT*=
637	*Bea*:	=>I *ME*- another ˏ*thing*< – is *I* have ˎ*my* u:m
638		(1.4) I *have* – *everything ready* to turn *in*
639		to *you* – to ˏ*day* – *except* for *my* u ˏ*nit*. °Can *I*
640		turn it *in* on *Thurs* ˏ*day*? – 'K there's°=

In the discussion that follows, Faye mentioned that she thought Bea had one more assignment due. If Faye wanted to leave, this was a tactical error. Bea was incredulous and queried Faye further (Transcript Fragment 4.5, line 666). Faye attempted to disengage from that contest (of whether or not there was actually another assignment due) at that time (lines 667–9). Bea persisted.

Transcript Fragment 4.5

659	*Faye*:	*YE:s* – but *I* have to °*get* back to ˏ*you* – I
660		*have* to *look* back through – your *file* and t-
661		t- con- I ma:rked it ˏ*down* and *penciled* ˏ*in*
662		– but *I* have *to* – >make *sure* – what ˏ*time*<°
663	*Bea*:	OˌK:
664	*Faye*:	theˈre's one – *more:* (0.3)
665		₍that you
666	*Bea*:	>I have anˈother one to ^*do*?<
667	*Faye*:	*well* – let me *talk* to *you* about *it* –
668		to ˏ*night* – *when* you ˏ*come*, – so I- – you can
669		*look* – *through* your *fold* ˏ*er*.
670	*Bea*:	ˏoh · ^O ˏK

Both stood and Faye moved toward the door.

However, Bea continued to call Faye to account until the end of their face-to-face encounter, until she made it out the door. Bea enumerated those assignments she had completed and turned in and those she had yet to complete. Faye's only defense (and, at the same time, her defenselessness) was that her records were at her office. The degree of contestation is evidenced in the following example (note the amount of overlap and competition for the floor):

Transcript Fragment 4.6

706	*Faye*:	*sure* ₁and s ee whether *I*: – *just* don't have
707	*Bea*:	OK ⌋
708	*Faye*:	it – *checked* on my ˄*list*, no- un- and *it*
709		would've *been* for ˄*last term* – it was *for*
710		your *incom*˄*plete*, 'cause I *star*˄*ted* – to
711		*cha:nge* your *incomplete* from ˄*la:st* term ·hh
712		*and* I *thought* (0.2) *wh*^*oops*: – ˄so: – *I'll*
713		talk to you to*night*, ₁WHEN I HAVE IT in
714	*Bea*:	all right – good⌋
715	*Faye*:	fr₁ont of – me
716	*Bea*:	˄ye:ah⌋ OK k- because I – *I* wasn't
717		awa₁re that there was *any thing* ˄*else*
718	*Faye*:	without being – *more*⌋ *explicit* about
719		^*it*
720	*Bea*:	OK₁
721	*Faye*:	th⌐ough ˄*Bea* – *don't* get *nervous* about *it*
722		– until *I*: – *check* it *out* ˄more.

Faye instigated a radical topic shift (a tactic Bea had used earlier). This was done through interruption, strengthened by asking a question in raised voice (Transcript Fragment 4.7, line 736):

Transcript Fragment 4.7

733	*Faye*:	and then we'll *do the* – uh – *fol*˄*der* (2.5)
734		Thurs˄day °OK° ˄your – curriculum=
735	*Bea*:	=I HA₁VE
736	*Faye*:	ARE⌋ YOU *DOING* – poe^try?
737	*Bea*:	>yeah<=
738	*Faye*:	=°good°=

This topic shift, while deflecting Bea's onslaught, did not get Faye out of the room. To do this, she enlisted me (Transcript Fragment 4.8, lines 754–7, 759) *and* referred to the group outside (lines 759–60, 762–3). Referring to the group outside reactivated Bea's role *vis-à-vis* her students. Bea responded affirmatively.

Transcript Fragment 4.8

754	*Faye*:	((to observer)) well *Dun*˄*can* – do you wanna
755		˄*go*: – or are you gonna ˄*stay*. Here I *am* –

756		*walkin'* outta *here* and ^ *he's* stayin' ˏ*here*
757		((laughs)) and *he's – watching me –*
758	*Bea:*	((to observer)) yeah, thank you ((laughs))
759	*Faye:*	*leave.* It's because – *I'm* thinking *you* need
760		to *be out* on *that play*ˏ*ground.*
761	*Bea:*	*I'm* going ˏ*out* – I'm gonna *take*=
762	*Faye:*	=I *SEE YOU* looking out *there* – *so* –
763		₍frequent ly
764	*Bea:*	I'm gonna t-⌋

We quickly said our good-byes and left.

Faye was aware of how Bea had manipulated her. Afterwards, she commented, 'I'm not going to win . . . because when I try to deal with problems, it becomes a personal assault' with Bea. 'So I just literally kind of backed away . . . [It works for her], she wins either way.' Faye was planning to return to her office to check Bea's course grades, because, as she said, 'There'll be a war if I don't. She really holds me to it' (fieldnotes, 6 June 1989).

The Nature of Teacher Resistance

Even if supervisory conferences can be characterized by their 'communicative hegemony' (Briggs 1986: 90), within the most hegemonic of systems there remains room for resistance (Foucault 1981; Lindstrom 1992). Bea's tactics are tactics of resistance, even if they form only one type of resistance,[13] and even if some of their characteristics still are ill-defined.[14] Others might take exception. Walker (1985: 65), for instance, prefers the term 'recusant' for that oppositional behavior which is not 'actually or potentially, consciously or unconsciously, contributing to progressive social change by undermining the reproduction of oppressive social structures and social relations' and reserves 'resistance' for those behaviors which are.

Other pedagogues, espousing a critical perspective, privilege the conscious, that is, rational (the Frankfurt School, for example) and/or the collective and progressive aspects (e.g. Giroux 1981, 1983; McLaren 1985) of oppositional behavior in their definitions of resistance. In defining terms such as resistance and hegemony, critical pedagogues must be cautious lest their attempts at definition fall prey to a totalization of the concept they seek to define. Commenting on this point, Terdiman (1985) notes that:

> Like any . . . Marxist concept, [hegemony] is particularly susceptible to epochal as distinct from historical definition, and to categorical as distinct from substantial description. Any isolation of its 'organizing principles', or of its 'determining features', which have indeed to be grasped in experience and by analysis, can lead very quickly to a totalizing abstraction. (Williams 1977: 112, as cited in Terdiman 1985: 55)

Definitions of resistance that privilege the conscious, the collective and the progressive often have been based on neo-Marxist analyses of power and dialectic based in class, race and more recently gender relationships. Such conceptions exclude considerations of other means of oppression and resistance and totalize personal experience in the process of assigning individuals to reductionistic categories. Fay (1977, 1987) recognizes that some of the problems critical theorists have dealing with resistance can be attributed to inadequate conceptualizations of the embeddedness of the subject and the limitations of agency. More recently, however, the multifaceted nature of oppression and resistance have been examined by such authors as Davis (1992), Ellsworth (1989), Hooks (1990), Lather (1991), Minh-ha (1986/87) and Shilling (1991).

In questioning the privileging of the rational, Shilling (1991: 666) suggests a 'need to recognise the body as a system capable of expressing and interpreting the nature of oppressive social relations'. Such work is based on the theory of embodiment (Bourdieu 1986) and reinstates the body (as opposed to the body politic, though this latter is not thereby negated) as a site of oppression and resistance.

The use of 'progressive' in definitions of resistance is highly subjective and assumes an unwarranted authoritative stance as regards historical moments (Fay 1977, 1987; Burbules 1986; Quigley 1992) and posits an impossible clairvoyance in regards to contemporaneity. No one is granted such an Archimedean position by which to judge contemporary moments.

Restricting resistance to the collective, aside from disenfranchising the body as noted above, almost by definition eliminates teachers from consideration. Organizational structures constraining teachers' lives heavily proscribe collectivity (Little 1990; Kanpol 1991: 139).

In a complex conceptualization of hegemony, resistance and the Other, Ellsworth came to see herself and her students as:

> inhabiting intersections of multiple, contradictory, overlapping social positions not reducible either to race, or class, or gender, and so on. Depending upon the moment and the context, the degree to which any one of us 'differs' from the mythical norm . . . varies along multiple axes, and so do the consequences. (1989: 302, fn. 13)

Ellsworth saw that '"there are no social positions exempt from becoming oppressive to others . . . any group – any position – can move into the oppressor role." depending upon specific historical contexts and situations' (1989: 322). Mills states that '[a] person's power relations in language are constantly the subject of negotiation' (1992: 7). Citing feminist analyses that stress power 'as a relation rather than as a quality or an imposition' (8), Mills concludes that '[i]f power is seen as a process, resistance to it is easier to consider than has been the case so far with feminist theorizing, which has run the risk of depicting women as passive victims' (1992: 8).

Likewise, Benhabib criticizes certain postmodern definitions of the Other:

any definition of a group's identity not in terms of its own constitutive experiences but in terms of its victimization by others reduces that group's subjectivity to the terms of the dominant discourse and does not allow for an appreciation of the way in which it may challenge that discourse. (1992: 83, fn. 5)

Teachers, supervisors and their respective roles must be re-examined in this light.

These more complex views of hegemony, resistance and the subjectification of the Other are actually more liberating than simpler, earlier definitions. Such views permit a constructed subjectivity in the place of normalizing categories and encourage an historical (both synchronic and diachronic) and relational examination of those structures and processes in which one is embedded and to which one contributes. It has been shown that not all teachers are passive victims at supervisors' hands, at least not this teacher with this supervisor, and if the possibility exists for one teacher to resist her supervisor, that potential must be said to exist for all teachers, whether they realize it or not.

Conclusion

From a deconstructed perspective of resistance Bea resisted her supervisor – whether or not she was conscious of what she was doing, whether or not she was part of a larger collective with a progressive agenda. Though supervision discourses may well be some of the dominant discourses in schools, Bea was able to invoke counter-discourses successfully in this case.

This teacher's resistance is ripe with implications for supervisors and supervision. Resistance, rather than being categorically and transcendentally defined, ought to be examined for its meaning and potential, that is, assuming supervisors are interested in emancipation rather than oppression for themselves and for teachers. Moments of resistance may take any of several trajectories. Supervisors and teachers might agree to concentrate on areas of agreement, rather than needlessly expending valuable time and energy in contestation. Teachers, knowing that the possibility for resistance exists, could become more active in the construction of their relationships with supervisors, even in defining supervision itself. Teachers need to take responsibility for supervision.

If the promise of this type of supervision was ever realized, conferences would then approximate Benhabib's moral conversation, 'in which the capacity to reverse perspectives, that is the willingness to reason from the others' point of view, and the sensitivity to hear their voice is paramount' (1992: 8). There must be a willingness on both parties' part to enter into such a dialogue, but supervisors, together with teachers, must work to establish the contexts and nurture the relationships conducive to such conversation. As Benhabib states:

In conversation, I must know how to listen, I must know how to understand your point of view, I must learn to represent to myself the world and the other as you see them. If I cannot listen, if I cannot understand, and if I cannot represent, the conversation stops, develops into an argument, or maybe never gets started. (1992: 52)

Such conversations are the subject of Chapter 6, and will be dealt with in much greater detail there, where the rationales for and principles of such supervisor–teacher conversations will be elaborated. This approach to supervision is termed dialogic supervision, and takes M. M. Bakhtin's writings on dialogism as its starting point. However, before attempting that project, the reader will be treated to a midpoint theory or approach to supervision, situationally-contexted supervision. Both these approaches take what has been learned from the previous studies and apply it; the first, Chapter 5, is a much more practical application, the second, Chapter 6, is more theoretical.

Notes

1 Deconstruction is used not in the strict Derridian sense, but in a more colloquial one: '[D]econstruction . . . [is] an attempt to grasp the conflicting heterogeneities of language, rewriting its heteroglot difference as precisely the impossibility of a master-discourse, the impossibility of an invulnerable metalanguage' (White 1984).
2 It is Giroux's belief that resistance must also be intentional.
3 There are, fortunately, a few notable exceptions; see for example Blumberg (1980), Blumberg and Amidon (1965), Blumberg and Jonas (1987), Munro (1991) and Smyth (1991a, 1991c).
4 These three processes – objectificaton, rationalization and commodification – are what West (1990: 35) refers to as 'major impediments of the radical libertarian and democratic projects of the new cultural politics'. Objectification transforms living beings into manipulable objects. Rationalization fosters and supports 'bureaucratic hierarchies that impose impersonal rules and regulations in order to increase efficiency, be they defined in terms of better service or better surveillance'. Commodification makes teachers susceptible to 'market forces . . . that centralize resources and powers and promote cultures of consumption that view people [teachers] as mere spectorial consumers and passive citizens'. Commodification of the original form of clinical supervision is discussed at length by Noreen Garman (1990: 202–3).
5 Goodman (1988: 213), incorporating critical theory and a feminist perspective on the disenfranchisement of teachers, notes the irony that 'much of the recent blame for the shortcomings of our present education in this country has fallen on teachers (rather than on community leaders, economic funding priorities, cultural values, etc.) who happen to be mostly poorly paid working women with little power in schools or society.'
6 'Critical theory' is used here as an inclusive, umbrella term. Others delineate the differences between 'critical theory', 'critical pedagogy' and 'emancipatory education' in far more detail than I can here (e.g. see Ellsworth 1989; Burbules and Rice 1991; Burbules 1992).
7 Recall that Goodwin and Heritage (1990: 288) define an acknowledgment token as use of 'uh huh', 'OK', 'uh hum', and so on that 'projects (but does not require) the

continuation of another speaker's talk. Simultaneously it usually displays an analysis of the other speaker's prior talk as being incomplete so far.'

8   The readily available us/them distinction of teacher culture is one available counter-discourse. These notions of (supervisory) discourses and (teacher) counter-discourses might be cases of what Friedrich (1989: 307) terms 'linguacultural ideology': 'Linguacultural ideology . . . [is] located in the unconscious or subconscious of the speaker and speaker collectivities'.

9   This particular segment also highlights the collective group estimation of Faye's role as supervisor and hints at a normative response to it: that subterfuge was permissible in protecting oneself from the potentially negative supervisor's gaze.

10 Hargreaves (1990) and Kanpol (1988) describe the tensions between teacher and administrator 'cultures'. Kanpol found teachers' perceptions to be that teachers are adept and administrators are inept. Kanpol (1991: 140–1) writes that this group norm reinforces what teacher solidarity was evident in the group of teachers he studied. Such taken-for-granted beliefs may, however, serve hegemonic ends when they stereotype and thereby constrain others', for example, supervisors', self-determination (see Burbules 1986: 97).

11 This particular comment reflects the heteroglossia, or 'multivoicedness', of Bea's positionality (Bakhtin 1981a). Both the internal and the external dialogic nature of this utterance are apparent, for as Bakhtin wrote: 'The word in language is half someone else's' (Bakhtin 1981a: 293).

    For more on Bakhtin and application of a Bakhtinian perspective to supervision, see Chapter 6.

12 See McDermott and Tylbor (1983) for a discussion of collusion as a necessary condition of conversation.

13 In his foreword to de Certeau's (1986) *Heterologies: Discourse on the Other*, Godzich comments on de Certeau's project of demonstrating there to be *multiple* discourses and *multiple* oppositions to them. He writes: 'This other, which forces discourses to take the meandering appearance that they have, is not a magical or a transcendental entity; it is discourse's mode of relation to its own historicity in the moment of its utterance' (p. xx).

14 I hesitate to delineate, once and for all, the transcendental characteristics of resistance, of any type of resistance. I have shown, I believe, how teacher resistance to supervision can be *accomplished*. I have not, nor will I, list the defining, essential elements.

Chapter 5

Instructional Supervision from a Situational Perspective

Veteran supervisors, having matured in their professional role, often reach a plateau and may have trouble advancing beyond it. The field of supervision, its advocates and theorists, is partially responsible for this state of affairs. This responsibility also must be extended to the wider contexts within which supervisors and teachers work, however. Theorists' promotion of models of supervisory practice as panaceas, and practitioners' overreliance upon such models limits the horizon of possibility of what supervision may accomplish. This is the 'mindscape' of supervision (Sergiovanni 1985).

However, reflective practitioners correctly perceive that any model of supervision is only a step on the path to a fuller conceptualization of both supervision and classroom life. This seems true both for the individual supervisor and for the field of supervision as a whole. As one veteran central office supervisor told me, 'You need to begin where you are; and, hopefully, you'll move on from there.' This maxim has become widely accepted regarding the developmental growth of teachers (Glickman 1990). It is an assumption of the present work that this maxim also holds true for supervisors and supervision.

In recent years, educational theorists and researchers have begun to examine school occurrences by paying close attention to their situational particulars (i.e. the numerous contexts and moment-to-moment processes of school life). Within the domain of instruction, this perspective has been informed by ethnographies of classroom life and the moment-to-moment accomplishment of pedagogical strategies, both tacit and explicit (McDermott 1976; Bremme and Erickson 1977; Mehan 1979; Dorr-Bremme 1990). Recent efforts in curriculum theory have examined curriculum implementation from a situational perspective, leading Catherine Cornbleth (1990: 13) to refer to curriculum implementation a 'contextualized social process'.

Though curriculum and instruction – particularly their development – are within the action domain of supervisors (Oliva 1989; Glickman 1990), supervision has yet to incorporate approaches or methods that address all the complexities of curriculum and instruction as they actually unfold in real classrooms, in real time. As if by definition, a model of supervision highlights a certain epistemology and its related pedagogy, while neglecting or rejecting others. While it is doubtful that any model of supervision could capture *all* situational particulars, what is needed is an approach to supervision that more closely honors the complexity and uniqueness of each classroom, teacher and the interpersonal relationships of those involved – in short, one that is responsive to the numerous contexts of schooling.

In this chapter, I introduce just such an approach to supervision, 'situationally-contexted supervision'. This term is, at best, problematical. Although other terms such as 'ecological supervision' were considered, I think the term 'situationally-contexted supervision' captures the essence of the approach I propose here (though it doesn't roll off the tongue especially easily). It is unfortunate that, as my colleague Ed Pajak (personal communication, April 23, 1991) has pointed out, this formulation may be dismissed out-of-hand by those who may equate situationally-contexted supervision with utilitarian supervision – an amoral approach that encourages use of whatever works simply because it works. That is definitely not the case here, where the actors' beliefs and feelings, informed by philosophical and moral considerations, are included in the concepts of 'situation' and 'context'.[1]

Throughout the remainder of this chapter, I will develop the rationale for the situational perspective and conjecture how such an approach may be operationalized. First, I will present a *brief* history of supervision (an extension of the discussion begun in the introduction). Second, I will detail the rationale for a situational approach, including examination of beliefs about teaching, learning and supervision. Third, I will present a vision of what supervision from a situational perspective may look like. This is the 'what' and 'how' of situationally-contexted supervision. Included in this section is a discussion of the 'action domains' of supervisors, teachers and others, as well as suggestions as to how an interested, reflective practitioner may proceed to incorporate this new approach in his or her work. Finally, I will present some of the implications of such an approach. These implications include, but are not limited to, those for professional relationships in schools, school–university collaboration, professional development (for example, preservice and inservice teacher education), shared governance and site-based decision making, and the redesign or redefinition of teachers' work.

The Evolution of Supervision and Supervisory Thought

The history of supervision profoundly affects current supervisory practice. This is especially true in the US (a case with which I have firsthand knowledge), where newer approaches never completely banish older approaches from the field – they just seem to push the older approaches underground. Still, the history of supervision illustrates a growth in the complexity of the process and its theoretical underpinnings (Karier 1982; Bolin and Panaritis 1992). Early supervisory efforts, known as supervision by committee and later, administrative monitoring, were quite simple compared with supervision today. In earlier days, the person(s) designated as supervisor(s) simply observed a teacher and decided on the spot to fire or retain that teacher. No reasons needed to be given and no documentation was required.

Slowly, administrative monitoring gave way to other forms of supervision. A turning point in supervisory practice came with the dissemination of the practice referred to as clinical supervision (Goldhammer 1969; Cogan 1973; Garman 1990; Acheson and Gall 1992). Most recent innovations in supervision have incorporated aspects of the clinical model. For example, Hunter's (1973, 1980, 1983) supervisory model, Glatthorn's (1983) differentiated supervision, and Glickman's (1990) developmental supervision have evolved from clinical supervision, as have the various approaches termed 'peer coaching', 'peer supervision', and 'peer consultation'.

Noreen Garman (1990), a student of Morris Cogan – who, along with Robert Goldhammer popularized clinical supervision – has critiqued recent developments of the clinical approach. Both she and others (e.g. Retallick 1986; St Maurice 1987) have criticized these adaptations of the clinical model for being overly technicist or, as Garman wrote, 'narrow instrumental versions' (1990: 202) of the original.

Though Garman (1990) leveled the same criticism at both Glatthorn's (1983) differentiated supervision and Glickman's (1990) developmental supervision, to my mind these two approaches represent progress within the larger field of supervision. Glatthorn presented a number of options to those with supervisory responsibilities. Under the term differentiated supervision, Glatthorn brought together administrative monitoring, clinical supervision, collegial professional development and individual professional development, thus allowing teachers, administrators and supervisors some choice. True, there was nothing new in this constellation, but Glatthorn's contribution chipped away at the 'one-size-fits-all' mindset.

Glickman (1990) encouraged supervisors to consider both individual *and* collective staff readiness when selecting a supervisory approach. This was one of his contributions to the field. Additionally, Glickman expanded the tasks of supervision from the three conventional tasks – staff development, instructional development and curriculum development (Oliva 1989) – to five, with his inclusion of group development and action research.

Although the models discussed above represent advances in the theory and practice of supervision, they do not address the current complexities of schooling and the supervisor's role in relation to them. Nor do they take into account the contextual or situational factors which figure prominently in teachers' and students' intellectual growth and the role of the school in that growth. The role of school in children's lives and the processes of schooling were examined, 20 years apart, by Carl Rogers (1971) and Elliot Eisner (1991) in 'Can Schools Grow Persons?' and 'What Really Counts in Schools', respectively.

How far have we really come in that time? What is the work needed to be done in order to give supervision theory and practice currency within modern contexts and modern schools? These are the questions that propel the discussion throughout the remainder of this chapter and the next.

Relationships Between Teaching, Learning and Supervision

That teaching, learning and supervision are interrelated is not at issue. What is of interest is how they are related and what the ramifications of that relationship might be for supervisors.

Relationships between Supervision and Teaching

As has been reported in previous chapters, one of the most widely accepted definitions of supervision is 'the improvement of instruction' (Weller 1971: 4). Though this definition begs the question of what constitutes instruction, it is illustrative of a long history of attempts to define supervision. Most of those attempts at a definition have focused on the teacher's behavior; relatively few have been concerned with students' behaviors; and fewer still concerned themselves with the learning environment or opportunities for engagement by the student.

Various authors within the field have used the previous definition, or others like it, to justify their inclusion (or exclusion) of various tasks when writing of the role or function of the supervisor. For example, it is not too difficult to justify including curriculum development and staff development with instructional development (Oliva 1989), considering the profound effects the former have upon the latter. The extension of the tasks of supervision to include group development and action research (Glickman 1990) is certainly justifiable given that these processes have an impact on what happens in the classroom. However, as can be seen from this brief treatment, supervision's ultimate impact has generally been envisioned as influencing instruction, teaching. Such conceptions of supervision, with their focus on *teachers' behaviors*, are unfortunate because they erroneously equate teaching with learning.[2]

Beginning supervisors are often faced with the dilemma of deciding what to talk about in a conference with the teacher.[3] They may be befuddled by the complexity of the classroom when viewed from the observer's perspective, or they may naively weight all classroom occurrences equally. Anthropologist Frederick Gearing and co-author Wayne Hughes (Gearing and Hughes 1975) have written of classroom observation that:

> About any human scene as complex and as fast-moving as a classroom there is an incredible amount of information to be had. Presumably any thinkable item of accurate information is potentially important to some theoretical purpose. Of all that, however, only a small proportion is practically important . . . [W]hat to the practical man [or woman, teacher or supervisor] is useful information? The answer is reasonably clear. Useful information is *strategic*, that is, it is information about critical moments which reoccur in a place like, in this instance, a classroom; and useful information is *pointed*, that is it is

precisely focused on some specific feature of all that is going on at those critical moments. (p. 15; emphasis in original)

There are so many interesting things happening in a classroom that any one of them could become a topic for a supervision conference, but are all those occurrences equally pertinent? I think not.

Veteran supervisors, with the knowledge gained through observing thousands of classroom hours, may begin to sense what matters in teaching and learning. Some few are able to see through all the hubbub to what matters. Some never do. Supervisors who rely solely upon the *techniques* of supervision and their complementary models may in fact become developmentally blocked – unable to move to more advanced stages of conceptualization. For such supervisors, supervision may become mere ritual (Garman 1990) and of little use to teachers or students. These 'blocked' supervisors may even hamper teacher development (Grimmett and Housego 1983).

Teachers' reactions to supervisors' intrusions are legion, but not unworthy of comment:

my principal and I are seeing the same events, but, like two witnesses to anything, we see them differently. Put us together and you might have a winning team – theoretically. But, while I have seen my classroom through his eyes, I don't think he has seen it through mine . . . I want him to stop writing and simply sense the rightness or wrongness of what's happening in my classroom. (Juska 1991: 470)

Supervision based solely upon paper-and-pencil classroom observation techniques often misses the mark, according to teachers, and evaluation systems based on such observations fare no better. 'Spot checks, check lists, and standard measures of learning (predictable artifacts of institutionalized monitoring) tend to gloss over the important intellectual nuances of classroom interaction' (Kilbourn 1991: 735). This inability to capture the 'important intellectual nuances of classroom interaction' results, in part, from the unreflective application of models of teaching and their supervisory counterparts, the 'one size fits all' mindset. Even systems of peer coaching or supervision suffer to the extent that their advocates and practitioners blindly (i.e. unreflectively) adopt such models of teaching and observation (Smith and Acheson 1991; Fullan 1992).

The shortcomings of observation systems and teacher evaluations based on them can also be explained by concepts borrowed from the field of social psychology. Roadblocks to observers' perceptual accuracy result from: fundamental attribution errors (Ross 1977; Gardner 1991: 171); errors due to the 'actor–observer effect' (Brehm and Kassin 1990: 115–7); and errors resulting from the 'cognitive busyness' of 'active perceivers' (Gilbert *et al.* 1988: 733).

A fundamental attribution error occurs because observers are prone to attribute causes of events to the actor's inherent characteristics (e.g. he is a bad teacher, or she doesn't like children) and to ignore the situational influences. (Teachers, too, are prone to the negative effects of these errors when observing and assessing students.) It is interesting, though, that as actors we generally characterize our own actions as responses to situational factors, while attributing other's actions to inherent personal factors. This is the actor–observer effect (Brehm and Kassin 1990). Actors are more cognizant of situational causes than observers. These negative effects are amplified by 'cognitive busyness' (Gilbert *et al.* 1988) on the observer's part, as when an observer is not only observing, but recording, coding, categorizing and analyzing as well. These negative consequences of observation and attribution are remedied by correctives the observer applies as part of the perception process. The correction requires that the observer adjust his or her attributions with situational information. If the normal process is hampered by cognitive busyness or by a lack of time for reflection, erroneous attributions are likely to stand uncorrected. This is because the characterization or attribution process is more automatic than the correction, which involves more deliberate reasoning and is a 'higher order process' (Gilbert *et al.* 1988: 738). A situationally-contexted approach to supervision inverts the typical ground/figure frame for observation by highlighting the ground to a greater extent. At the same time, situationally-contexted supervision holds the promise of being able to empower supervisors and other participants to action within a much broader arena than had heretofore been the case.

Supervision, Teaching and Learning: Understanding the Context

Liston and Zeichner have contributed to a situational understanding of classrooms for those involved in teacher education and curriculum development. They wrote:

> If we can explain an occurrence in the classroom by appealing to the actions and intentions of the teacher, student, or any other relevant actor, then we feel as if we have understood and adequately explained the situation . . . [However] as former elementary teachers and now as teachers of teachers, we rarely have found the individualistic orientation to provide an adequate account of classroom life. In order to act effectively we have had to recognize the influence of the social context. (1990: 611–2)

Though their intended audience was university teacher educators, the relevance of Liston and Zeichner's remarks for supervisors (and teachers) is clear. Atomistic views of the teaching–learning environment that privilege teachers and teachers' intentions are no longer useful. This carries profound implications for the supervisor's role in curriculum and instructional development.

Research that highlights the contextual or situational nature of teaching and learning has generally benefited from a grounding in sociolinguistics (e.g. Green and Wallat 1981) or educational anthropology (e.g. McDermott 1977) and the related methodologies of conversation analysis, ethnomethodology, ethnography of communication and symbolic interactionism. What these studies have in common is their demonstration of teaching and learning to be moment-by-moment accomplishments in relation to a dynamic context or situation (i.e. that the context is ever-unfolding). These studies show how the participants both contribute and orient to the contexts of learning. Specifically, participants in an interaction such as a school lesson orient to 'contextualization cues' that are 'recognizable to a researcher' (Dorr-Bremme 1990: 382) and that let them know what is happening now. In addition, such studies examine the relevance participants' assumptions and behaviors have for how situations, acts, scenes or lessons unfold. The relevance of these research perspectives for supervision should not be underrated. As Bremme and Erickson wrote:

> A participant must 'read' others' verbal and nonverbal behaviors together, simultaneously, to make sense of what they are meaning and to make sense of what social situation is happening now . . . But newcomers to a classroom may have difficulty doing all this in the ways experienced members do. *The tacit and often subtle rules these members know and use in making sense may not be immediately accessible to the new student, the occasionally visiting supervisor, the educational researcher, or other neophytes* . . . They may not see immediately what behaviors are appropriate when, according to those *microcultural* rules in use among this particular classroom group. (1977: 154; emphasis added)

Office-bound supervisors, or those who lack intimate knowledge of teachers, their students and the conditions and assumptions under which they operate, are prone to misinterpret classroom occurrences.

Education as a field has just begun, through the work of a few, to address the issue of what students need to knew in order to act appropriately in learning situations, and how to teach those skills (e.g. Sternberg *et al.* 1990). Those skills, though seldom addressed explicitly, are powerful determiners of scholastic success or failure (McDermott 1976; Mehan 1980). Research has yet to address what it is teachers (or supervisors) need to know to act appropriately in those same learning situations so as to be judged competent.

Expanding the Mandate of Supervision

Unfortunately, those of us who teach and write about supervision have offered precious few alternatives to teachers, supervisors and other classroom observers who are interested in affecting what goes on in schools.[4] To that end, I suggest that a situationally-contexted supervision approach would address those shortcomings inherent in conventional models of supervision. Such an approach broadens the supervisor's mandate to include attention to the contexts of learning, broadly defined. Indeed, in ethnographic studies I have conducted (Waite 1990/91) supervision practitioners understood their mandate to be that of ensuring students' physical *and* psychological well-being. This shift in emphasis away from attending solely to *teachers' behaviors* opens the supervisor's action domain to consideration of classroom climate, the hidden curriculum and its effects, issues of equity, participant structures (Phillips 1972),[5] functions of language, and issues of social control and reproduction (Dorr-Bremme 1990; Liston and Zeichner, 1990), along with the more traditional focuses of supervision. Such a reconceptualization of supervision allows the supervisor to pay attention to what seems to matter in the school-life of children *and* their teachers. Such a broadened view of supervision would also increase the amount of attention teachers give these important aspects of life in school. There have been a few supervision theorists, however, who proposed that the supervisor's mandate include consideration of learning environments and/or opportunities (e.g. Wiles 1950; Goldhammer 1969). Goldhammer broached a number of these issues in the first chapter of his seminal work. Unfortunately, these issues have largely been ignored or forgotten by subsequent theorists in the field.

The Situational Supervisor

The folk wisdom of teaching holds that each year is different, that every new day brings its own trials and cause for wonderment. This is a manifestation of the belief that each situation is unique. What are the elements that contribute to the uniqueness of situations and what is the relevance for supervision?

One of the assumptions of the present work is that *every* aspect of a context or situation has *possible* relevance for teaching and learning and thus for supervision. This is not to say that *all* contextual considerations have relevance, or an *equal relevance*, for what goes on in schools and their classrooms. Some contextual considerations have a disproportionate influence, negative or positive, on the academic lives of children.

The supervisor's principal task in the situationally-contexted approach is to augment those situational factors that have a positive influence on learning and to seek to diminish those whose influence is negative. The supervisor cannot, however, assume beforehand which factors are important, as would be the case with an indiscriminate application of any observational instrument or supervision model. Teasing out the relevant situational factors must be done inductively by honoring the uniqueness of situations. The action a supervisor takes to remedy situational deficits must be taken in response to the situational particulars.

Consider an example from my own experience. As a supervisor of interns, a 'clinical professor', I had occasion to work with a mature returning student who was also a mother of two. This teacher already had had a successful career as a social worker, where, in her own words, she had worked with 'juvenile delinquents in a juvenile detention center'. I judged her to be knowledgeable of curricular issues, instructional techniques and cognitive development, as well as professionally competent, energetic and concerned. In short, there was not much I could show her about teaching. However, she had been placed in a rural setting. The teacher-administrator at the site was due to retire at the end of that year and, by all accounts, was deeply conservative.

Due to my supervisee's assertiveness and her profound belief that she knew what was right for her students, she often found herself at odds with her administrator. Besides attempting to get this teacher to practice more cooperative interpersonal skills, I knew that my major focus was to be in working with/on the administrator, trying to neutralize her so the teacher could teach without interference and not suffer any negative consequences. Though the relative success of my efforts is open to question, I have no doubt that I proceeded in the only professionally responsible way that I could, given the situation. Clearly, I could have discharged my responsibilities at less psychic cost to myself by simply observing the teacher and conferencing with her. To my mind, however, this strategy simply would have been ritualized supervision.

Reconceptualizing supervision along situational lines increases the number of action domains open to the supervisor. Traditionally, supervisors' power has been defined as stemming from a *staff* relationship with teachers as opposed to a *line* relationship, the latter being hierarchical in nature and bureaucratically grounded (Pajak 1989, 1992). According to this view, supervisors are in no direct line of authority over teachers, yet they report to other administrators. Consideration of alternative notions of power, such as 'facilitative power' (Dunlap and Goldman 1991), and other redefinitions of power brought about by feminist thinkers, permits a re-examination of the conventional top-down power configuration. Facilitative power is different from *power over* and can be considered to be *power through* or *power with*. Facilitative power, according to Dunlap and Goldman, 'reflects a process that, by creating or sustaining favorable conditions, allows . . . [others] to enhance their individual and collective performance' (1991: 13). Supervisors, borrowing from this concept, influence *all* those with whom they are in contact, not just teachers.[6] As the personal example above shows, supervisors can and should work to affect key actors no matter what their position may be, for all these actors have an effect upon the situation, the context, of teaching and learning. Situationally-contexted supervision, as I have portrayed it here, is a modified form of organization development (Schmuck and Runkel 1985). Of all forms of teacher professional development, including the various peer models, organization development is the most respectful of teachers' autonomy and the least prescriptive (Smith and Acheson 1991).

In proposing a situational perspective on supervision, I am encouraging supervisors to be aware – to the extent humanly possible – of all contextual factors. These factors have a chronology, and supervisors must attempt to see the big picture, holistically and over time. They must understand the past and envision the future. Supervisors must first negotiate the local culture in order to achieve their positions of responsibility (Waite 1992c, and Chapter 1, this volume). 'Culture', of course, has several dimensions or levels: national, community, professional, school, interpersonal and intrapersonal.[7] Each of these dimensions also has historical roots of which the supervisor should be aware. Supervisors already know, at a tacit level at least, much of what they need to know. I suggest that they make this knowledge explicit.

Self-knowledge on the supervisor's part is especially important in the situational perspective because the supervisor is considered to be part of the context, so the supervisor's effect upon the scene and its actors becomes relevant. Once the supervisor's tacit knowledge has been made explicit, the supervisor operating from a situational perspective would concentrate on aspects of the situation yet to be discovered.

Practicing a situationally-contexted approach, the supervisor could begin at the macro-level in an investigation of what matters to the participants in their teaching and learning. Following such a procedure, the supervisor would examine national, state, community and school norms for their influence upon instruction. This method of supervisory investigation, though informative, would leave the supervisor with a near infinite number of factors and considerations, only a few of which may have a local impact upon learning. Though all professionals should be consciously aware of the environment in which they operate, micro-level observation and analysis is more apt to yield immediately relevant insights into problems and suggestions on how to proceed toward solutions.

This type of observation and analysis may be done through involvement of participants in ongoing action research (McCutcheon and Jung 1990) or participatory research (Hall 1984; Latapí 1988). These methods involve the participants in a systematic examination of their situation, as well as their role in that situation. Difficulties may be encountered by the shift from hierarchical role definitions engendered by a commitment to action research, especially by autocratic supervisors and administrators. The ethnographic literature is replete with references to the attitude the researcher should take. Agar (1980) alternately referred to the ethnographer's role as a 'one-down position' or as a 'student' or 'child' role. He wrote that the advantages for a (qualitative) researcher in adopting these roles is that 'both child and student are learning roles; they are roles whose occupants will make mistakes . . . They can be expected to ask a lot of questions. They need to be taught' (1980: 69). These roles strike me as antithetical to many administrators' self-perceptions. Ethnography, as an example of a method supervisor and teacher-researchers may choose, has the advantage of being

> of all forms of scientific knowledge . . . the most open, the most compatible with a democratic way of life, the least likely to produce a

world in which experts control knowledge at the expense of those who are studied. (Hymes 1981: 57)

The consideration of who controls knowledge and its forms of production is apropos to the current discussion. Traditionally, the knowledge generated from supervisors' classroom observations served the supervisors' (i.e. bureaucratic) ends.[8] Even today, in innovative programs such as the Program for School Improvement – a Georgia-based program started by Carl Glickman and built on the ideas of shared governance and action research – when school teams are encouraged to practice action research, they overwhelmingly opt to consider only quantitative data (e.g. attendance records and standardized test scores).

McCutcheon and Jung (1990) have written of action research and the perspectives informing it. According to these authors, there are three distinct traditions within action research: the positivist, the interpretivist and the critical science traditions. Simply to engage in action research does not ensure democratic participation in the selection of its focus and control of the knowledge it generates. I suggest that schools practicing positivistic action research and using only quantitative data may disenfranchise the majority of their teachers and students. Depending on their genesis and nature, such data and methods may prove inaccessible to most teachers and students and hence not inform immediate local concerns.

In action research in schools the supervisor may serve as leader, facilitator, resource or 'critical friend' (Ingvarson 1986). This new supervisory role is strikingly similar to the researcher role adopted by Elliott (1990) in his work with teachers in their examination of their classrooms and pedagogy, and similar to the supervisory role suggested by Grimmett *et al.* (1992). This role involves the supervisor as a co-equal participant, devoid of hierarchical power.

Action research projects may include various methods and focuses and are highly appropriate for school settings. Hymes (1982: 104) stated it well in his rationale for 'ethnolinguistic' studies of schooling: 'In any given case, of course, everything depends upon discovering which dimensions are relevant and active.' He cautioned, however, that local knowledge is seldom sufficient in the examination of situations or cultures:

It is never the case that knowledge is served adequately by accounts solely from self-study. The 'native' or insider has invaluable insights and interpretations to make that the outsider may be unable to provide. The outsider has a distance and strangeness to the situation that may provide necessary insights and interpretations as well. (Hymes 1982: 8)

The supervisor has a place as an outsider, or, perhaps more accurately, as an insider/outsider. Outsider knowledge is never sufficient without the complementary insider's perspective. The supervisor, then, should seek to make explicit those rules, norms, members' understandings and strategies operant in each scene witnessed. This, as I have suggested, must be done with the members' participation. The degree of members' participation should be problematic for the supervisor. Should participants direct the study? Should the supervisor direct the study? Or should it be a negotiated process? A possible answer is found in the process of participatory research where all actors would have a say in what to study, what tentative solutions to implement, and how to evaluate them.

Getting at the participants' taken-for-granted beliefs and actions requires a commitment of time. There is no room for hasty judgment, just as there is no ready observational instrument that will always be relevant. In fact, the supervisor may take some time in simply fashioning a situationally relevant observation instrument or protocol, or in combining several already at hand when appropriate.

Gearing and Hughes (1975) have provided three versions of the ethnographic method for self-study by teachers, principals and supervisors. These different versions of ethnography for educators are distinguished both by the amount of time educators can devote to them and by their depth or fidelity to the ethnographic method. Briefly, the most simple process begins with the identification of a concern, for example, students who talk too much. The next step is to specify the *actors*, the *behaviors* and the *context*. Do only working-class boys (or some other readily identifiable children) talk too much? When? What is the interactional environment? What follows is an observation and provisional mapping of a routine associated with the concern – those actions by those actors that immediately precede the 'problem' and those that follow. This step is repeated until the researcher – teacher, student or supervisor – is fairly certain that what is found is an accurate analysis of the routine. This mapping is then assessed, and possible solutions should recommend themselves. Gearing and Hughes point out that possible solutions should be judged as they bear 'on your professional goals, your personal morality, and the political realities of your situation' (1975: 27). Future actions or solutions should then be monitored, possibly with the ethnographic protocol already developed.

This is one approach to the study of the situational reality in schools and classrooms, action research is another, and 'force field analysis' is still another (Schmuck and Runkel 1985: 222–3 Johnson and Johnson 1991: 239–42). Further study and 'self-work' may be needed by the supervisor seeking to operate from a situational perspective. Such a supervisor may wish to take courses at the local university in qualitative research methods or consult the voluminous literature base on qualitative research in education (see Erickson 1986a).

Implications of the Situationally-Contexted Approach

Implementation of a situationally-contexted approach carries with it implications that range from the immediate and local to the long term and holistic.

The first implication is the change in thinking about supervision, what it entails and its scope, or action domain. Supervisors come to a situationally-contexted understanding because they see that atomistic thinking about effective teaching captures only a minute part of 'effective learning'. Supervisors operating within the conventional paradigm have become as deskilled as teachers have (Apple 1986). In order to 'reskill' supervisors and teachers, supervisors must come to a more mature, that is, political, sense of their action domain and their part in it. Supervisors must communicate this understanding to those with whom they work, as, at the same time, they must operate from that understanding.

Also, the change in the supervisory mindscape prompted by adoption of the situationally-contexted approach – which, after all, is simply another way of seeing – frees teachers (and students) from blame and its associated guilt. Both these negative affective states can freeze teachers, preventing them from acting to better the conditions of schooling. The situationally-contexted approach views teaching, indeed all interaction, as 'collusional' (McDermott and Goldman 1983) – the result of conditions that organize participation. In such a view, blame has no utility.

Supervisors must also understand the arena of teachers' work. They must understand teachers, their personal and professional biography – a facet of the context within which both operate. Such an understanding allows the supervisor insight into how to involve the teacher and what to expect. Supervisors need to take the time necessary to understand the teacher's philosophical and pedagogical (ontological and epistemological) frames of reference. Rather than talking past each other in ritual exercises, conferences then become constructivist exercises in the sense that each party accepts and respects the phenomenological stance of the other with respect to the classroom and lesson. Often, as practiced now, the supervisor's reliance upon data collection or classroom observation instruments privileges the supervisor's evaluation of the lesson and the resultant conference demonstrates a power differential in the supervisor's favor (as discussed in Chapters 2 and 3).[9] Such an approach takes time, however, supervisors will need to redesign their work to allow for such intensive interaction. Supervisors must become versed in the research skills spoken of here. Eventually, teachers and students may also practice those same skills.

Implementation of the situationally-contexted approach to supervision would necessitate, as well as foster, certain conditions in schools. This approach is highly suitable for schools with multicultural populations and those involved in reform and restructuring. Situationally-contexted supervision would encourage and inform efforts in decentralization, for example, site-based decision making and shared governance, transformational leadership, and teacher and student empowerment. The degree of adoption of a situationally-contexted approach would depend on personal, political and moral propensities, needs and desires. In its most basic form, a situationally-contexted supervisory approach may be enacted solely at the classroom level and involve discovery of and action upon the interactional processes constituting the local contexts of learning. In its most complete and radical form, situationally-contexted supervision could involve entire schools and their populations in social activism.

The situationally-contexted approach entails a fundamental change in the definition of the nature of school, and participants' roles and relationships. An essential dynamic present here is that of reflexivity, that is, that changes in parts affect changes in the whole. This being the case, attention to any or all of the following areas would move schools toward the ideals I envision. A point of clarification: I am not proposing that action be exerted equally on all areas simultaneously. The amount and focus of participant action should be determined by an examination of the situational factors, their relative effect and the possibility of successfully influencing those factors. Some constraints are more resistant to change.

Implications for the Nature of School

The nature of school is one of the most fundamental questions addressed by the situationally-contexted approach. In line with Sarason (1990), the situationally-contexted approach promotes classrooms and their schools as centers of inquiry. Knowledge generated in this manner is not generated simply for its own sake, but to inform and better the educational efforts of all. The situationally-contexted approach highlights the *processes* as well as the outcomes of participatory, action-oriented research. Such research flattens the hierarchies of knowledge production and control (Deforge 1979) inherent in traditional supervisory relationships, encourages the redefinition of schools as communities (Sergiovanni 1992), and, at the same time, invites connection with other communities (McTaggart 1991a, 1991b). Schools could become centers of inquiry not only for their resident populations, but for the larger society as well.

Constraints: Time and Freedom

Time becomes a primary concern. Teachers today are constrained by time and space (see Chapter 1, this volume; also Hargreaves 1994) and suffer from 'intensification' of their work (Hargreaves 1991). Intensification results in teachers who have less time for relaxation, less time to keep up with their field, fewer opportunities for collegial interaction, a dependency on outside experts, and who cut corners (Hargreaves 1991: 5). These space/time restrictions limit, among other things, teachers' access to information, and information is a facet of power.

If teaching and learning are hindered by traditional images of teachers standing in front of classes and holding forth, these notions need to be 'demythologized' (Palmer 1969: 28–30, 44). Schools and districts attempting innovative educational programs soon come up against constraints imposed by conventional thinking about time, space and the nature of teaching and learning. Such schools often seek to 'buy time' to loosen the shackles of the clock to allow more flexibility for teachers and students. For example, some schools now operate flexible lunchroom schedules and brownbag 'carry out' service, where student messengers take lunches back to their classrooms so everyone may eat and learn without disruption. Other alternatives need to be considered as well.

Teachers need greater freedom of movement inside and outside of the school, with and without students. As mentioned, if teachers are to participate in knowledge production, that is, research, then they must have access to information. Granting teachers access to information might finally permit them to have telephones within easy reach in their classrooms (not to mention access to other communication technology).[10]

The situational approach to supervision would require community education regarding the definition of teaching, learning and teachers' and students' work. This may be accomplished by engaging the community and its members in dialogue concerning the nature of school and the roles, responsibilities, and relationships of students, parents, teachers and others. In this way, educational leadership, the current term for administration, might actually fulfill the promise implied by its name and truly become educational leadership, activism, for the community.[11]

Integration and Democratization of Roles and Relationships

Out of necessity, supervisors must renegotiate their role *vis-à-vis* both the teacher and the administration. Supervisors are carriers of culture (as shown in Chapter 1). In traditional societies this role is granted much status. However in schools change, not maintenance of tradition, is the most often promoted priority. The danger here is that schools and newer generations of teachers and students may embrace change for the sake of change and, in a move toward the nihilistic, abandon those cultural ways that serve a positive end. Supervisors may be in the unique position both to encourage change and to preserve what is valuable in a school or community. This is another facet of the insider/outsider role mentioned earlier. Supervisors are in the position of perceiving broad goals and alternative futures and how particular schools, classrooms, teachers and students relate to these goals. Supervisors communicate across school sites and synthesize the information gained. They do this because of the position they hold in school organizations, but teachers could assume this supervisory function just as well, if able to redesign their work. This position could be filled by a teacher chosen on a rotating basis, just as some schools are experimenting with rotating principalships. Whoever assumes this role, however, must be able to see and communicate the whole, while also attending to the particular moment-to-moment and day-to-day practices.

The supervisor practicing a situationally-contexted approach should be able to see, and encourage others to see, how particular practices relate to the whole, theoretically and practically.

Administrators, too, must change or at least not openly and actively resist such change. If supervisors of instruction are the only administrators interested in the situationally-contexted approach, however, they must not be afraid to proceed. Other administrators then may become the focus of action – negative or positive contextual factors needing to be addressed.

If schools become centers of inquiry, they could assume a greater role in teacher training. Schools would gain status *vis-à-vis* universities and may actually engage university professors in research and teacher education on site, and in collaboration with students, teachers, supervisors and others. Such an approach has radical implications for staff development and would ameliorate the discontinuity presently found between preservice and in-service professional development (Holland *et al.* 1992).

True, this is an ideal end state. Initially, schools might wish to draw on the expertise of university professors in training supervisors and teachers to conduct research. Universities may grant certain teachers adjunct professor positions. Universities need to redefine for themselves what constitutes valid knowledge – would participatory, action-oriented research be appropriate for masters or doctoral-level study? Universities may wish to emphasize research skills in their teacher education programs. A loosening of credentialing requirements may be required if the lines between university and school are to be blurred. Schools may even look to credential their own teachers.

In this, the 'era of reform', such notions as those presented here have currency. What I propose is more than just another model of supervision. It is actually an alternative view of school, its relationship to those whom it purports to serve, and the relationships among its many populations. Supervisors and other concerned educators may begin locally, at the classroom level. Yet the situationally-contexted approach reaches beyond classroom walls. The ideal end state is to make of education a process at once reflective, democratic and a life-long activity, not just for students but for teachers as well.

Unfortunately, adoption of the supervisory processes outlined here will not make the supervisor's job easier, at least initially. It will, however, prove effective in addressing teachers' concerns about the relevance of supervisory intervention. For until supervision addresses the day-to-day and moment-to-moment particulars of teaching and learning in a way that respects the dignity of the participants, it will remain simply a ritual exercise in administrative meddling.

In the next chapter, I shall attempt to draw in broad strokes the next conceptual step toward the visions of school I have painted here. In discussing dialogic supervision, I push the limits of popular conceptions of supervision by drawing on ideas connected with postmodernism, communitarianism and feminism. Through that discussion, I offer some concrete, practical steps supervisors can take to bring supervision into the (post)modern world.

Notes

1   The term 'situationally-contexted supervision' certainly may, however, suffer from connotative associations with Hersey and Blanchard's (1982) 'situational leadership' (an approach that I read as overly behavioral).

2   For a discussion of teaching and its definitions, see Kilbourn (1991) and Nolan and Francis (1992). Gardner (1991) discusses various types of learning.

3   The discussion in this chapter will be concerned primarily with the 'what' – what to look for in classrooms and schools etc.; the next chapter will be more concerned with the 'how', that is, how can a supervisor interact with a teacher in face-to-face encounters in such a way that carries more potential for opening up, rather than shutting down, the dialogue.

4   Welcome exceptions are Nolan and Francis's (1992) 'Changing Perspectives in Curriculum and Instruction', with its implications for supervision, and Grimmett *et al.*'s (1992) 'The Transformation of Supervision'.

5   Participant structures are the resultant interactional forms – as occasioned by the norms, mores, rules etc. – in a particular milieu.

6   This notion is in keeping with an interactionist perspective (McDermott and Church 1976; McDermott 1977), whereby people in interaction jointly construct both their own and the other's identity and, through repeated and patterned interactional processes, contribute to the forms of larger social structures (Giddens 1984; Wilson 1991). Following this line of reasoning, students, teachers, principals and central office staff influence and are influenced by whomever they interact with, regardless of the other's social or institutional status.

7   See Wolcott's (1991) discussion of 'propriospect' for the distinction between shared and individual culture.

8   In all fairness to Keith Acheson and Mark Gall (Acheson and Gall 1992), they have consistently advocated the teacher's 'ownership' of the data.

9   To facilitate more collegial interaction between supervisor and teacher I propose a form of supervision I term 'dialogic supervision' (see Chapter 6), fashioned after the work of Mikhail M. Bakhtin (1981b), in which supervisors would forsake the use of an 'instrument' to simply be witness to a teaching episode. Supervisor and teacher would then mutually (re)construct the past lesson in dialogue, each from their own egocentric position with respect to the other.

10   Ironic, isn't it, that teachers (and their students) may not have access to the so-called information highway simply because their rooms don't have phone lines!

11   Such a stance by educators is not without risks. Witness the repressive reaction to such community activism visited on those educators in Chile, Guatemala, El Salvador, Haiti, Kenya, China and others who have had the courage to leave behind their ivory towers for participation in their communities' efforts at education and social justice. A situational perspective should aid in the discovery of barriers and the appropriate paths around them in response to local conditions.

Chapter 6

Dialogic Supervision, or, Re-embedding Supervision within the Contexts of Change

So how can we be strangers, he's got no personality. He's just a clever imitation of people on TV. A line for every situation, he's learning trivia and tricks, having sex and eating cereal, wearing jeans and smoking cigarettes . . . I can be you and you can be me, in my mundo, mundo mambo. Everyone's happy and everyone's free, in my mundo, mundo mambo . . .

David Byrne, *Make Believe Mambo*

Introduction

In this chapter, supervision and supervisors are placed within their current contexts – contexts of reform, and contexts of what Anthony Giddens (1990) refers to as a radicalized modernity (other authors prefer terms like postmodernism and postmodernity to describe the current state of affairs). Seen within its current ambiance, supervision is lacking and in need of rehabilitation. A new way of thinking about supervision and supervisor–teacher realtionships as well as a process born of that new way of thinking are introduced here. That process is dialogic supervision.

Contexts

School reorganization takes many forms, some of which require redefinitions of conventional roles, relationships and responsibilities.[1] Within the contexts of reform, supervision and supervisors' roles must be re-examined and reconceptualized if supervisors are to participate in the dialogue of reformed and reforming schools. Profound systemic change must be accompanied by different forms of thought *and* action, and at all organizational and conceptual levels, if reform is to amount to more than a reactive patchwork of local remedies (Sarason 1990).

To this end, some authors have suggested fundamentally different visions for schools. Sergiovanni (1992) and Etzioni (1993: 89–115), for example, apply communitarian ideals to schools and their reorganization. However, some serious considerations are neglected or glossed over in these communitarian visions of schools. For example, the words 'community' and 'communication' share the Latin root, *communis* (common).[2] Yet communication is neither explicitly addressed nor problematized in these idealized and romanticized treatments of community.

Anthony Giddens (1990) in *The Consequences of Modernity* warns us to 'avoid the romanticized view which has often surfaced in social analysis when traditional cultures are compared with the modern' (p. 101). He continues:

> In conditions of modernity . . . human activities remain situated and contextualized. But the impact of . . . the separation of time and space, disembedding mechanisms, and institutional reflexivity . . . disengages some basic forms of trust relation from the attributes of local contexts . . . Place has become phantasmagoric because the structures by means of which it is constituted are no longer locally organized. The local and the global . . . have become inextricably intertwined (p. 108).

Some problematic aspects of community have entered the dialogue of postmodernism, neo-colonialism and discussions of the radical alterity of the Other. The relation between community and communication has been recognized by some. Lyotard (1993) claims that 'in theory, the human "we" doesn't precede but results from interlocution' – such interlocution being 'authorized by respect for the other'. In other words, communities result from communication (and other interrelational processes), not the other way around.

In defining the common, communities establish borders, borders which include some and exclude others. Sergiovanni (1992) writes of the establishment of norms in school communities, but fails to mention that norms are as likely to be repressive as they are to be nurturing, enabling or empowering.[3] Instructional supervisors, teacher-leaders, and administrators involved in establishing, nurturing and maintaining school communities need a deep understanding of communication, for communication – understanding and employing it appropriately – is at the heart of change.[4]

Conceptions of communication have become more complex recently (Duranti and Goodwin, 1992), and yet there has been little application of these more complex communication concepts to schools, school leadership and supervision. The need is especially urgent today for schools are embedded within the contexts of modernity. Within the contexts of modernity, supervision is flawed – the systems, models and practices of conventional supervision are inappropriate to deal with teachers, instruction etc. today.[5]

A model of communication-based supervision derived from the work of the Russian scholar Mikhail Bakhtin (1981b) is here proposed as a corrective for the shortcomings of supervision as it is currently conceived and practiced.[6]

The proposed remedy is termed 'dialogic Supervision'. Bakhtin's work has particular relevance for the study and practice of educational supervision. This is especially true within the contexts of reform and modernity. For Bakhtin, contexts are important considerations. The contexts of modernity, their instantiation in schools, and their effects on school leadership make relevant discussion of global movements that impinge upon today's schools (Giroux 1992; Smyth 1992). Where previous supervision research has favored micro-analysis of supervisor–teacher dyads (e.g. Blumberg 1980) over larger units of analysis, application of the dialogic principle to supervision links all contexts in an organic whole, re-embedding supervision within the changing contexts of modernity. Thus, application of Bakhtin's work on dialogue and context has profound implications for supervision theory, research and practice.

Locating Supervision

Theories and practices of supervision reflect the times in which they operate (Bolin and Panaritis 1992). Times change, and changes are occurring with greater rapidity now. Astute observers remark that we have entered a period characterized by the crises of modernity (Giddens 1990; Hargreaves 1994). Schooling, teaching and learning are undergoing profound changes (Nolan and Francis 1992). Constructivism, cooperative learning, Foxfire, global education, technology, site-based management, multicultural education, and applications of business reorganization techniques such as Total Quality Management are but a few of the many innovations discussed in staff rooms, universities and education journals.

Where does supervision fit into a context of change? Is supervision still viable? If schools decentralize, is there no longer a need for supervisors, or only no longer a need for central office supervisors? If teachers professionalize further and become reflective practitioners, researchers and leaders, will supervisors become superfluous?

The Crises of Modernity

The German philosopher Jurgen Habermas (1976) has written that a condition of modernity is the legitimation crisis, a questioning of authority. Others have written on the conditions of modernity, especially as these conditions affect schools (Hargreaves 1994). Hargreaves and Macmillan (1992: 30) note that the modern world is 'fast, compressed, complex and uncertain' and that the conditions of modernity place organizations 'under pressures of multiple innovation requiring rapid and responsive change'. Other characteristics of modernity include: 'globalization of trade, information and communication'; 'multicultural migration'; 'constant upgrading *and questioning of knowledge*'; and 'new patterns of production' (p. 30; emphasis added). In summarizing and applying the conditions of modernity to teaching, Hargreaves and Macmillan state:

> The challenge of change for teachers in the postmodern world, then, are ones of intensification and innovation overload, *the need to define new missions and purposes, the search for justifications for practice when scientific certainty cannot supply them, and the struggle to create and define collaboration and self-management in ways that enhance collective empowerment instead of reinforcing administrative control.* (1992: 31; emphasis added)

These are also the supervisor's challenge with/in the postmodern.

The malaise of modernity has brought a deep and pervading questioning of, among other things, science and scientific certainty. People all over the western world in all walks of life have begun to question basic assumptions, the previous bedrock upon which modern society has been built. Such profound questioning extends to, for example, science and the scientific method, government and government (dis)information, nature and people's relationships to it, and characteristics of and relationships among individuals and between individuals and their communities.

These phenomena are consequences of modernity. Briefly, the modern period, an extension of the Enlightenment, has been depicted as a response to the medieval period (Sale 1990), the period in western European civilization and history known for its dogmatism and the utter and pervasive power of the Roman Catholic church in peoples' lives. Sale (1990: 40) wrote that 'the task of achieving this triumph of European rationalism was immense, and it took a whole range of disparate talents . . . and decades before it was ascendant, centuries before it was commonplace.' It was during this time that early scientists such as Galileo Galilei were condemned by the Church as heretics and forced to recant or face death or imprisonment.

Gradually, with the assistance of certain technological developments (gunpowder and refinements in the emerging science of geography, for example), the Enlightenment ascended to supremacy over the dogmatism of the Church (Harding 1990; Sale 1990). This was the dawn of the modern age. Harding writes that 'objectivist discourses are not just the territory of intellectuals and academics; they are the official dogma of the age' (1990: 88). A certain degree of people's religious fervor transferred to a belief in science and the possibilities it promised. It was during this time that the 'new world' (neither new nor a world) was 'discovered' and colonized and its peoples subdued (chiefly, I might add, with the assistance of those technological developments, like gunpowder, that had helped supplant the supremacy of the Church).

Technological developments came rapidly: the steam engine, the Industrial Revolution, the locomotive, the telegraph, the telephone, the electric light, the internal combustion engine, the motorcar, the airplane and the computer.

These technological developments, heralded as the benefits of science, had dramatic impacts on people and their ways of life.

Philosophies also changed. There were radical ontological and epistemological changes abroad, followed by bloodletting revolutions. Fueled by new conceptions of human and individual rights primarily influenced by Kant, Hobbes, Locke, Leibniz, Martin Luther, Schleiermacher and other western European philosophers, great social and political movements engulfed whole countries and their people. The effects were, and still are, felt around the globe.

These movements in science, philosophy and politics continued and intermingled, and the philosophies of Marxism-Leninism and German Socialism (Nationalism) were born. Was it coincidental that the German Fascist government of World Was II perfected the jet-propulsion engine and nearly completed the atomic bomb? Such militarism prompted Anthony Giddens (1990: 10), to comment that:

Not just the threat of nuclear confrontation, but the actuality of military conflict, form a basic part of the 'dark side' of modernity in the current century. The twentieth century is the century of war, with the number of serious military engagements involving substantial loss of life being considerably higher than either of the two preceding centuries.'

Some so-called advances in science began to trouble people's moral sensibilities severely. For instance, what are we to make of genetic engineering? What of the effects of even a relatively simple, taken-for-granted diagnostic procedure such as amniocentesis – by which, among other things, fetal gender is revealed – upon societies and cultures where there is tremendous pressure on women to bear males? Each of these developments has produced a counter-discourse. Genetic engineering, fetal neuron transplants and similar technological 'advances' in bio-medicine have produced outrage in some and swelled the ranks of the religious Right; unexamined importation of certain technological and medical procedures has produced a whole field of study called 'ethnobiology'. Ethnobiology generally denotes a field of study in which certain practices are examined for their degree of fit with different cultures. Included in this field is examination of, for example, agricultural techniques (not usually thought of as a cultural practice), pest control and medical practices (Harding 1993).

The culmination of crises brought about by the unexamined and pervasive application of modern technologies and modes of thought has created what several writers refer to as 'the postmodern condition' (Lyotard 1985). This term, even the concept itself, is problematic. There are those, like Seyla Benhabib (1990, 1992) and Anthony Giddens (1990), who suggest that this cannot be a postmodern epoch because we are still so firmly entrenched with/in the modern. Other philosophical quibbles revolve around the issue of whether the postmodern is a unique, discrete period whose primary trait is anti-modernism, or whether the so-called postmodern is simply a logical extension of the modern, built upon its foundation. In place of 'postmodern', Giddens (1990: 3) writes of the radicalization and universalization of modernity.[7]

Giddens (1990: 16–17) examines the dynamics that contribute to the radicalization of modernity: the separation of time and space, the disembedding of social systems and the reflexive ordering and reordering of social relations. What follows is a discussion of two of the crises of modernity – the crisis of scientific certainty and objectivity and the crisis of representation – and the ramifications of these crises for supervision. Also, poststructuralist discourse on the Other becomes relevant to the discussion of supervision with/in the modern.

The Crises of Scientific Certainty and Objectivity

Feminist philosophers of science have for some time been involved in demythologizing the western European, predominantly male, rational, objective and value-neutral posture of modern science (Harding 1990, 1993). Within contexts of modernity, science becomes problematic, due primarily to the phenomenon of the double hermeneutic. In Giddens's (1990: 17) discussion of modernity he refers to 'the reflexive ordering and reordering of social relations in light of continual inputs of knowledge affecting the actions of individuals and groups'. This double hermeneutic, Giddens believes, affects modern conceptions of knowledge and of science in that even as we gain some measure of understanding of a social phenomenon, we change the phenomenon because of our understanding. Science, it seems, has succeeded too well at its own game. Science usurped tradition and replaced it with rationalism, positivism. In so doing, the sense of greater certitude offered by science

> actually subverts reason, at any rate where reason is understood as the gaining of certain knowledge . . . We are abroad in a world which is throughly constituted through reflexively applied knowledge, but where at the same time we can never be sure that any given element of that knowledge will not be revised. (Giddens 1990: 39)

Thus, writes Giddens,

> In science, *nothing* is certain, and nothing can be proved, even if scientific endeavor provides us with the most dependable information about the world to which we can aspire. In the heart of the world of hard science, modernity floats free.

Application of these ideas to supervision and educational leadership problematizes classroom observation. In conventional instructional supervision, the supervisor observes a lesson, takes 'data' through some observation instrument, and reports on the 'findings' of the observation in a post-conference. Questions of what constitutes data, whose data they are, and what values are embedded in the instruments and models chosen are relevant here – though seldom asked and never answered (Garman 1990: 202). Conditions of modernity also belie the certainty of teacher evaluation systems.

The Crisis of Representation

The second crisis of modernism with direct practical importance for supervision is what has been termed 'the crisis of representation' (Benhabib 1990: 109–13, 1992: 205–11; Harding 1990: 94–99). Harding's critique of positivism's claims at representation draw her to advocate 'feminist standpoint theories' in their stead. Benhabib (1990: 109) foresees the 'demise of the classical episteme of representation' and credits Jurgen Habermas with identifying four trends of modernity which contribute to the irrationality of modern society. These trends have particular relevance for supervision and educational leadership with/in the modern. They are:

> [F]irst, access to the public sphere has always been limited by particularistic considerations of class, race, gender and religion; second, *increasingly not the consensual generation of norms but money and power have become modes through which individuals define the social bond and distribute social goods*... Third, as money and power become increasingly autonomous principals of social life, *individuals lose a sense of agency and efficacy*... Fourth, *the demands of increased role-distance* and continuing subjection of tradition to critique and revision in a disenchanted universe *make it difficult for individuals to develop a coherent sense of self and community* under conditions of modernity. (Benhabib 1992: 80–81; emphasis added)

Applied to supervision, this means that supervisors practicing conventional techniques may inadvertently contribute to power differentials and an incoherent sense of community, in short, to the alienation, atomization and disenfranchisement of teachers (Waite in press).

Benhabib (1990: 110) notes that the 'classical episteme of representation presupposed a spectator conception of the knowing self, a designative theory of meaning, and a denotative theory of language'. In the classical positivist tradition, 'meaning was defined as "designation"; the meaning of a word was what it designates, while the primary function of language was denotative, namely to inform us about objectively existing states of affairs' (Benhabib 1992: 206). Benhabib details three distinct directions of critique which, when taken together, lead to the rejection of the classical episteme: 'the critique of the modern epistemic subject ... the critique of the modern epistemic object, and ... the critique of the modern concept of the sign' (Benhabib 1990: 110).

The third line of critique, begun with Ferdinand de Saussure and Charles Sanders Pierce and extending through Wittgenstein, posited 'the public and shared character of language as a starting point' (Benhabib 1990: 112). Benhabib might have added Bakhtin to this list, for his work integrates all these lines of critique within his conception of 'translinguistics'.[8]

Dialogic Supervision as a Corrective

There are many authors in the area of supervision who privilege the objective nature of supervisory observations and feedback. Acheson and Gall (1992: 12), for example, hold that a goal of clinical supervision is 'to provide teachers with objective feedback on the current state of their instruction'.[9] This mindset perpetuates not only certain worldviews, but respective teacher and supervisor roles that are inflexible and unresponsive (Waite 1992a, 1992b, 1993; Hargreaves 1994).

What is the role of the teacher in supervision? What is the role of the supervisor? What purpose does supervision serve? The classical episteme would posit teachers as passive recipients of supervisors' expert knowledge. This way of thinking results in the fatalistic find-what's-wrong-and-tell-them-how-to-fix-it phenomenon assumed by many practicing administrators to be the core practice of supervision (Holland *et al.* 1991: 6).

Research on teacher–supervisor conferences (Waite 1992b, 1993, in press) has demonstrated power balance shifts between teacher and supervisor from the pre-conference to post-conference. Equal relations in a pre-conference often become unequal in the ensuing post-conference, with power accruing to the supervisor. This is understandable given that in a pre-conference it is the teacher who generally holds the information and the supervisor who is in the role of learner, answer seeker. One can easily see how this is the case. Acheson and Gall (1992: 102) suggest that the supervisor ask four basic questions of the teacher during the pre-conference: What is the lesson to be about?; What will you (the teacher) be doing during the lesson?; What will the students be doing during the lesson?; and what would you like me (the supervisor) to look for? The only intervening variable which could account for the power shift from the pre-conference to the post-conference seems to be the addition of the observational record, the data.

The power-shift phenomenon between the pre and post-conference should come as no surprise to those familiar with the literature concerning the nature of science and objectivity, and the power of these discourses to persuade and convince. Science, scientific research, and its findings are more often used to settle a question, to end a debate or discussion, than they are used to free up discussion. In this regard, use of 'hard' data in supervision may in fact close down discussion rather than open it up.

Conventional supervisory observations and their subsequent conferences are reductionistic (see Figure 6.1). That is, the supervisory process, as

Figure 6.1:   Schematic representation of reductionistic tendencies in conventional clinical supervision

School Contexts

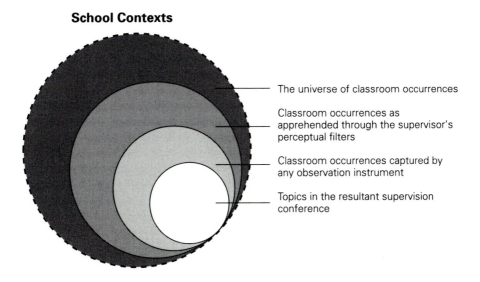

The universe of classroom occurrences

Classroom occurrences as apprehended through the supervisor's perceptual filters

Classroom occurrences captured by any observation instrument

Topics in the resultant supervision conference

traditionally practiced, reduces what gets seen and talked about. These reductionistic practices, whether intended or not, serve particular aims and ignore or exclude others. It is generally the teacher who gets short shrift in the conventional clinical supervision cycle. This is so because, as illustrated in Figure 6.1, classrooms are busy places, cognitively and perceptually dense. No one can see all that goes on in a classroom, and some of what goes on in classrooms is invisible (Erickson 1986b). Of the processes that can be visually or auditorially perceived, the supervisor's (or another observer's) biases and perceptual filters omit important occurrences. Further reductions in what gets recorded and talked about result from the use of an observation instrument, any observation instrument. Even the best observation instrument, the least selective, cannot capture even a small percentage of what the supervisor's perceptual filters allow to pass through to conscious recognition. This phenomenon is at the root of discussions of the crisis of representation. What finally gets discussed in a supervision conference is reduced further still.

Further reductionism is occasioned by the interactional face-to-face processes of the conference itself, as was made evident in Chapters 2 and 3. Usually the supervisor shares or reports the data from the observation to the teacher. This is often done in compressed time. The teacher may comment on or respond to what the supervisor reports. Seldom is the teacher allowed to speak his or her mind, to say anything he or she wants. All teacher contributions in such a conference are responses to the supervisor's report of the data. The supervisor, whether he or she wishes to or not, controls the entire conference. Even in the most collaborative of conferences, it is the supervisor's data that frame the interaction.

Teachers are disempowered through the normal supervisory process because, in part, conversations are sequential (and linear); seldom are they holistic or gestalt experiences. No one can talk about everything at once. As an example, how often in a conversation such as a class discussion does the talk move on to make now irrelevant the contribution the student with his or her hand raised wished to make? In order to make relevant a now irrelevant comment, the potential speaker needs to do a lot of interactional work (e.g. 'Remember when you said . . .').

Supervision conferences flow and topics become interactionally irrelevant. If a teacher wants to bring up an issue, he or she must do the necessary work ('You said that . . . but I feel that . . .'). This is not always possible and seldom likely. The press of the moment proscribes against it, the conversation moves on, the teacher and supervisor have other (more important?) things to do. The end result is that teachers seldom can bring up their concerns, free and unencumbered, except maybe with other teachers in informal settings. In supervision conferences, owing to their formal and ritual nature (Garman 1990: 211), not any and all topics are sanctioned as legitimate ones for discussion. In a free and open discussion, in the dialogic supervision process, *any* topic is appropriate, any assumption or authority can be questioned.

If the goals of supervision and supervisory conferences include teacher reflection, participation, empowerment and change, then we ought to seek alternatives to the traditional supervision pre-conference–observation–post-conference ritual. One alternative, with liberatory potential for teacher and supervisor alike, is 'dialogic supervision', based on the work of M. M. Bakhtin.[10]

Bakhtin and the Dialogic Principle

Bakhtin was a Russian intellectual, internally exiled during Stalin's reign, who wrote and taught from the early 1900s until his death in 1975.[11] Possibly due to the time in which he was writing or the tardiness of his translation into English, Bakhtin's influence is still cresting in American academia. His most influential works are *Rabelais and His World* (1968), *Problems of Dostoevsky's Poetics* (1973), and *The Dialogic Imagination* (1981b).

Bakhtin's application to the field of supervision, especially, is to be found in his exegesis of dialogue, the dialogic and dialogism, and his notion of unfinalizability.[12] He has been characterized as a philosophical anthropologist (Todorov 1984: 94–112) and his notion of the dialogic principle as a distinct epistemology (Holquist 1990: 14–17). More specifically, Gardiner (1992: 170) terms Bakhtin's project a 'proto-existentialist philosophical anthropology', while White (1984: 142) credits Bakhtin's dialogism with establishing a 'critical socio-linguistics of culture'. Holquist, however, sees Bakhtin's contribution as much more than an epistemology. He makes the claim that dialogism is also an axiology, concerned with 'social and ethical values as the means by which the fundamental I/other split articulates itself in specific situations'. Furthermore, Holquist believes dialogism to be a science of building, an 'architectoncs' – that is, in so far as 'the act of perception is understood as a patterning of a relation' (1990: 33).

As best as can be described in this short space, the dialogic principle refers to the notion that an utterance takes place in already inhabited inter-actional zones. A word is already always inhabited with others' meanings, an utterance, more so. Bakhtin (1981a: 293) wrote that 'the word in language is half someone else's', in that 'language, for the individual consciousness, lies on the borderline between oneself and the other'.

The world for Bakhtin is known for its 'heteroglossia', its multivoicedness. This is an important concept for Bakhtin and marked a radical departure from the dominant Saussurian linguistics of his day. *Heteroglossia* is the influence of another's word upon an utterance, the stylization of it in a novel, for example, 'involves a sideways glance at others' languages, at other points of view and other conceptual systems, each with its own set of objects and meanings' (Bakhtin 1981a: 376). Heteroglossia is a 'social diversity of speech types' (1981a: 263).

Language processes include, for Bakhtin, *centripetal* and *centrifugal* forces – forces acting to pull the language to a unified center and opposing forces acting to pull a language apart. Centripetal forces (those associated with monologism, another important theme for Bakhtin) include movements to-ward standardization and centralization, a 'correct language'. (Bakhtin 1981a: 270). Much more is at stake than linguistic norms for Bakhtin, who conceives language as

> ideologically saturated . . . a world view, even as a concrete opinion, insuring a *maximum* of understanding in all spheres of ideological life. Thus a unitary language gives expression to forces working to-ward concrete verbal and ideological unification and centralization, which develop in vital connection with the process of sociopolitical and cultural centralization. (p. 271)

These forces socially stratify language into languages that are 'socio-ideological: languages of social groups, "professional" and "generic"' languages, languages of generations and so forth' (p. 272).[13]

Operating concurrently with the centripetal forces are the countervailing centrifugal forces of language, the forces of 'decentralization and disunification' (Bakhtin 1981a: 272). Slang, parody, humor in general, and the carnivalesque aspects of speech are examples of centrifugal forces at work on language.

At any given moment, both these forces are at play simultaneously, cre-ating a 'contradiction-ridden, tension-filled unity of two embattled tendencies in the life of language' (Bakhtin 1981a: 272). It is these two forces acting upon an utterance that produces heteroglossia:

The authentic environment of an utterance, the environment in which it lives and takes shape, is dialogized heteroglossia, anonymous and social as language, but simultaneously concrete, filled with content and accented as an individual utterance. (1981a: 272)

The dialogic principle explains how words mediate understanding, how words are encrusted with others' meaning even as they are directed at another's conceptual horizon and that other's 'future answer-word' (Bakhtin 1981a: 280). The word, the utterance, 'structures itself in the answer's direction' and forms 'itself in an atmosphere of the already spoken, the word is at the same time determined by that which has not yet been said but which is needed and in fact anticipated by the answering word' (1981a: 280). Going much further than traditional Saussurian linguistics, Bakhtin posits an active responsiveness on the speaker's part. Rather than positing an ideal speech situation with a passive listener, Bakhtin believes speakers and their words are directed to active understanding, 'one that discourse senses as resistance or support enriching the discourse' (1981a: 281).[14] In Bakhtin's terms:

this contradictory environment of alien words is present to the speaker not in the object, but rather in the consciousness of the listener, as his (*sic*) apperceptive background, pregnant with responses and objections. And every utterance is oriented toward this apperceptive background of understanding, which is not a linguistic background but rather one composed of specific objects and emotional expressions. (1981a: 281)

The speaker orients himself or herself to the specific, concrete 'conceptual horizon' of the other when in a dialogical relationship. In Bakhtin's (1981a: 282) admittedly overly militaristic language: 'The speaker breaks through the alien conceptual horizon of the listener, constructs his (*sic*) own utterance on alien territory, against his, the listener's, apperceptive background.' 'The word', in the sense which Bakhtin conceives it and its interaction, 'lives, as it were, on the boundary between its own context and another, alien, context' (1981a: 284).

Thus, dialogization has internal and external aspects. Externally, dialogization takes place between two alien conceptual horizons using words encrusted with still others' meanings. Internally, dialogization takes place within a single speaker or self, using these same already invested words, and takes place between different speaker states and/or at different times (between past and present selves).

In sum, we have then the definition of dialogization provided by Caryl Emerson and Michael Holquist (Bakhtin 1981b: 426) in the glossary companion to their translation of *The Dialogic Imagination*:

Dialogism is the characteristic epistemological mode of a world dominated by heteroglossia. Everything means, is understood, as part of a greater whole – there is a constant interaction between meanings, all of which have the potential of conditioning others. Which will affect the other, how it will do so and in what degree is what is actually settled at the moment of utterance. This dialogic imperative, mandated by the pre-existence of the language world relative to any of its current inhabitants, insures that there can be no monologue.

Dialogism and its opposite, monologism, relate various poles on the continuum of authority, and on the nature of power.

Bakhtin sought to explicate literary genres and, in doing so, contributed to the complexity of the meanings of authorship. What are the sources of authority on which authors and their characters draw? What are the relationships between genres – contemporary and historical – between the author and the text's characters, and between the multiple characters within a single work? These are essential questions for Bahktin. Bakhtin's work has been extended to include examinations of 'authorship . . . [as] a form of governance' (Holquist 1990: 34).

In order to understand the work of Bakhtin and the relevance it holds for supervision better, it might be advantageous to oppose two of his fundamental concepts. The first, dialogism, we have touched upon briefly; the second, opposing principle, monologism, is worthy of further discussion here. In explicating the distinctions between these two opposing concepts, their relevance for supervision, indeed any face-to-face encounter, should become apparent.

Monologism[15] can be thought of as the movement toward a unitary language: 'Totalitarian government always seeks the (utopian) condition of absolute monologue' because the aim of such a government is 'the suppression of all otherness in the state so that its creator alone might flourish' (Holquist 1990: 34). Authoritative language borrows from the monologic. In supervision conferences or wherever, authoritative language reifies the word: 'only a single and unitary language, one that does not acknowledge other languages alongside itself, can be subject to reification' (Bakhtin 1981a: 336).

Bakhtin (1981a: 342) described an ideological dynamic between the forces he termed 'authoritative discourse' and 'internally persuasive discourse'. Both these forces contribute to the development of the individual ideological consciousness:

> The ideological becoming of a human being . . . is the process of selectively assimilating the words of others . . . The authoritative word demands that we acknowledge it, that we make it our own; it binds us, quite independent of any power it might have to persuade us internally; we encounter it with its authority already fused to it. The authoritative word is located in a distanced zone, organically connected with a past that is felt to be hierarchically higher. It is, so to speak, the word of the fathers. (1981a: 341, 342)

The authoritative word 'is indissolubly fused with its authority – with political power, an institution, a person' (1981a: 343). The domains of the authoritative word are the 'religious, political, moral; the word of a father, of adults and of teachers, etc.' (1981a: 342); one might hasten to add 'the words of supervisors and other administrators'. In supervision, such authoritative discourse is usually signaled by such phrases as: 'according to the superintendent . . .'; or 'the district guidelines state . . .'; or 'research says . . .'; or 'the whole language process (or whatever) is done like this . . .'; and so on. 'Authoritative discourses may embody various contents: authority as such, or the authoritativeness of tradition, of generally acknowledged truths, of the official line and other similar authorities' (1981a: 344). The authoritative word is distant from the zone of contact and cannot be separated, cannot be divided up and appropriated piecemeal – one cannot choose which parts to accept and which to reject. It is reified and monologic in that one does not enter into a dialogic relation with the authoritative word, though, as will be shown later, one *can* enter into a dialogic relationship with authorities.

Set against the authoritative word is the internally persuasive word and its discourse. The internally persuasive word also embodies the language of others; however, it enters into an internal dialogue within the hearer's consciousness. The advent of a unique individual ideological consciousness is brought about through dialogue with the internally persuasive word:

> When thought begins to work in an independent, experimenting and discriminating way what first occurs is a separation between internally persuasive discourse and authoritarian enforced discourse, along with a rejection of those congeries of discourses that do not matter to us, that do not touch us. (Bakhtin 1981a: 345)

The dynamic tension between authoritative and internally persuasive discourse is characteristic of Bakhtin's epistemology. That epistemology is a fluid, forceful interplay of opposing forces taking place at the site of the individual, be it the individual utterance or consciousness: '[T]here is a struggle constantly being waged to overcome the official line [the authoritative] with its tendency to distance itself from the zone of contact, a struggle against various kinds and degrees of authority' (Bakhtin 1981a: 345).

Internally persuasive discourse, on the other hand, is 'denied all privilege, backed by no authority at all, and is frequently not even acknowledged by society (not by public opinion, nor by scholarly norms, nor by criticism), not even in the legal code' (Bakhtin 1981a: 342).[16] It is 'tightly interwoven with "one's own word"' and

> its creativity and productiveness consist precisely in the fact that such a word awakens new and independent words, that it organizes masses of our words from within, and does not remain in an isolated and static condition. It is not so much interpreted by us as it is further, that

is, freely, developed, applied to new material, new conditions; it enters into interanimating relationships with new contexts. More than that, it enters into an intense interaction, a *struggle* with other internally persuasive discourses. Our ideological development is just such an intense struggle within us for hegemony among various available verbal and ideological points of view, approaches, directions and values. The semantic structure of an internally persuasive discourse is *not finite*, it is *open*, in each of the contexts that dialogize it, this discourse is able to reveal ever newer *ways to mean*. (Bakhtin 1981a: 345–6)

Unique to the internally persuasive discourse is its relation to the context and the listener. Where authoritative discourse is static and distant, internally persuasive discourse is marked by its contemporaneity:

The internally persuasive word is either a contemporary word, born in a zone of contact with unresolved contemporaneity, or else it is a word that has been reclaimed for contemporaneity . . . [W]hat is constitutive for it is a special conception of listeners, readers, perceivers. Every discourse presupposes a special conception of the listener, of his (*sic*) apperceptive background and the degree of his responsiveness; it presupposes a specific distance. (Bakhtin 1981a: 346)

Framing of internally persuasive discourse, its transmission and its contexts, 'provide[s] maximal interaction between another's word and its context, for the dialogizing influence they have on each other, for the free and creative development of another's word, for a gradation of transmission' (Bakhtin 1981a: 346). These methods of transmission and framing the internally persuasive discourse in its context

govern the play of boundaries, the distance between that point where the context begins to prepare for the introduction of another's word and the point where the word is actually introduced (its 'theme' may sound in the text long before the appearance of the actual word). These methods account for other peculiarities as well . . . such as that word's semantic openness to us, its capacity for further creative life in the context of our individual consciousness, its unfinishedness and the inexhaustibility of our further dialogic interaction with it. (1981a: 346)

For Bakhtin, the ideological development of an individual consciousness, the movement away from authoritative, monologic discourse is one of struggle:

The importance of struggling with another's discourse, its influence in the history of an individual's coming to ideological consciousness, is enormous. One's own discourse and one's own voice, although born of another or dynamically stimulated by another, will sooner or later begin to liberate themselves from the authority of the other's discourse. (1981a: 348)

When viewed in this way, supervisory dialogue, indeed all dialogue within schools, takes on a new identity and purpose. If, as is the assumption here, supervision is concerned with the development and growth of people in schools, their fulfillment and realization of potential, then the struggle with the authoritative word must be joined by supervisors and teachers alike. This, according to Bakhtin, is the path to the realization of the individual's ideological consciousness within a community of voices.

The Dialogic Principle and Supervision

Supervisors and other school leaders must first recognize the diversity within even the most seemingly homogenous staff, school situation and context. Heteroglossia is more the norm than the exception.[17]

Supervisors and administrators need to examine the role they play in perpetuating the status quo (Blase 1993) – the accretion of others' words in their own, and the authoritarian side of school organizations within the wider society – their monologism and centripetal force. Along the lines suggested by the dialogic principle, supervisors must examine their own actions and words for the degree to which they are already always inhabited by others' ideas. For example, we sometimes say something and wonder where the words came from. 'I'm beginning to sound just like my mother' (or father), is a common parental meta-linguistic reflection. Supervisors, too, internalize other authorities' words and views, often without realizing it, without consciously choosing to do so.

Just as Bakhtin discusses the emergence of a consciousness – the ideological development of the individual consciousness, phrased by Bakhtin in terms of struggle – it is presumptuous to think this applies only to children or teachers. Supervisors develop too. They develop globally, in cognitive complexity and in personality, and they develop in interaction with others. Supervisors develop in their role (Waite 1994b), they develop ideologically, and they develop the political savvy to survive in that role. What aspects of this development are taken from others, out of their mouths, so to speak? Which of these borrowed thoughts and phrases actually run counter to what a supervisor believes deep in his or her heart? What can be jettisoned and what needs to be met on the ideological battlefield of already inhabited words and others' perceptual horizons? How can a supervisor be true to herself or himself and to the teachers with whom she or he works?

The first step in dialogic supervision, obviously, involves self-work, not that this work needs to be done in isolation or before assuming a supervisory role. That would run counter to Bakhtin's notion that the Self is developed in response to or in conjunction with others. The Self is not an atomistic, pre-existing entity, a *tabula rasa*, to be written at one's will. The Self is socially constructed. What is required is continual reflection on one's practice and beliefs. Others may lend assistance in this effort – teachers, superiors, other supervisors. In short, anyone with whom one comes into contact may provide the dynamic for self-reflection. One cannot do it oneself. Bakhtin writes that one cannot know the totality of oneself. I cannot see the whole of my life. I cannot see my death. I cannot see all the contexts that influence me even as I influence them. I cannot perceive the totality of the event in which I am emerged. The Other is needed for that.

This notion that the Other is needed to help one begin to perceive the whole of oneself is ample justification that there be supervisors, or someone to perform that role, in today's schools. Teachers cannot see the whole. This is not to suggest that supervisors are in a superior position *vis-à-vis* teachers, just that they are in a position of Other. Any Other could perform this service.

For matters of clarity and brevity, let us say that anyone performing this service – that of entering into a dialogic relationship with a teacher in order to grant that teacher an Other's perspective on their teaching, their embedded Self, is performing the services of a supervisor, that he or she is, in fact, and at that instant, a supervisor. How should a dialogic supervisor proceed?

In the Classroom

In order to see how dialogic supervision is enacted in the classroom it may be best to contrast it with other approaches (a decidedly Bakhtinian project). Acheson and Gall (1992: 12) privilege the objective nature of the data supervisors gather in classroom observations and the non-judgmental feedback supervisors give teachers. Indeed, these authors provide supervisors with no less than 35 supervisory 'techniques', 17 of which are classroom observation techniques!

One classroom observation technique not proposed by these authors is the 'null technique' – observation of a classroom by a supervisor or Other where *no* explicit data gathering technique is used.[18] Rather than risking reification of the supervisor's perceptions through the process of objectifying complex classroom contexts and occurrences as 'data', the dialogic supervisor or peer observer becomes a witness to a teaching episode in order to enter into a dialogue with that teacher. Of course, data may be gathered through paper-and-pencil instruments or other means at various times, but dialogic supervision seeks to focus on and enhance the quality of the teacher–supervisor conversation, the dialogue, rather than focusing on the data. When the supervisor witnesses in this way, both teacher and supervisor have a better chance of coming to the table on an equal footing, having participated in a shared experience (to the extent that is possible) to which they may refer in the ensuing discussion.

Of course, there must be a context already established for such supervisor–

teacher conversations to take place. One of the ground rules of dialogic supervision is that participants are free, indeed encouraged, to question anyone's assumptions. This is done within a relationship of mutual trust and reciprocity. Another underpinning of the dialogic approach, an essential element for the approach to succeed, is that dialogic supervision is to be employed for reflection and growth (i.e. for its potential to foster freedom and liberation) and *not* for monitoring for control. Monitoring for control, surveillance, is a bureaucratic function, one of the dangers or dark sides of organizations within a radicalized modernity.

> In respect of administrative resources, tendencies towards increasing democratic involvement have as their dark side possibilities for the creation of totalitarian power. The intensifying of surveillance operations provides many avenues of democratic involvement, but also makes possible the sectional control of political power, bolstered by monopolistic access to the means of violence. Totalitarianism and modernity are not just contingently, but inherently, connected . . . (Giddens 1990: 172)

Such uses of the knowledge and rapport gained through implementation of dialogic supervision must be avoided by the dialogic supervisor. Coming to the conference with no explicit data allows for the possibility to emerge that the supervisor's assumptions and biases are laid bare, revealed and examined instead of having them embedded within some supposedly neutral scientistic observation record.

An explanation by way of an example may help clarify this last point. An often used observation instrument, known to most supervisors and some teachers, is that called the 'At Task' instrument (Acheson and Gall 1992: 127–33). With this instrument, the supervisor codes students' behaviors as to whether they are on or off task and may capture other behaviors as well. Embedded within this instrument and its use are various assumptions, tenuous at best, about the nature of tasks in general and beliefs, extrapolated from the literature on effective teaching, that time on task somehow equates with improved student learning. A moment's reflection reveals that the problematic nature of defining the task undermines whatever objectivity is presumed for this instrument.

First of all, only overt student behaviors are available to the supervisor for coding. Use of this instrument, with its embedded assumptions, neglects the fact that humans are polyphasic (i.e. multiphased) or able to do many tasks at once. We are able to walk and chew gum at the same time, for example, or do homework with the television on. Students actually may or may not be attending to a lesson whether or not they seem to be; their overt, observable behavior is often a poor indication of their attentiveness.

Another problematic aspect of using this instrument is in getting the teacher to define the task the supervisor is to observe. Lessons have varying degrees of complexity at any one time, and lessons change over time. Getting teachers to make explicit in a pre-conference all of their implicit assumptions of the tasks the students are to be engaged in is nearly impossible, or at least highly improbable, in a conventional supervision pre-conference. A dialogic approach, however, stands a much better chance of getting at these assumptions.

Still another problematic embedded within the use of this particular instrument has been discussed by educational anthropologist Fred Erickson (1986b: 139). This has to do with who defines the task . Briefly put, everyone is on task all the time. The question for the anthropologist or any classroom observer becomes what is the task?

Other Dialogic Alternatives

The dialogic supervisor could supervise in the manner described above, through use of the 'null technique', though the process actually begins much earlier. For example, Diane Wood (1992) suggests that supervisors assist teachers in developing the teacher's narrative. This represents an important first step toward a dialogical relationship, though it falls short of establishing the multivoicedness which is the ideal goal of dialogic supervision.

Wood (1992) proposes a supervision and evaluation process of nine phases. The process of facilitating teachers' narratives begins with an interview in which the teacher is asked to recount 'a critical incident or particular memory of his or her teaching or learning experience' (p. 537). The development of the narrative proceeds through collaborative interpretation of that account, to the naming of a theme in the teacher's professional life, and the establishment of goals for the teacher's professional development based upon that theme. The process includes another interview and a classroom observation by the supervisor, with feedback. Finally, the process culminates in a written self-evaluation by the teacher, an evaluation of the teacher by the supervisor, and a joint discussion of further professional growth opportunities. Wood justifies this process with her belief

> that omitting subjective knowledge and personal knowledge from conceptions of what can be known denies us access to truth. The way teachers experience their lives as professionals matters, and the way they interpret and make meaning of their work can and should be grounds for inquiry, research, and theory in education. (1992: 545)

As stated, this supervisory facilitation of the development of teaching narratives offers an important first step toward a more dialogical relationship. However, enactment of Wood's process does not guarantee a symmetrical power relationship between supervisor and teacher. It is still the supervisor who acts on the teacher; the roles are never reversed. The teacher is the only agent asked to disclose her or his psyche. If the supervisor and the teacher each were encouraged to facilitate the development of the narrative of the other, the power differential has a better chance of being redressed. The assumption here is that, in a dialogical, egalitarian process both parties benefit. The *supervisor* gains valuable insights into both her or his own and the teacher's ways of making sense, and the *teacher* benefits from the intimate knowledge gained of the supervisor and of himself or herself.

Another weakness of the Wood approach, from a dialogical perspective, is that it assumes an individualistically-oriented agency; that is, the belief that the teacher can construct her or his narrative uninfluenced by the supervisor. This notion runs counter to constructivist and interactionist notions of both discourse and meaning making. From the Bakhtinian perspective, all tellings are interactional constructions. The word for Bakhtin is formed in anticipation of the other's conceptual horizon, his or her answerability. The assumption that the narrative belongs solely to the teacher is fallacious.

Other weaknesses of the Wood (1992) approach – more likely to be rectified by a dialogical approach – are those shared by narrative inquiry generally (Bourdieu 1977a; Hargreaves 1993; Waite 1994a). Privileging one person's narrative (or phenomenological episteme) over another's contributes to power differentials. Historically, supervisory discourses were the privileged ones. In this light, supervisors facilitating the telling of teaching narratives can be viewed as a necessary corrective. However, it would be wrong to believe that the process of addressing power imbalances should necessarily end with the ascendancy of the teacher's point of view; especially if this means privileging one point of view to the exclusion of others.[19] The threat here is the potential for simply substituting one form of monologism, the supervisor's, with another, the teacher's. What about the student's point of view? Is the teacher's phenomenological construction to eclipse the student's (Hargreaves 1993)? What about other stakeholders in the educational process – parents, supervisors, administrators, other community members? Are they to be sacrificed at the altar of teacher narrative?

The answer is no. Following Bakhtin's dialogic principle, a teacher's voice is one among many, one voice in a heteroglot community of voices. Supervisors too have only one voice (not that supervisors speak with the same voice, nor teachers for that matter).[20] The project of the dialogic supervisor is to bring all those voices together on an equal footing.

Ideally, supervision conferences and their dialogue should approximate a moral conversation (Benhabib 1992: 8, 53–54). A moral conversation is a process 'in which the capacity to reverse perspectives, that is, the willingness to reason from the others' point of view, and the sensitivity to hear their voice is paramount' (1992: 8). The underpinnings of moral conversations are 'norms of universal moral respect and egalitarian reciprocity' (Benhabib 1992: 30), whose procedural steps include:

1   A philosophical theory of morality [the moral conversation] must show wherein the justifiability of moral judgments and/or normative assertions reside.

2 To justify means to show that if you and I argued about a particular moral judgment . . . and a set of normative assertions . . . that we could in principle come to a reasonable agreement (*rationales Einverständnis*).

3 A 'reasonable agreement' must be arrived at under conditions which correspond to our idea of a fair debate.

4 These rules of fair debate can be formulated as the 'universal-pragmatic' presuppositions of argumentative speech and these can be stated as a set of procedural rules . . .

5 These rules reflect the moral ideal that we ought to *respect* each other as beings whose standpoint is worthy of equal consideration (the principle of moral respect) and that furthermore,

6 We ought to treat each other as concrete human beings whose capacity to express this standpoint we ought to embrace by creating, whenever possible, social practices embodying the discursive ideal (the principle of egalitarian reciprocity). (Benhabib 1992: 30–31)

The goal of such moral conversations

> is the process of such dialogue, conversation and mutual understanding and not consensus . . . In conversation, I must know how to listen, I must know how to understand your point of view, I must learn to represent to myself the world and the other as you see them. If I cannot listen, if I cannot understand, and if I cannot represent, the conversation stops, develops into an argument, or maybe never gets started. (1992: 52)

Egalitarian reciprocity would be difficult for a teacher (or teachers) and a supervisor to achieve if each remains encrusted with layers of taken-for-granted beliefs about themselves, about schools and about children. A critical, reflective and receptive disposition must be kindled and nurtured throughout the dialogic supervisory process. (It is to be hoped that each party to the supervision process would maintain a critical and reflective disposition toward one's conditions, yet a caring and accepting attitude toward one's colleagues.) A deep respect for the Other is the background of the dialogic process, an authentic drive to understand is the dynamic.

An important aspect of the dialogic approach is that everything is held as being open to scrutiny and to question:

> a universal-pragmatic reformulation of transcendental philosophy . . . is postmetaphysical in the sense that truth is no longer regarded as the psychological attribute of human consciousness, or to be the property of a reality distinct from the mind, or even to consist in the process by which 'givens' in consciousness are correlated with 'givens' in experience. In the discursive justification and validation of truth claims

no moment is privileged as a given, evidential structure which cannot
be further questioned. (Benhabib 1992: 4–5)

For supervision, this would mean that each of the conferees could raise
any issue which he or she felt relevant, from any perspective, and based upon
any evidentiary claim thought substantial.

In the continuing and potentially unending discourse of the community of inquiry there are no 'givens', there are only those aspects of
consciousness and reality which at any point in time may enter into
our deliberations as evidence and which we find cogent in backing
our statements. (Benhabib 1992: 5)

In practice, upholding these ideals would mean authoritarian discourse is
interrogated and questioned, whether the authoritative discourse is spoken by
the teacher or supervisor. Though Bakhtin believed that the authoritative word
could not be taken apart and appropriated segmentally, nor interrogated
because of its distance from the site of interaction, the authorities *can* be
questioned. For example, if the supervisor states that a district rule is such-and-
such, or that the superintendent said so-and-so, these statements do not need
to be accepted at face value. The rules can be found, the superintendent can
be interviewed. Even the rule-making body can be approached and questioned about the policies it has set; the policies can be questioned. Of course,
within an open system, these interactions are much more probable and positive. Even within more closed, or monologic systems, however, the limits can
be tested and, hopefully, made more flexible through application of the dialogic
approach. The assumption here is that many, though not all, administrators,
at whatever hierarchical level, would welcome open communication. The disadvantages of the modern school organizational structure include its rigidity,
its inflexibility and unresponsiveness (Hargreaves 1994). Often those at the top
of hierarchical chains of command are insulated from and out of communication with everyone else in the organization except for those few with whom
they have formal relations, i.e. their immediate subordinates (Scollon and Scollon
1986).

Teachers' authoritative discourse is open to question also. If a teacher
says in conference that 'these children are lazy and don't do their work', this
statement is subject to refutation and/or verification. Simple action research
projects can be set up to analyze and affect the situation.

Obviously, much of the authoritative discourse could not be interrogated
at the moment of the utterance, within the context of the immediate supervision conference. Time will be needed to take one's concerns to the supposed
author/authority. The supervisor could do this simply because in his or her
role it is usually the supervisor who has greater mobility and, perhaps, easier
access to the author of the authoritative discourse, but this need not always be
so. The teacher may be empowered to carry the questions generated to others.

In this way one of the goals of dialogic supervision, that of moving toward a heteroglot community, is initiated. A truly heteroglot, multivoiced community remains an ideal; not all superintendents and boards of education would be open to justifying themselves to teachers and supervisors. Without this type of activism on educators' parts, however, it is less likely that policy makers and others would take responsibility for those decisions that are made at a distance which affect teachers and students and their lived experiences daily.

Also, because of the distance of the authoritarian voices from the scene, it may take some time for there to come a reply, or no reply may be forthcoming. This should not deter conference participants, teacher and supervisor, from seeking to dialogue with the authors of authoritarian words, nor should it keep them from acting while awaiting a reply. The teacher and supervisor should not become frozen in anticipation of a reply. The questions raised and the replies anticipated become but one voice, one avenue of inquiry and growth in the tapestry that is the life of the classroom and school.

Another strategy with the potential to foster dialogic supervisory relationships is for the teacher and supervisor to reverse roles. One possibiity is for the supervisor to generate some data using an appropriate observation instrument, but in the conference, the teacher assumes the traditional role of the supervisor while the supervisor assumes the role of teacher (see Chapters 2 and 3 for a discussion of more conventional roles). In such a reversal, the teacher would then report on the data and the supervisor would respond. Use of this procedure would allow for the reversal of perspectives prized by Benhabib.

Another possible procedure is that which was briefly described above. Here, the supervisor uses the 'null technique' and simply witnesses a teaching/learning episode. Then, after agreeing on the ground rules, the two co-construct the lesson with neither's perspective being the privileged one. The ground rules to be agreed upon are Benhabib's procedural steps for a moral conversation – the search for reasonable agreement in a dialogic process replete with mutual respect and characterized by reciprocal egalitarianism.

The search for understanding is one of the main goals of dialogic supervision.[21] The goal is for the teacher to understand the supervisor's perspective and for the supervisor to understand the teacher's perspective. Understanding, though it sounds inconsequential, is a difficult goal to attain. Often teachers and supervisors are more interested in immediate action and stop-gap solutions than they are in authentic communication. To strive for understanding, the actors may have to delay action until some semblance of understanding is attained. This is difficult to do.

Other possible processes to experiment with in aspiring to a dialogic ideal of supervision include having others' portrayals of classroom occurrences frame the interaction between teacher and supervisor. Using others to do the initial classroom observations mitigates some authors' criticisms that clinical supervision is too time and labor intensive (Glatthorn 1983). Other teachers, classroom aides, student teachers, students themselves, even parent volunteers and school auxiliary staff (custodians, lunchroom workers, bus drivers, etc.) could be taught classroom observation and recording techniques in order to generate the data that might stimulate teacher–supervisor dialogue. (These others might even be invited to join the table during the discussion, if desired.) The use of others to generate the data informing the teacher–supervisor dialogue accomplishes several goals of a dialogic approach. It brings other perspectives, other voices, to the conference and it relieves both the teacher and the supervisor from the onus of the expert role. This process equalizes relationships (no one has an investment in the data *per se*) and dampens objections to the claimed objectivity of scientific data gathering. These third-party perspectives could easily be interrogated by both the teacher and supervisor. The likelihood of a confrontation over interpretation of classroom occurrences between the supervisor and teacher is lessened by using data gathered by some third party.

Conclusion

A dialogic supervisor could take the process as far as is possible and as long as it is of some benefit. The question of how far to take the process of inclusion must be addressed at some point since the contexts of supervision conferences are multilayered and the potential contributors, the multiple voices possible, are nearly infinite. It is recommended that supervisors wishing to begin the dialogic supervision process begin locally, with oneself and with one's immediate partner. Establishing the norms of egalitarian reciprocity and mutual respect between teacher and supervisor while discussing teaching and learning is a worthy project with which to begin.

Notes

1 See the comments of Phil Schlechty in Brandt (1993a).
2 This point has not been lost on Flinders (1991), who, writing on changing supervisors' relationships with teachers, wrote that: 'This concern is in keeping with the etymology that connects the word *communication* with the word community . . . communication implies a process of coming together' (p. 105).
3 'The idealized image of community' also bothered the Russian anthropological linguist, Mikhail Bakhtin, upon whose writing much of this chapter is based. Caryl Emerson (1993) states that Bakhtin was 'reluctant to grant any authority to group identity' and was 'suspicious of organization and "tediology"'.
4 For example, note the success the women's movement has had in changing not only popular language, but popular thinking as well. Such changes are recursive and occur at fundamental levels of consciousness.
5 Though this is held to be true for *all* current and past models or approaches to supervision, the critique here will center mainly on the approach known as clinical supervision, perhaps the most benign and responsive of supervision models, the implication being that if the criticisms here apply to clinical supervision, then they are true for the other approaches as well.

6   Recent interpretation, analysis and application of Bakhtin's work has propelled renewed academic interest in language, culture and cultural studies. See for example Todorov (1984), Hirschkop (1986), Hirschkop and Shepherd (1989), Barsky and Holquist (1990), Holquist (1990), Gardiner (1992), Hall (in press).

7   This convention, that of writing of modernity rather than of the postmodern, is employed throughout this book.

8   Todorov (1984) equates translinguistics with the current term 'pragmatics' and its meaning. Todorov refers to Bakhtin as 'the modern founder of this discipline' (1984: 24).

9   These authors write of the differences between '"hard" data' and '"soft" data' (Acheson and Gall 1992: 186), privileging the former. True, they do provide the qualification that 'all data are more or less subjective', but that is as near as they come to admitting that all so-called data are value-laden, and therefore suspect.

10 Granted, some may view the present project as an appropriation or colonization of Bakhtin and his work. After all, Bakhtin was concerned with text and discourse in the text. However, the extension of the dialogic principle to real-life dialogue is natural and, in fact, may be said to have been anticipated by Bakhtin himself. He, perhaps more than others, was aware of the subsequent readings and rereadings, interpretations and reinterpretations a text goes through – a process he referred to as 're-accentuation': 'Every age re-accentuates in its own way the works of its most immediate past. The historical life of classic works is in fact the uninterrupted process of their social and ideological re-accentuation. Thanks to the intentional potential embedded in them, such works have proved capable of uncovering in each era and against ever new dialogizing backgrounds ever newer aspects of meaning; their semantic content literally continues to grow, to further create out of itself. Likewise their influence on subsequent creative works inevitably includes re-accentuation' (Bakhtin 1981a: 421).

Others have looked to Bakhtin for support in their ideological projects. Hirschkop (1986: 104) adroitly describes the ideological tug-of-war that politicizes Bakhtin's work resulting, he believes, from the ambiguity of the original: 'Conditions of ideological struggle, rather than subjective attitudes, define the shape of dialogism and monologism. Not surprisingly, differences in the political inflection of Bakhtin interpretation derive from this central ambiguity. For the liberal theorist, the novel [or the dialogic principle] symbolizes the ideal condition of discourse we would all enjoy if only we recognized our constitutively social nature. For the Left, however, dialogism tends to be the local tactic whereby the popular subverts the ideology of that part of the social, the ruling class, whose function is exploitation.'

Though in the present work I am more inclined toward Hirschkop's caricature of the liberal project, I am not about to neglect the ideological (i.e. political) implications of Bakhtin's terms and concepts within the real-life contexts of supervision.

11 See Todorov (1984: 3–13) on Bakhtin's biographical particulars.

12 Emerson (1993) notes Bakhtin's three major concepts, or contributions to the world of ideas:

1   *prosaics,* 'that deep preference for irregularities of prose' as opposed to the regularities of poetry, and 'also a view of the world that sees messiness and particularity';

2   *dialogue and understanding of the creative process,* that 'any genuine consciousness requires for normal growth the continued interaction of at least two embodied voices'; and

3   the belief in *unfinalizability,* particularly 'the virtues of surprise and creativity in everyday life', the belief that one could 'never start anything over fresh', and that 'the past always leaked into the present and left traces'.

13 A more recent discussion of this phenomenon is offered by Pierre Bourdieu (1977b) in 'The Economics of Linguistic Exchanges'.

14 In his attack on Saussurian linguistics, Bakhtin wrote: 'A passive understanding of linguistic meaning is no understanding at all' (1981a: 281).

15 Each of these concepts represents an ideal end-state, hardly ever realized in actuality.

16 These two concepts, the authoritative and the internally persuasive discourses, are roughly equivalent to Bruner's (1985) paradigmatic and narrative modes of thought respectively.

17 Hargreaves (1990) writes on the differences between teacher and administrator cultures, especially as regards different perspectives on time. Administrators, notes Hargreaves, tend toward a monochronic view of time; teachers, especially elementary teachers, are enveloped in a polychronic environment.

See Hall's (1983) *The Dance of Life* for a complete discussion of the many different types of time and the effects differing views of time have on how people both organize their lives and interpret others' lives.

18 Nolan and Frances (1992) encourage supervisors to gather data through other than paper-and-pencil means. I am not so sure that they would go so far as to recommend that the supervisor gather no explicit (external) data.

19 Thanks to John Elliott (personal communication, April 9 1993) for planting the seed of this cognitive dissonance in me.

20 Thanks to Andy Hargreaves (personal communication, May 1993) for clarifying this for me.

21 Understanding the teacher and the teacher's perspective was one of the original goals of clinical supervision (Goldhammer 1969), since lost in the press of modernity.

Chapter 7

Creating Environments for Moral, Egalitarian Dialogue: Supervisors and Teachers As Partners in a Professional Community

As we have seen, instructional supervision is an interactional achievement and more. It is also a thought process, and can be a thoughtful process, involving administrators, supervisors, teachers, parents, auxiliary staff and students in discussions about and changes in learning, on everyone's part. To paraphrase Gregory Bateson's (1972) notions, the system learns from the feedback it receives. All parts of that system can and should contribute to the feedback, to the input into decisions affecting the systems of which they are a part. To do otherwise would to be to deny and negate strides made in participatory decision making and democracy in schools. Just how to amplify the systems' feedback and what such processes would mean for schools and those within them is the subject of this chapter.

First, no one should be excluded a priori from the decision making/ learning process, no one should be excluded by definition. To do so assigns real people to the category of the Other, marginalizes them and places them beyond the pale. Rather, instructional leaders (however they choose to define themselves) must spend time in deciding what consitutes a particular community (that is, the stakeholders) for any arena of decisions to be agreed upon and enacted. This question is at the heart of Glickman's (1993) book, *Renewing America's Schools* (though Glickman concentrates more heavily on areas of instructional decisions). Not only should these areas affecting instruction be decided upon and those decisions reviewed periodically, the *processes* by which the decisions are made and, perhaps more importantly, those processes by which the decisions made are implemented should also be open to the purview of those affected.

These decisions, those of who constitutes the immediate and appropriate community, are not to be entered into lightly. Indeed in other fields much discussion has centered around just how to define a community (Bloomfield 1933; Benhabib 1992; Sergiovanni 1992; Etzioni 1993; Lyotard 1993). Often, it is not known who will be affected by any particular decision until after it has been implemented for some time, and only upon thoughtful reflection on the implementation's consequences. That is why decisions must always be open to reconsideration, and not only the decisions themselves, but who is to be allowed input into them, at what stage, how they are to be implemented, their effects assessed and changes made.

Supervisors and other educational leaders can facilitate these processes. At the heart, these issues really are issues of communication, issues of voice. One way in which supervisors can facilitate this process is for them to act as advocates for those who will be affected, as champions of the disempowered. In operationalizing this maxim we encounter our first major problem, for putting this idea into practice may entail large amounts of time on the instructional leader's part and often taking time to, for instance, research a problem and delineating who the affected stakeholders are, runs counter to prevailing modes of operation in schools, where leaders are valorized for 'thinking on their feet' and where professional educators are socialized to an action, rather than a cognitive, orientation (see Hargreaves 1984, 1990, 1994). Time is a problem.

Schools are ruled by time, its cycles, and perhaps most of all, the way we conceive of it and its effects (Hall 1983; Clandinin 1985; Hargreaves 1990, 1994). We are slaves to time. Bells, clocks, schedules, age-graded cohorts,[1] standardized assessment, teacher evaluation, bus routes, lesson and unit plans, and adages such as 'don't let them see you smile til Christmas' and 'it's a full-moon day, the children are crazy', *all* and more reflect our obsession with time and the imposition of our culture's standard conception of time on our institutions, especially schools. Though it is true (from a functionalist perspective) that our conception of time performs some function, allows us to operate in a certain way, it is also true that it inhibits other ways of acting. (As examples, think, if you will, of the sanctions visited upon a teacher if his or her children are consistently late arriving to physical education classes, or if they don't progress through the texts at what is considered an appropriate rate.) Opening up our schools and their organization will require that we open up our thinking about time.[2]

Size of schools and other organizational features will need to be rethought if schools are to become, as Hargreaves (1994) so poignantly puts it, more flexible and responsive to changing times and changing demands. Size and the number of participants in an interaction are limiting features of communication (Scollon 1981b). The more people you have in an interaction, the less each is able to negotiate the type of interaction he or she desires. (Think of the difference between, say, a lecture and a seminar.) The debate about class size essentially centers on this issue, but the issue is relevant for the size of organizations as well as the size of classes.

Educational leaders have been experimenting with the 'school within a school' concept, and other variations on standard time and space their apportionment. As Hargreaves (1994) and Giddens (1990) argue however, time, along with space, are two of the primary casualties of a radicalized modernity. The trend to distantiation through time and space is not likely to abate. Yet schools and school leaders are simply tinkering with alternative models of school organization in seeking to bend time and space to grander purposes of schools and schooling. This is hardly enough. What we are in dire need of are educational leaders, true visionaries, who will put into place radically different organizations with their fundamentally different organizational structures so that those grander purposes of schooling will be protected, no, nurtured, in postmodern time(s).

One of the first consequences of the distantiation of time and space wrought by radicalized modernity is the erosion of relationships and community, in a word, humaneness.[3] Others have written about the affective side of education and the conditions necessary for the affective development of students (Rogers 1971; McDermott 1977; Noddings 1984; Eisner 1991). In applying the under-standing gleaned from studies of the affective development of students to that of adults, teachers and supervisors, it is obvious that attention needs to be paid to the contexts – the structures and processes – in which adults work if hu-mane, caring and egalitarian relationships are to flourish between supervisor and teacher and between teachers themselves. Often times, unfortunately, these environments are *not* attended to in any systematic way.

Simply put, the institutions in which teachers and supervisors work should become flexible and ever-renewing, yet supportive. Ecologists speak of biodiversity as a desirable goal. Yet such diversity must be planned and man-aged. It will not come about haphazardly and by coincidence. In human sys-tems, diversity is a strength which also needs to be thoughtfully managed, nurtured and protected. Eugene Odum (1994), the so-called 'father of ecol-ogy', speaks of systems that are mutualistic. He gives as an example the coral reef, where resources are limited and where the ecological systems and the species within them have evolved to be mutually supporting. The lessons to be learned for humans from systems like coral reefs, says Odum, is that when faced with questions of limited resources, we must 'think positive and suggest alternatives. Don't say "no" all the time . . . If you get crowded, you have to get more mutualistic.'

Fostering alternatives is a worthy goal for school leaders, supervisors and other administrators alike. Realization of this goal is a measure of how far the field of supervision has come.[4] With this end in mind – that of seeking out and fostering alternatives – the present book and alternative models or approaches presented herein should *not* be taken as simply another new orthodoxy. These alternative approaches are simply a few of the many possible alternatives available. Still, supervisors and other instructional leaders must act to identify alternatives to instructional development and school organization. Once iden-tified, these alternatives must be nurtured. They must be assessed and, per-haps, reworked based upon that feedback.

Simply identifying and initiating alternatives to traditional instructional improvement and conventional school organizational structures is but the beginning. These alternatives, like the biodiversity spoken of above, must be thoughtfully managed. This thoughtful management involves many processes – processes that include some traditional supervisory tasks such as curriculum development, staff development and instructional improvement (Oliva 1989);

some extensions of the traditional supervisory tasks, such as group development and action research (Glickman 1990); some other processes such as
those discussed in Chapters 5 and 6; and some supervisory processes that have
yet to be conceived.

The moral, thoughtful management of instructional development, of
supervisory *systems*, may entail conscientious resistance by supervisors themselves to regimes of domination and hegemony. (This again is another indication of how far the field of supervision has come.) It may be, as suggested in
Chapter 5, but really only hinted at there, that supervisors may serve as buffers, power buffers, to protect teachers from regimes of domination. Indeed,
'fending off interference from the environment' has been listed as a task function of the leadership role, along with those of

> initiating group action, predicting outcomes for various actions, train-
> ing group members . . . keeping members' attention on the goals, clari-
> fying issues, evaluating work done, [and] making expert information
> available. (Oja and Smulyan 1989: 144)

As an, albeit mild, example of this in practice, I can offer my ethnographic
observations of supervisors in the state of Georgia. Supervisors and other
administrators in Georgia are charged with observing and evaluating teachers
with an instrument based on Madeline Hunter's (1973) model of instruction.
According to the state-level mandate, these supervisory observations are to be
'drop in' observations, unannounced. You can only imagine the consternation
even the threat of one of these observations causes teachers. The stories of the
underground communication systems in place to notify one's fellow teachers
when the supervisor is roaming the halls with the infamous yellow pad are
legion. Conscientious and sensitive supervisors, principals among them, sub-
vert this system by scheduling their observations and, sometimes if the teacher
being observed is obviously not functioning at the level the supervisor knows
he or she is capable of, these conscientious souls will scrap the observation,
and offer to return some other day.

I question why these supervisors do not organize, rise up, protest and
throw off this unrealistic and inhumane system. That's a question to which I
have no ready answer. What I am suggesting is that these subversions be
documented and legitimized. In fact, I would suggest that supervisors go even
further in resisting administrative mandates and processes, like undue amounts
of paperwork and unreasonable demands on teachers' time, in fostering diversity among teaching staffs, and go further in identifying and nurturing alternative pedagogies. I suspect that such is the case now, though it is probably the
best kept secret in the field of supervision. For as de Certeau (1986) and others
(Terdiman, 1985; Lindstrom, 1992) have written, (and as I pointed out in Chapter
4) for each and every ideology, there is a corresponding discourse of resistance.

No doubt, and to the extent that what has been written here can be
appropriately termed an ideology, these words will engender resistances also.
It is interesting to contemplate what form those resistances might take.

Still, I stand behind what I have written here: that supervision is more than an expert system designed solely to aid in the improvement of instruction. All systems in our schools must be instantiated by living, breathing human beings. Such systems are far from mechanistic, and as such, are imbued with human dreams and aspirations, human feelings and frailties. Such systems are more flesh and blood than mechanistic or bureaucratic.

It is high time that everyone, from governmental education leaders to the schoolchildren and their parents themselves, come to realize the human in what schools and schools' systems do. Recognition of the human in our schools' systems permits recourse to the social sciences (i.e. the humanities) when explanations and understandings are sought in the design, description and reinvention of schooling, supervision included. Sole use of a mechanistic or bureaucratic paradigm to conceive of such systems blinds us to the humanity – with all its glories and potential for atrocity – of those who populate those systems and which, by definition, must enact them. Such blindness not only limits the possibilities of schooling, but does symbolic violence to teachers, students, supervisors and other school leaders.

What I have tried to do in these pages is to show just how truly human supervision is. After exposing the humanity of supervision, I have suggested several approaches which I entrust will make supervision even more human, more just, and more equitable. For it is my firmly held belief that supervision, indeed schooling itself, should be about the project of liberating human beings, not subjugating them as in the past.

Notes

1   When someone is 'ready' for school more often is felt to be associated with his or her chronological, as opposed to developmental or cognitive, age. Recently I experienced firsthand the effects of educators' intransigence concerning this phenomenon as my wife and I wrestled with the decision to promote our daughter, Tamara, from first grade to second in the middle of the academic school year. Fortunately, and to their credit, the local school officials gave us the major responsibility for making the decision. But, as I anguished over the decision, I was involved in a series of consultations with teachers in another district. Seeking input, I queried all with whom I came into contact and, not surprisingly, though it's still puzzling, to the last person, all recommended my daughter *not* be promoted. Reasons were given as to the fact that she will be able to drive a car a year after her compatriots, date later, etc. I believe we acted in my daughter's best interest in working to get her promoted; she's happy in her current classroom. However, to the educators I asked, this seemed almost an abomination of nature, that a 6-year-old should be in second grade, and they warned me of the horrors they saw which were to be visited on her and me in time to come.

2   See Hall (1983) for various conceptions of time.

3   Giddens (1990) writes of the movement to trusting in expert systems over known individuals and their expertise in this regard.

4   Recall that historically, supervisors were charged with enforcing curricular mandates, with standardization and normalization (see Introduction).

Appendix: Teacher–Supervisor Conferences

Bea and Faye: 6 June 1989

```
 1  Faye:  ((first few seconds missed)) (   ) why?
 2  Bea:   u:::h=
 3  Faye:  -in what ^way?
 4  Bea:   Well (1.9) ((noise of students in class)) hh
 5         huh (2.0) I think – we were doing that with
 6         and- real (feel inside) getting – o:ver the
 7         fact that that's their ^peers: up there
 8  Faye:  ye- oh I ˄see: ₍I s-    I hea₍rd you men
 9  Bea:                 yeah Iˡ       I am         ˡ
10  Faye:  tioning that ₍way: >like< are you talking
11  Bea:                  y eah ˡ
12  Faye:  about the ^sce:ne, are you talking about the
13         prob˄lem.
14  Bea:   and ^then the other=
15  Faye:  =reality of °the prob˄lem.°
16  Bea:   yeah then the other thing is >is< (1.1) u:m
17         – not knowing really what – questions to
18         ˄ask, so – the respons:e – from the kids >I
19         felt like< someˆtimes – >I just< (1.4) that:t
20         I wasn't asking ((electronic bell)) the
21         right ques˄tions, – to get the responses
22         that we – that were necessary. But I wasn't
23         really sure – how ˄to – ₍so
24  Faye:                      yeˡah – I hear
25         ˄you. – Where's ^your: – little crib˄sheet –
26         BECAUSE – UH (1.0) it should have – ^eVOLVED
27         ˄ba::ck,
28  Bea:   uh huh
29  Faye:  and (0.4) uh – I noticed – that you – forgot
30         to do ₍˄that
31  Bea:           >yeah<ˡ I >and I know I was doin'
32         it, but I didn't know how to< change: it hh
```

33	*Faye:*	·h and *th-* – *the* in*tent* of *this* ques⌄*tion*
34		(0.5) is – to *de*⌄*al*: (0.7) *sometimes* you the-
35		it *helps* me to word *'em* into another °(kind of)
36		question° – *what* you *want* to ⌄*do* – what
37		you ∧*want* – from *this question*, is *simply*
38		>*kids* have *you* seen *this* happen ⌄*before?* –
39		see you *wanna*< – *F:OCUS* 'em on the *scene*.
40		(1.0) *A:nd* get ⌄*away*. from the *enactment*,
41		and- they'll *say* – ·h *no*:: and then you- –
42		and *you* say *no* >have you *ever* seen this –
43		∧*kind* of ⌄*thing*< – happen – ⌄*before*=
44	*Bea:*	=°OK°
45	*Faye:*	SO (0.3) *the answer* – to *this* is ∧*yes* or
46		⌄*no*:.
47	*Bea:*	°OK°
48	*Faye:*	EITHER (0.2) *yeah* *this* kind- – and- – if
49		*they're* saying oh – *that* person – *never* –
50		∧*I'd* *never* see *some*⌄*body* (0.4) talk like
51		⌄*that,* or I'd
52		ne₍*ver* see *somebody*
53	*Bea:*	um hum¹
54	*Faye:*	do *it* like *that* >or *whatever* lit₍tle *th* ing
55	*Bea:*	um hum¹
56	*Faye:*	they ∧*are*< ·h *then* you know you've – *got* °to
57		do *intent* and use – (then you back up some)°
58		– UH >let me *see* if I can ask *it* another
59		⌄*way*< – ∧have you seen *this* kind of – *whole*:
60		thing (0.6) ∧*un*∧*fold* – >°in *front* of your
61		⌄*eyes?*< – *this* whole ⌄*scene?*°=
62	*Bea:*	=um=
63	*Faye:*	=Is this ⌄*scene*. – realistic? Is *what* you're
64		just *a:*sking (0.2) and *then* – if you *just*
65		write up *here* – *yes*: – or ⌄*no*. (0.2)
66		>*Whatever* they ⌄*say*< – if they *say* –
67		*N::OBODY* would do *that* – °they're *making* a
68		*value judgment* – right ⌄*there*° – when you
69		say – ⌄*no*:
70	*Bea:*	OK:
71	*Faye:*	*because* – ⌄*no*: – I don't *see* this kinda
72		⌄*scene*: – in the *real* ⌄*world*. – *that* kinda
73		stuff ∧ *ne*:⌄*ver*: happens – and *so* – *then* you
74		*write* – no – *right there* (0.4) AND *you* would
75		*expect* them ∧*not* to *be* able to *finish* – the
76		⌄*rest* – *because* – they've *never* seen any
77		₍such *thing* HAP ∧*PEN* ₍in the *real*

78	*Bea:*	O-OK so th-] I see:]
79	*Faye:*	ˏworld. – ^OˏK so then – *what* are the
80		^*fee*ˏ*lings* of the *play*ˏ*ers?* – you should've
81		ˏ*ba:d* – *two:.* – *feelings* (0.3) the ^*tea*ˏ*cher:*
82		– an:d – the – *stu*ˆ*dent.*
83	*Bea:*	OK
84	*Faye:*	AND – *you* should've *named* – na-un- – you
85		*don't* name *that* person a – *thief* –
86		((laughter in voice)) *pick out a name* –
87		*other* than *thief.*
88	*Bea:*	OK hhh
89	*Faye:*	*and* I d- – uh °I don't *know* whatchu'd call
90		*that* person° >but *somethin'*< – >I *mean just*
91		*write* down< *every* time *they* say – this
92		*person* may have *felt* – ^*this* ˏ*way:* – *this*
93		ˏ*way:* – *just* jot it ˏ*down.*=
94	*Bea:*	=OK=
95	*Faye:*	=*How* would the *teacher* ˏfeel? –
96		₁ (angry)
97	*Bea:*	*those* were ˏ*my*] *in*ˆ*ten*ˏ*tions* – but I *didn't*
98		do *it.* hhhhh ((laughs))
99	*Faye:*	°well you *will* – next *time*°
100	*Bea:*	^*yeah*
101	*Faye:*	AND ˏ*THEN*:: (0.3) *WHAT* WAS ((another teacher
102		enters asking for stopwatches)) THE *RESULT*
103		OF THIS (1.0) *WHOLE SCENE?*
104	*Bea:*	On my ^*desk.*
105	*Faye:*	That's ^*all right*
106	*OT:*	I'm sorry.
107	*Bea:*	hhhhh
108	*Faye:*	*WHAT YOU* WOULD expect *here,* – is *both* are
109		ˏ*mad.* – I *think* – one *thing* that's °gonna
110		help *you* the *most* – is *clarify* the *intent* of
111		*these* questions.° (0.7) >When you sit ^*back*
112		and *look* at this< – *whole* *sce*ˏ*ne::* (0.5)
113		*what's* gonna *hap*ˏ*pen?* – How are *these* people
114		gonna – *f::eel* about what *went on* – la*ter?*
115	*Bea:*	um hum
116	*Faye:*	^*Like* – the *tea*ˏ*cher's* not gonna *trus:t* –
117		*that* kid *later.*
118	*Bea:*	°um – hum°
119	*Faye:*	The *KID'S* gonna – *thi:nk* – they can – *keep*
120		*stealing* 'cause they got *away* with *it.*
121	*Bea:*	um hum ˏ(OK)
122	*Faye:*	⌈So th⌉*at's what* you would *expect*

123		as a *result* of *that* first ⌄*scene, so see* it
124		*really* does – *fo:llow* in a=
125	*Bea:*	=*yeah* – *it does*=
126	*Faye:*	=*FIRST* – *PREDICT* WHAt's gonna *happen* as a
127		*result* of this ⌄*scene* – now when *Dorothy* did
128		^*hers*, she *predicted* (0.2) *another way*, like
129		you *did* – and so *that* was the next ⌄*sc:ene.*
130		– *Well* that *kinda* gotchu into ^*trou*⌄*ble* –
131		when they – *predicted* – that *they* were gonna
132		*punch* ⌄*ou:t* – *and* – I – *could not* (0.6)
133		°*lis*⌄*ten*° – I *tried* to stay *out* of *it*, but I
134		⌐*could* NOT leave ⌄*it* ⌐I could *n ot*
135	*Bea:*	OH I'M *GLAD* – you *d*┘*id* tha *t's* fine ┘
136	*Faye:*	*lea*⌐*ve* – *that* because *it* – *e:* ^*volved* so
137	*Bea:*	°*that's fine*°┘
138	*Faye:*	– *naturally* – *that* – >*it* got ⌄*worse*<
139	*Bea:*	um hum um ⌐hum um ⌐hum
140	*Faye:*	>*th*┘*at* it ^*es*⌄*calated*< once┘
141		you *use* an ^*escala*⌄*tion:* – whether it
142		*involves* t- I mean *they* were just ^*thrilled*
143		– *because* here's a *scene* they hadn't *seen*
144		⌄*before*=
145		((Bea goes to window))
146	*Bea:*	=I'm *jus*- *concerned* that *my kids* are out
147		⌄*there* ((at recess)) with no *supervi*⌐*sion*
148	*Faye:*	*OH::*┘
149		*well* you'd *better* get out^*the*⌐*re,* ⌄*then.*
150	*Bea:*	^*no*┘ *he's*
151		*still* out ⌄*there* – *that's* good (1.2) >*just*
152		let me ⌄*check* and make ⌄*sure*< – ^O⌄K=
153	*Faye:*	=*the* – *intent* of *this question* – *is:* (0.8)
154		*if:* – *you* wer:e=
155	*Bea:*	=oh, I *forgot* to take
156		⌐my ( )
157	*Faye:*	*IF* – YOU WERE ⌄*TAKING*┘ – °a *pen*⌄*cil* – at the
158		*end*° see what you're *after* ^*here:* – *IS:* –
159		*THEM* to *th:ink*
160	*Bea:*	UM HU:M=
161	*Faye:*	=about *each scene.* – and the *result* of *each*
162		⌄*scene.* (0.2) And to *jus:* – *decide* right
163		⌄*now* (0.5) °if *you* were in the *position* of
164		*taking* a *pencil* (⌄now) – you ^*did* – you
165		*thought* you *needed* a *pencil* and – *took*
166		⌐it *outta* the ⌄*desk* – you
167	*Bea:*	hum ┘

168	*Faye:*	were *caught* red ˰*handed*° – you ^*NEEDED* ˰*it.*
169	*Bea:*	hum
170		(1.1)
171	*Faye:*	*And* (0.7) the *teacher* saw *you* do ˰*it.* (0.6)
172		*May.be* you took *it* because *you* were just –
173		*borrowing* it for a *minute* – >you were *gonna*
174		to put it ˰*back*<
175	*Bea:*	um hum
176		(0.7)
177	*Faye:*	*but* the *teacher* – saw *you* do ˰*it.* ^*How* would
178		you *res˰pond?* (0.8) *Right* ^now – *to˰day*
179	*Bea:*	u:m 'K – *I've* got *that* part –
180		*com*₍*pletely*
181	*Faye:*	°*and* try ˰*tho*│*se.*° – SO YOU JUST ˰*ge:t* – a
182		₍*quick* (0.8) *re˰view::* of ^*ALL* the
183	*Bea:*	OK │
184	*Faye:*	˰*sce:nes* – in the ˰*minds* – of the ˰*kids* – *and*
185		(0.6) *not* a *real* ˰biggie – but a
186		*commit˰ment.*
187	*Bea:*	OK (0.4) ·h >and *I* don't know
188		*wh*₍*y* I forgot *it*<
189	*Faye:*	And *ask* – *them*│ – to *re˰spond.* (1.0) *U:H*
190		– *bu-* – *what* you ˰*did* – *was* you laid your –
191		*sta˰ges,* (2.2) *the kids* were – ^ *mo:derate˰ly*
192		*in˰volved* – and the *rea˰son* °*I* think *they*
193		were *not*° ^ *more* ˰involved than they ^*were* –
194		*was* – >*because* of *that* – *first quest˰tion.*<
195	*Bea:*	O^K
196	*Faye:*	I *think* they *jus-* (0.9) u::h got ^*off* – *on*
197		the *reality* of the ˰*scene,* like you *said* –
198		you *picked* it ^*up* – and I *think* they ^*did* –
199		they – *they* said – *oh this* – *teacher* – *a*
200		teacher °*never* ( )°=
201	*Bea:*	=um hum=
202	*Faye:*	=and *they weren't* – LOOKing at the ˰*whole*
203		picture –
204	*Bea:*	₍they were n't?
205	*Faye:*	they were-│ they ˰*weren't* –
206		*contextua*₍*LIZING THOSE*
207	*Bea:*	(well I)│
208	*Faye:*	*ROLES.* ·h
209	*Bea:*	*what* do I ^*do* if *that* hap₍^*pens?*
210	*Faye:*	YOU sta│*bilize* it
211		*right* ˰*here:* (0.4) *you* – *say:* (0.3) *you::*
212		*say* – *yea:h* ther- *they* – acted – *like* –

213		^*this* – *but* – *look* at *the* whole ˏ*thing*
214		((knock)) – *have* you ever ˏ*seen* – a
215		^*tea*^*cher* –
216	*Bea:*	°ʻK°
217	*Faye:*	accuse a ^*child,* and the ^*child* denies ˏ*it.*
218	*Bea:*	((Bea gets up to speak to person at door))
219		*do* you *need* – to go ^*in?*
220		.
221		.
222		
223	*Bea:*	*no* – 'bout *three* or *four* minutes – is *all* I
224		ˏ*need* ((door closes))
225	*Faye:*	*so* – ˏ*so:* – the *kids* were *moderately*
226		in ˏvolved
227	*Bea:*	um ₍hum
228	*Faye:*	*only*⌉ because – *they* got *off* on the
229		*reality* of the *character:*s – and – *ra:ther*
230		than the *whole* °ˏscene°
231	*Bea:*	OK ₍
232	*Faye:*	AND⌉ YOU HAve to *redirect* that ₍*early* –
233	*Bea:*	uh huh⌉
234	*Faye:*	or they're *gonna* lose *it* the *rest* of the
235		*way* ˏ*through*=
236	*Bea:*	= >couldchu *gimme* an *exam*ˏ*ple*< – ₍*how* I'd do
237	*Faye:*	·hhhh ⌉
238		ˏ*right* ^*here.*
239	*Bea:*	*that?* just go ₍*back* – and *say*
240	*Faye:*	You'd *SAY* – *WH*⌉*EN* THEY –
241		*START TELLING* YOU ˏ*no* (0.3) that- with *your*
242		first *ques*ˏ*tion* – *after* the ^*enact*ˏ*ment* – if
243		they *start* (0.4) *giving* you *feed*ˏ*back* – *that*
244		the *tea*ˏ*cher* would *never* hold *their* hand
245		that ˏ*way,*
246	*Bea:*	uh huh
247	*Faye:*	*I* would never *see:* – a *kid* (0.2) *keep* saying
248		ˏno ˏno ˏno=
249	*Bea:*	=oh OK
250	*Faye:*	use- – *you* correct *it* right h₍*ere* >y ou *say*
251	*Bea:*	OK ⌉
252	*Faye:*	*no* look *at* the *whole:*< picture (0.6) be ˏ*fore*
253		in your ^*life* – have you – *ever* – *seen* – in
254		this ^*school* – a *tea*ˏ*cher.* – *say* to a
255		^*child,* I saw *you* do *some*ˏ*thing* >the *child*
256		*says*< ^*no::* – the *teacher* says – *I saw you*
257		doing °ˏit.° >The *child* says< ^*nO::* – a –

258   *CHILD* totally *deny*:: (0.5) *taking* some*thing*
259   when *someone's* seen *him* do *it.* Oh
260   ₎then *they'll* say – ^*sure:*
261   *Bea:*   OK   ⌐
262   *Faye:* because *they've* seen *that* hap⌐*pen.*
263   *Bea:*   >OK.<
264   (0.9)
265   *Faye:* SO ⌐*HERE'S* where you *have* to *set* the ⌐*stage*
266   with *th*₎*at* first *question* again
267   *Bea:*   all right ⌐   u₎m hum
268   *Faye:*   so   *th*ˡ*at's*
269   where *you'd* make your *correction* ⌐then°
270   *Bea:*   °OK°
271   *Faye:* UH – >*did* the *students*< *des*^*cribe* the
272   *charac*⌐*ters,* – na:h °*you* forgot *that*
273   ₎^part°
274   *Bea:*   (° I   ⌐ – *forgot* that part°)
275   *Faye:* WERE – ALTERNA*tive* ⌐beha^*viors yes*:. ^*Were*
276   the *enact*⌐*ments* – *discussed* and *ana*⌐*lyzed* –
277   °ye:s° (0.2) *didchu* make the *kind* of –
278   *mo:ves* – didch- *did* they *re*⌐*flect*:? – ^*And*
279   *did* they *summa*⌐*rize.* – ^*Have you* seen *that*
280   happen *be*⌐*fore* – now *that's* a *key*:: –
281   *discussion* °strategy° (0.7) *HAVE* you *seen*
282   that *hap*⌐*pen?* – ^*think* ⌐*back* – ^*is* this a
283   *real* ⌐scene (2.2) *what* hap⌐*pened* – so *these*:
284   – *two* discussion *skillls* are °*critical* to
285   your – *role* play° – the *analy*^*sis* of the
286   *fee*⌐*lings* – you *did* get *to* (1.2) >*UH*< – it
287   would've *been* – m:*ore* – *explicit* – it
288   would've *gotten* you *where* you – ^*wan*⌐*ted* –
289   to ⌐*be*: – if *you* – *hadn't* talked *about* – the
290   *feeling* about – the ⌐*scene.*
291   *Bea:*   OK₎
292   *Faye:*   *ta*ˡ*lk* about the – ^*reality* of the ⌐*scene*
293   *Bea:*   °O₎K°
294   *Faye:*   andˡ the *f:eelings* of the *people*
295   *play*⌐*ing.*
296   *Bea:*   OK
297   (0.7)
298   *Faye:* U:M (0.7) *the analysis* of the *behaviorial*
299   *reali*⌐*ty:* °*yeah* they *talked* about *that a*
300   *lot* hhh° ·h an- the *consequences* – *OF* the
301   *ac*⌐*tion*: – now in*STEAD* of *saying* – *what* was
302   the *reSULT* of *this* – *whole* ⌐*scene,*

303   *Bea:*   um hum

304   *Faye:*   *you* got – uh – ˏ*they* thought of another ˏ*way*

305   *Bea:*   um hum=

306   *Faye:*   =to ˏ*act.* – So you *went* to *another* ˏ*way* –

307   *rather* than the *consequences* of °*this* –

308   *whole* kind of uh *sce*ₗ*nario*°

309   *Bea:*   OK ˥

310   *Faye:*   U::*h* – *did* they *genera*ˏ*lize* >*whatda* you

311   ^*think?*< do *you think* your *kids* left *here*

312   with – *a* (1.0) °*way:* – of *dealing* with *that*

313   *prob*ˏ*lem?*°

314   *Bea:*   °*No* – *I* don't ^*think* they ˏ*did*° – *because* I

315   *th*- *I* don't *think* they *were* in *tune:* with

316   *what* was goi- I don- th- *I* ^didn't feel

317   *comfor*ˏ*table*

318   (0.4)

319   *Faye:*   I *think* it's °*right,*° and I *think* you're

320   *right* – I think *it* was right *here*=

321   *Bea:*   =yeah=

322   *Faye:*   =*I* think *we* °got *off* right *there*°

323   *Bea:*   um hum

324   *Faye:*   and they *needed* – uh – EI^*ther* – *explanation*

325   °at the *beginning,*°

326   *Bea:*   um 'K

327   *Faye:*   *it's:* – *realistic* to *tell* ˏ*'em* (0.4) *that*

328   you're gonna *play* something *you've* ˏ*seen*

329   (0.6) *you've* seen ₗ*kids*

330   *Bea:*   >*SEE*˥ I didn't *know*

331   whether- a- because *see* – *the boy* that was

332   in the very *back:*< (0.9) *Cody?* – um – *he* –

333   *he is.* I mean *I* have a huge *ba:g* – *he's* – *he*

334   has done ˏ*that.* Aₗlot

335   *Faye:*   um hˡum

336   *Bea:*   ˏand the *reason* – I didn't call on him ˏ*today*

337   is *just because* he's been *totally off* the

338   ˏ*wall:* and so (0.6) *ha:ving him* up *there* –

339   *participating* >*would've been* a *very* bad<

340   ˏ*choice:.* Because – *he* would *have* – *just*

341   been (0.4) *more obnoxious* – that he *was* by

342   *sitting* back *there* – stac^*king:* – ˏ*books*

343   *around* and doing the *things* that he's- ^IN

344   ˏFACT – *he's* been *so bad* throughout the

345   whole *schoo:l* – *that* – *some*body *said* – if

346   *Faye's* coming to *watch* – to*day* you *don't*

347   wanna be *sabotaged* by *Cody* – >*send* him *outta*

348		the ˏroom – and *I* didn't – *do that*
349	Faye:	do – uh – yet – but – *some^ti:mes* – his –
350		*thorough – involvement* in *it*
351		(0.9)
352	Bea:	*well* we *tr͵ied* ₍al ˏready
353	Faye:	*cut*⌐ ou ts⌐ the *behavior*. –
354		*But you're* saying *that* wouldn't *work* f₍or
355	Bea:	*it*⌐
356	Faye:	₍( )
357	Bea:	Di dn't w–⌐ *it* hasn't *worked* so ˏfar: –
358		*today* – >an *I'd<* – 'cause *I* was *really* going
359		to ^*use:* ˏhim.
360	Faye:	is ^*HE:* – the *reason* you *picked* °the
361		prob ˏlem°?
362	Bea:	yeah (0.9) ˏhe ^*is*=
363	Faye:	=SO *he's* the one *it* would've been – *most* –
364		re₍*leva nt* to
365	Bea:	right⌐
366	Faye:	*act* ˏ*ually*.
367	Bea:	but – *so* far *to* ˏ*day::* – in every*thing* I-
368		I've ₍tried
369	Faye:	DID HE⌐ *VOLUN^TEER?* I *didn't* – ˏsee:.
370		*Did* he *volunteer* to be *a play* ˏ*er*?
371	Bea:	he came ^*up* – to *the* – ^*class* ˏ*room* and *said*
372		– I *want* ^*to* – >°*be* one of the *play* ˏ*ers.*°<
373	Faye:	°hh uh huh – *So* he *really wanted* – but *you* –
374		*didn't* want *him* to *be, because* of his
375		*behav^ior* ₍today°
376	Bea:	(be *cause*⌐ – of *his*) – *behavior*
377		today – be ˏ*cau:se* – *I'd already* given him –
378		*many- chances* – (then) *he* – *he* – *hit* a *kid* –
379		in the ˏ*head.* (0.4) he – un=
380	Faye:	=right=
381	Bea:	=*you* know – *just* – *totally* off the *wa:ll* –
382		*witho-* uh- – he *took* – the *time* ˏ*clock* –
383		s:*pun* it *around* – *knocked* somebody in the
384		ˏ*hea:d* – ₍(an-)
385	Faye:	°un hun° DO YOU ⌐ *TH:INK* – *BEING* A
386		*PLAYER* WOULD'VE MAde – *this:* – um –
387		>*situation*< – *meaningful* to ˏ*him*?
388	Bea:	no – *not to* ˏ*day* – be ˏ*cause* – *he:* ((clears
389		throat)) (2.3) *he* would *have* made a *cir* ˏ*cus*
390		– >*a* three-ring *circus*< *out* of ˏ*it* – ^*up*
391		*there* – to ˏ*day. He* would *have* – um
382	Faye:	So ₍you can say

393	*Bea:*	just gone – o:.⌐*ff* – the *wa*₍*ll*
394	*Faye:*	EVˑEN THOUGH
395		*THIS* – you – real⌐*ly* – *picked this* – *because*
396		– *he's* >the *one*< – >I'll *tell* you *what*< the
397		reason *I'm* – ˔*saying this* is – *many times.* –
398		˔w:hen there's >*been* a *problem*< in the
399		ro:˔om, – it is be˔cause – of the *target*
400		^ *kid.*
401	*Bea:*	um hum
402	*Faye:*	And – *almost invariably* – *they* wanna *be* in
403		the ˔*play,*
404	*Bea:*	>um hum and *did*chu *see* the *other* little *girl*
405		that – *raised* her *hand* and said *yes she*
406		wanted to *do* the *argu*^ *ment* with the
407		*tea*˔*cher?*< – >but *then* she *said*< ˔*no* (0.5)
408		*sh:e argues* with *me* – e::*xact*˔*ly* that *way:*
409	*Faye:*	°um h₍um°
410	*Bea:*	in fa⌐ct wer- – we *have* an *a*^ *lert* – for
411		the um
412	*Faye:*	um hum
413	*Bea:*	*owl* squad ˔*today.*
414	*Faye:*	=°um hum°=
415	*Bea:*	=And her *parents* have been *called* – and
416		*aler*˔*ted*=
417	*Faye:*	=°um hum°=
418	*Bea:*	=because – of ˔*her*
419	*Faye:*	AND – *SOME*˔ti:mes – when the *play*˔ers – ARE
420		– the *real* peo˔*ple* – but *you'd*- – *you never*
421		*call* on 'em un*less* – *they* wanna ˔*play,*
422	*Bea:*	°yeah° *see* sh₍e RAISED *HER* ˔*HAND* T-
423	*Faye:*	but THEY KNOW HOW TO⌐ Do ˔it –
424	*Bea:*	₍˔yeah
425	*Faye:*	*real ly* ˔we⌐*ll*=
426	*Bea:*	=um hum
427	*Faye:*	and – *when* the *play*˔*ers* are the *real* peo˔*ple*
428		(0.9) a:*nd* – a *kid* will ˔*say* – *they* act like
429		*that*
430	*Bea:*	u:m:
431		(0.9)
432	*Faye:*	*this* isn't a ˔*scene* – *that* person *really*
433		acts like ₍˔*tha:t*
434	*Bea:*	u m hum⌐
435	*Faye:*	and *it's* – *very revealing* to the *person*
436		th₍at the *kids* –
437	*Bea:*	um hum⌐

438	*Faye:*	can – pre⌄dic₁t ₁so
439	*Bea:*	I¹ *wish* I ha¹dn't – been – so –
440		*afraid* to do ⌄*that* – I *wish* I hadn't had
441	*Faye:*	we:ll – it *isn't* like *this* is gonna to go
442		a⌄*way* – you *can* try *it* again
443		so₁meTIME hhh
444	*Bea:*	oh ye¹s >oh the thing is -s *that*<
445		they *wa-* – the *kids* an- and the *kids* – I
446		*think* they *do* wa^nna try it *again*, >I *got*
447		the *feeling*< *they'd* like to *do*: – *try* it
448		^*again*,
449	*Faye:*	uh huh=
450	*Bea:*	=an₁d I-
451	*Faye:*	>I th¹ink they do< ⌄*too* >ahh< >*try* a
452		*different* ⌄*prob⌄lem* ₁so it's a – *whole* – *new*
453	*Bea:*	um hum¹
454		right
455	*Faye:*	and *then* – *try* getting *these* ques⌄tions *so*
456		that *you* focus more into *the* – *actual*
457		₁*pr* ocess of the ⌄*sc*₁*ene*
458	*Bea:*	yea h:¹ ·hh¹
459		and ^*I:* wanna *try* it *again*, because ⌄I
460		^think *it* – ⌄*I* think – it can- – could ⌄*work*
461		really ^*well*. (0.3) *as* long as *I* –
462		₁if (_____) di dn't *fe*₁*el*
463	*Faye:*	it *really can* ¹ – be¹ ⌄*use*^*ful.* You
464		know *how Dorothy talked* about *her* kids
465		^*tattling?*
466	*Bea:*	>um hum<
467	*Faye:*	The *thing* that came *out* in her ro:*le play* –
468		°*she* had 'em *lined up* at the ⌄*door* (0.3) and
469		– to go: – to:° li⌄*brary* – and – *what* they
470		*do* is take ⌄*cuts*
471	*Bea:*	um::
472	*Faye:*	and *the* thing *that* – *resulted* in (0.8) from
473		her ^*role* ⌄*play*, – wa:s – in the *second*
474		^*sce:ne* – *whe:re* – the *students* – >come in<.
475		A *fri:⌄end* – who'd *allow:ed* a kid to *come*
476		take ⌄*cuts*: – and *then* – the *two* kids
477		be⌄*hind* (0.7) *this* kid went and *told* a
478		^*tea⌄cher*
479	*Bea:*	um::
480	*Faye:*	and when *they* discussed *that* – they *said* –
481		*how* did *this* kid ⌄*feel*
482	*Bea:*	um hum

483	*Faye*:	*kid said* – pretty ^*good*
484	*Bea*:	um hum
485	*Faye*:	*he – feels like – he got* ⌄re^venge
486	*Bea*:	um::
487	*Faye*:	so: the *tattling prob*⌄*lem in her* fifth:
488		*gr*⌄*ade –* the ^*class* recognized ₍as a *way*: –
489	*Bea*:	u m:]
490	*Faye*:	o:*f* >getting *even* with the *kid without*
491		getting in *trouble* with the *figh*⌄*ting*<
492		°because in the *previous* one the *kid*
493		⌄*fought.*
494	*Bea*:	°yeah: ₍I: see::°
495	*Faye*:	And they *both* got] in *trouble*° – so
496		if *YOU* wanna *get-* (0.6) if *you* wanna *get*
497		re⌄*venge*:, – *you* go *tell* the *tea*⌄*cher.*
498	*Bea*:	um::
499	*Faye*:	And *then* you *stay* outta *trou*⌄*ble* – and (0.8)
500		°this kid gets *it*°
501	*Bea*:	I see – ₍and I'd- – *that* felt *good*
502	*Faye*:	in fact – look how this i]s – I
503		mean – *look* how *re*^*vea:ling* the₍se k ids *are*
504	*Bea*:	yeah]
505	*Faye*:	₍when *they*: >when *they* give
506	*Bea*:	yeah]
507	*Faye*:	you< *feed*°*back* in *this* way.°
508	*Bea*:	·h *I* wish *I* had done *this* – I wish *I* had
509		done ⌄*this* – *I* woulda been *able* to do ⌄*it* –
510		*four* weeks *ago, because* I *think* – that t-t-
511		their *reaction* to it *all* an- – re⌄*sponse* –
512		*every*⌄*thing* that would *be* taking ⌄*place* –
513		*would've* been – *dif*⌄*ferent* – than *today*:
514	*Faye*:	°um hum°
515	*Bea*:	*next* to the *last* day of *sch*⌄*ool* – *today's*
516		the first school ( ) meeting and the
517		sched- – t- *the* kid's *not* having the s-
518		*scheduling* and stuff=
519	*Faye*:	=°yeah°=
520	*Bea*:	=maybe I'm ⌄*wrong,* maybe *it* wouldn't ⌄*be,*
521		but *it* would be *intere*₍*sting* to *see* how it
522	*Faye*:	WEll-]
523	*Bea*:	⌄*did*=
524	*Faye*:	=sometimes this ∧*works* – *like* it *did* with
525		*Doro*⌄*thy,* it *reveals* a lot of=
526	*Bea*:	=uh huh=
527	*Faye*:	=*the kids'* – fee⌄*lings* ·h *that* you have

528		*changed* any ˎthing – *particularly* that ˎ*day*
529	*Bea:*	uh huh
530	*Faye:*	I mean – at the *End* of the ˎ*day* – the *Kids*
531		*didn't say* – *we're* gonna use *conflict*
532		*resolu*ˎ*tion.* They said we're gonna *punch* ya
533		*out* if yoᵢu *tell* the *tea*ˎ*cher*
534	*Bea:*	(laugh) ⌉ um hum
535	*Faye:*	a:nd they – *still* ^felt *that* ˎway – but *it*
536		lets *her* know *where* they ˎare.=
537	*Bea:*	=um hum
538	*Faye:*	An:d – *it* let's ^*them* kinda ˎsee: – *where*
539		they *are* >but-< ᵢthey *did* *n't* con*text*ualize
540	*Bea:*	°um hum°⌉
541	*Faye:*	^ *it,* – *they* didn't ˎ*see* –
542	*Bea:*	°um hum°
543	*Faye:*	*they* didn't ^*see*: *this* kid's *fee*ˎ*ling,* they
544		*didn't see this* kid's *fee*ˎ*ling,*
545	*Bea:*	°um hum°
546	*Faye:*	*they* didn't *see* any ^*reason* for the ˎ*ru*ˎ*le*
547	*Bea:*	um hum
548	*Faye:*	BUT *IT* – *tells you* where *you* need to gᵢo
549	*Bea:*	um:⌉
550	*Faye:*	when you're *through* with *this*=
551	*Bea:*	= >*I thought*- I *just* feel *comfortable* 'bout<
552		a *couple* of ˎ*things* – the *respon*ˎ*ses* from
553		*some* of the *kids* that=
554	*Faye:*	=*YES*=
555	*Bea:*	= >an' I *also* felt *comfortable*< – with – the
556		*way*: – *Ernie handled* – being a *tea*ˎ*cher* and
557		*his* replies t- *the* kids >a lot< *'cause* I
558		think *he* came- *i-it* showed *that* he um-
559	*Faye:*	*Yes*:
560	*Bea:*	kᵢnew ᵢthe riᵢght
561	*Faye:*	*Yes*:⌉ ye s: ⌉ you⌉r players -=
562	*Bea:*	=um hum=
563	*Faye:*	=*I*: *thought* your *play*ˎ*ers* revealed a^*lot*=
564	*Bea:*	=um hum=
565	*Faye:*	=when you *s*ˎ*ee*: – that your *play*ˎ*ers* – *know*
566		the *sc*ˎ*ene* – so ^*well because they've* seen
567		*it* – you ^*can* come *right* in *here* and
568		*see*ᵢ– and SAY ˎTHAT
569	*Bea:*	I⌉ can- *say* that >OK<=
570	*Faye:*	=OH ^YEAH *feel* comfortable *saying* – ·h *these*
571		people seem to *know* – °*just* what to *do*
572		because *they've* seen *it* beˎfore.°

573	*Bea:*	umkay
574	*Faye:*	i ₁s-
575	*Bea:*	>AND YOU *KNOW* WHEN I ^*READ*< – ₓTHE – *the*
576		pac^ket thatchu *gave* us – *on* role *play*^*ing,*
577		it was *con*^*fu*^*sing* because *I* didn't –
578	*Faye:*	*it's* so *detail*₁*ed* that you- you'd go >^*on*
579	*Bea:*	ye¹ah:
580	*Faye:*	and ^*on* and ^*o*₁*n*<
581	*Bea:*	ye¹ah=
582	*Faye:*	=on *each little segment* – to the *point* that
583		you ^*lo:se* – almost – the *purpose* of the
584		*whole* con₁^cept
585	*Bea:*	and: *I* didn't¹ know – *exactly* how
586		*much* to *do* and how *much* – *not* to *do* and *then*
587		– with- *the* – *what* we *did* in ^*class* when we
588		*role* ^played. ₁(it li:-)
589	*Faye:*	it was ve¹ry
590		*abbrevi*₁*ated* I kno- ₁bu- *tha t's why we do*
591	*Bea:*	^yea¹h and so-¹
592	*Faye:*	it >*clear through*< in ^*class* ·hh is – the
593		^*pa*^*cket has* – more *informati:on* – than you
594		– ACTually need ₁but *i t's a good*
595	*Bea:*	OK: ¹
596	*Faye:*	*theoretical* pa₁cket
597	*Bea:*	yeah¹ I en- d- it was a you
598		know *I:*
599	*Faye:*	and it *gives you:* – °once you get *through*
600		that *packet* you have more o:p^tions on how
601		to use *role* ^*play* – because we *rea*₁*lly* do
602	*Bea:*	°yeah°¹
603	*Faye:*	it *up* pretty *good* and *try* to *get* to *the* –
604		*source* of the *prob*^*lem.*°
605	*Bea:*	but *I wasn't* really *sure* – which *op*^*tion* to
606		*take* – or *how* to *really* – ^mince it ^*down* –
607		so ^*that*
608	*Faye:*	°right°
609	*Bea:*	every*thing* t- plays ₁out B₁UT >*NOW* I HAVE
610	*Faye:*	right¹ W-¹
611	*Bea:*	A *BETTER*< i₁dea:
612	*Faye:*	>if *I*¹ were *you*< I'd ask *Nancy* –
613		t₁o: ju st SEE ^*HERS*
614	*Bea:*	^OK¹
615	*Faye:*	NOW SHE DIDN'T U::se >*reflection* and
616		*summary,*< she *used* – uh – *clarifica*^*tion*
617	*Bea:*	um ^hum

618	*Faye:*	*what's* another ^*one* – >what's another ^*one*,<
619		and *ex:tending* she kept (0.4) uh so *this* was
620		– *tricky,*
621	*Bea:*	um ⌊hum:
622	*Faye:*	for *h*⌉*er* to *get* to *this:* – *strategy* of
623		°*discussing*°
624	*Bea:*	um'K
625	*Faye:*	But – uh (0.5) *it* would be *g:ood* – for *her*
626		to be *able* to see ˰*your:s* – because *she*
627		would *say* – oh – >I *shoulda* done *that*< or –
628		*yep* – *that* worked *really* ˰*well* and *it* would
629		probab⌊ly be ^*good* – for ˰*you* to be *able* to
630	*Bea:*	ye^ah⌉
631	*Faye:*	see ˰*hers.* If ⌊IF she's *willing* to
632	*Bea:*	°um° *I'D* ^*LI KE* – to do ˰*that*⌉
633	*Faye:*	*ex*˰*change.*
634	*Bea:*	°yeah° ^O˰K – *we* can *talk* about
635		i⌊*t*-
636	*Faye:*	*ALL*⌉ RIGH*T*=
637	*Bea:*	⇒ I ME- another ˰*thing*< – is I have *my* u:m
638		(1.4) I *have* – *everything* *ready* to turn *in*
639		to *you* – to˰*day* – *except* for *my* u˰*nit.* °Can *I*
640		turn it *in* on *Thurs*˰*day*? – 'K there's°=
641	*Faye:*	=an⌊- – and *I'll* see *you* at
642	*Bea:*	fif-⌋
643	*Faye:*	*four*->˰*thirty*<
644	*Bea:*	at >*four* thirty< ·h I ^*have* to
645		*recopy* my *fi*˰*nal.* I've – it's in the rough
646		*stages.* I just have to *recopy* it for the- –
647		*I mean* – it's *all* – writ˰ten=
648	*Faye:*	=oh – OK=
649	*Bea:*	=and I haven't-
650	*Faye:*	I: can- – if: – that's not *ready* by to˰night
651		– *by* Thurs˰day
652	*Bea:*	˰o:h – >well I'm *gonna* try- I *think* I'm
653		*gonna* have some ˰*time*< this *after*˰*noon* – so
654		I thought *I* could go *ahead* and do ˰*that.* I
655		*have* it *here* – with ˰*me,* – and *then* – I
656		*ha:ve* – I *turned* in *my* thing ˰*that* – from
657		˰*last term:* – to ˰*you* – and *I* have *my* – u:m
658		(0.8) I turned in *the* – *time*
659	*Faye:*	*YE:s* – but *I* have to °*get* back to ˰*you* – I
660		*have* to *look* back through – your *file* and t-
661		t- con- I *ma:rked* it ˰*down* and *penciled* ˰*in*
662		– but *I* have *to* – >*make* *sure* – what ˰*time*<°

663   *Bea:*   O₁K:
664   *Faye:*   theʲre's one – *more:* (0.3)
665   ₁that you
666   *Bea:*   >I have anʲother one to ⌃*do?*<
667   *Faye:*   *well* – let me *talk* to *you* about *it* –
668   to-*night* – *when* you .*come*, – so I- – you can
669   *look* – *through* your *fold*.er.
670   *Bea:*   .oh ⌃O.K
671   *Faye:*   Go ahead and – .*check things*
672   *Bea:*   O.K: ((sounding deflated))
673   *Faye:*   and – and see ·h ₁(   )
674   *Bea:*   >(I know)ʲ but – I have
675   *Faye:*   ₁and see
676   *Bea:*   another oneʲ .*here*<
677   *Faye:*   *I have to*:: *go back through*
678   ₁>I w ouldn't *want* you to
679   *Bea:*   O.:Hʲ
680   *Faye:*   have a *fit*< – *until* I've gone *through* your
681   *fol*.der if there's any other *one* in .*there.*
682   *Bea:*   OK >because I ⌃*took*-< – I .*have* – *another*
683   one *han*.dy, th- – >*that* I *did* on .*Ka*⌃*ri*<
684   (0.2) O.K and *Kendra* – °yeah – I have
685   that° ((walks to desk)) and do you *need* all
686   that *stuff* too, or do you just,
687   ne₁ed the *fi* .*nal?*
688   *Faye:*   um humʲ
689   *Bea:*   OK=
690   *Faye:*   =you just need (*that*) and (*that*)
691   *Bea:*   OK – .great – one's done – and the:n=
692   *Faye:*   =got ⌃*this* one *outta* the .*way* ₁for ⌃*th is*
693   *Bea:*   um hum   ʲ
694   *Faye:*   .*term* – all .*right*=
695   *Bea:*   = >so that's *yur*-< – >and *then*< – >*then* – the
696   *other one's* o' the .*time*< – >*that* we *did* in
697   *Tech*.*town*< (0.2) *I* turned *that* in to you
698   last *time* >*with* the one< – from ⌃*last* .*term.*
699   *Faye:*   righ*t*
700   *Bea:*   OK ·hh
701   *Faye:*   I have *that*₁t
702   *Bea:*   Iʲ have *that.* And ⌃*then* (0.7) >so
703   you're *sayin'* – there's *one* mo⌃*re?*<
704   *Faye:*   uh *no*: le₁t ⌃*m e*: – .*check ba*:*ck* – and make
705   *Bea:*   oh   ʲ
706   *Faye:*   *sure* ₁and s ee whether *I:* – *just* don't have
707   *Bea:*   OK ʲ

708	*Faye*:	*it – checked* on my ∧*list*, no- un- and *it*
709		would've *been* for ∧*last term* – *it* was *for*
710		your *incom*∧*plete*, 'cause I *star*∧*ted* – to
711		*cha:nge* your *incomplete* from ∧*la:st* term ·hh
712		*and* I *thought* (0.2) *wh*^*oops:* – ∧so: – *I'll*
713		talk to you to*night*, ⌈WHEN I HAVE IT in
714	*Bea*:	all right – good⌋
715	*Faye*:	fr⌈ont of – me
716	*Bea*:	∧ye:ah⌋ OK k- because I – *I* wasn't
717		awa⌈re that there was *any thing*∧*else*
718	*Faye*:	without being – *more*⌋ *explicit* about
719		^ *it*
720	*Bea*:	OK⌈
721	*Faye*:	th⌋ough ∧*Bea* – *don't* get *nervous* about *it*
722		– until *I:* – *check* it *out* ∧*more*.
723	*Bea*:	sure ⌈('cause I feel)
724	*Faye*:	*it* just *looked* on⌋ my – *check sheet*
725		(0.2) *like* – *there* was *another* ∧*one* – °*s:o*
726		*wait* until I *check* it ∧*out* an- – have my
727		*facts* ∧*down*, O^K?°
728	*Bea*:	OK >*so* then *I'll* see *you* at< ∧*four thirty*
729		– *to*∧*night* – an- I- *I'll* ^have ∧*my* – >I
730		*have*:< – *I'll* bring ∧*my*
731	*Faye*:	ALL *right*
732	*Bea*:	*my* – ∧*write* ^ *up*
733	*Faye*:	and then we'll *do the* – uh – *fol*∧*der* (2.5)
734		*Thurs*∧*day* °OK° ∧your – curriculum=
735	*Bea*:	=I HA⌈VE
736	*Faye*:	ARE⌋ YOU *DOING* – poe^try?
737	*Bea*:	>yeah<=
738	*Faye*:	=°good°=
739	*Bea*:	=>I'M GOING TO ^*STICK* WITH ∧*IT* BECAUSE I
740		I ⌈I *REAL LY* LIKE ∧*IT* – AN- I *WANNA* –
741	*Faye*:	°good°⌋
742	*Bea*:	I *KNOW* ∧THAT ⌈I'LL GET
743	*Faye*:	IT'LL be *USE*⌋∧ful
744	*Bea*:	IT'LL BE *USE*∧FUL AND *I'LL GET* VALUABLE
745		^*IN*∧*PUT* FROM ∧YOU THAT I WON'T *GET* AT
746		ANOTHER ^*TIME* AND SO I *WANT* – YOU KNOW –
747		*THOSE* ∧THINGS THAT I LEAVE ∧*OUT* OR I ∧*DON'T*
748		DO *I'LL BE ABLE* TO – ^*find* out from ∧*you*
749		what *I* need to ^*change*.
750	*Faye*:	°Do you *know* how *easy* it *is* to teach (from
751		the beginning)?°
752	*Bea*:	Wow hh – it'd be ^*nice* ((laughs)) it's *gonna*

753		be *really* ^*nice* – and I'll *love* ⌄*it*
754	*Faye*:	((to observer)) well *Dun*⌄*can* – do you wanna
755		⌄*go:* – or are you gonna ⌄*stay.* Here I *am* –
756		*walkin'* outta *here* and ^*he's* staying' ⌄*here*
757		((laughs)) and *he's* – *watching me* –
758	*Bea*:	((to observer)) yeah, thank you ((laughs))
759	*Faye*:	*leave.* It's because – *I'm* thinking *you* need
760		to *be out* on *that play*⌄*ground.*
761	*Bea*:	*I'm* going ⌄*out* – I'm gonna *take*=
762	*Faye*:	=I *SEE YOU* looking out *there* – *so* –
763		⌊*frequent* ly
764	*Bea*:	I'm gonna t-⌉
765		.
766		. ((observer asks Bea to sign consent
767		. form and gives Bea a copy))
768	*Faye*:	*see* you to⌄*night*
769	*Bea*:	thank you *very* ⌄much
770	*Faye*:	good⌄bye

Kari and Kendra: 7 June 1989

Pre-conference

1	*Kendra*:	((first few seconds missed)) (did you write
2		these yourself?)
3	*Kari*:	^yeah (0.6) *gives* me *more* ^*ques*^*tions* (0.4)
4		and then (0.3) *hopefully* (0.5) we *can* get
5		through ⌄*that* then the *second* half of the
6		*period* will go: (0.5) how they *re*^*spond* to
7		⌄*those* ques^tions ((clears throat)) yeah
8		their – ^*questions* in the ⌄*book* are *like* –
9		>they're ^*all* – ^know⌄ledge ^*ques*⌄*tions*<
10		they're just
11	*Kendra*:	um hum
12	*Kari*:	and *they* have *really* nothing to *do* with the
13		*importance* of hhh ((laughs)) the hh *sto*⌄*ry*
14		(0.4) I mean *it's* >kinda ^*like*< (0.4)
15		⌄*didcha* ⌄*under*^*stand* what you ⌄*re:ad*, but it
16		*really* was⌄n't – any^thing more *in depth* than
17		that – *so* (0.2) I *don't* use ⌄*'em* (0.8) an
18		then; (0.7) *this* is just *another* – from the
19		^*fi*⌄*nal* ques⌄tion – *like* – to pre⌄*dict* –
20		*where* we're *going* w- °with the ⌄*story*° (2.4)
21	*Kendra*:	^*dis*⌄*courage*^ment to ^*en*⌄*courage*^ment –

22		interes^ting
23		(1.9)
24	*Kari*:	u::m (2.2) and ^I *don't think* I'm gonna to
25		˰do a *fish˰bowl* – ei˰ther (0.8) they *haven't*
26		done a ^*fish˰bowl* in *this* ˰class
27		an₍d I th ink- (0.2) I'm *tryin'* to *cover* –
28	*Kendra*:	um hum¹
29	*Kari*:	a ˰*lot* of mate˰*rial* – and *I* don't *wanna* to
30		in₍troduce anything ˰*new*
31	*Kendra*:	°(yes) °¹
32	*Kari*:	so – >they *ARE* familiar with ˰*it*< (0.2) (the
33		inquiry) – *sty:le* (0.4) of *discus˰sion* – so
34	*Kendra*:	great=
35	*Kari*:	=it's BEEN *AWHILE*: since *we've* done *this*
36		les-
37	*Kendra*:	°(I noticed it)°
38		(0.8)
39	*Kari*:	and so *these* are *just* some some uh ^*these*
40		are my ^ *brain˰storm^ing*
41		ques₍˰tions that ₍I've-
42	*Kendra*:	sure ¹ s ure ¹
43	*Kari*:	^*hey*: WELCOME TO CLASS – ^ BUDDY ((to student
44		entering)) (2.1) ((breathy, quiet laugh))

Post – conference

1	*Kendra*:	*I* just *took* ˰down ^*all* kinds of ^stuff ˰*here*
2		((excited voice)) (0.3) u:₍:m
3	*Kari*:	OK¹
4	*Kendra*:	I *first* I ˰started doing a little *break˰down*
5		of *ti:me* – for ˰*you*.
6	*Kari*:	°um ^hum°
7	*Kendra*:	just to ^*see* – kind of ˰how it's ˰*going* –
8		this is-s h- ha you – *got* – *right* into
9		*things* – ˰*very* ^quick˰*ly*
10	*Kari*:	um hum
11		(3.4)
12	*Kendra*:	*then* – when you *got* into your ˰*dis^cussion*
13		(0.5) I *started* ˰counting the – *different* –
14		*stu˰dents* – >*look at* ˰this:< (1.0) *five* >ten
15		fifteen twenty< *twenty* five – twenty ^*se˰ven*
16		– *you* called *on* – tw₍enty s even (0.2)
17	*Kari*:	>^good<¹
18	*Kendra*:	*different* kids

19	*Kari:*	just about – ˏevery^body
20	*Kendra:*	*that's ˏjust ^about ˏevery^body >except* for
21		the ˏ*ones* that *wouldn't* 'ave ₁respon ded
22	*Kari:*	>great<⌉
23	*Kendra:*	ˏ*anyway* I mean< ·hh you *took* a ^little –
24		str.*etch* – break (0.8) um (0.4) *HOW* DIDCHU
25		*FEEL* about the – *discus*ˏ*sion* – ^af.ter – the
26		(0.2) ₁stretch ^break
27	*Kari:*	stretch ^break⌉
28		(1.2)
29	*Kari:*	It's *going* down ˏ*hill* – >I mean< – it was
30		*kinda* – I think *that's* an a *lo:::ng time* to
31		dis₁ˏcuss
32	*Kendra:*	um h⌉um
33		u₁m hum ₁um hum
34	*Kari:*	and I⌉ *pro bably* w⌉ould do *that*
35		^diffeˏrent^ly (0.3) um (0.5) ^sometimes you
36		can haˏv:e (2.4) a ˏ*long* discussion if *kids*
37		are *really* into the *sto*ˏ*ry:* (0.8) um:
38		(1.3)
39	*Kendra:*	*they did* ^well – I ˏthou₁ght
40	*Kari:*	the⌉y did *O*ˏ*K* –
41		but *I* think *they* were *getting* kinda *restless*
42		>and I *don't* blame ˏ*them*< hhh ((laugh)) I
43		mean I think – I just *ex*ˏ*pect* that *they're*
44		gonna get a *little* ˏrest^less and (0.4)
45		u::m- I *could've::* – *maybe* opted to have
46		*them:* (0.5) *talk* about the *second* ^quesˏtion
47		– ( ) more
48		(1.2)
49	*Kendra:*	w₁*rite* – individual *an*₁*swer* s ^yeah?
50	*Kari:*	°yeah°⌉ (provide)⌉
51	*Kendra:*	or *e*^*ven* – I suggested *maybe* down ˏ*here* this
52		is *jus*- – *these* are *just* – uh some ˏ*other*
53		^*WAY:S* – if *YO:U* get *up*=
54	*Kari:*	=um hum
55	*Kendra:*	and *change* (0.2) *you* move *around*
56	*Kari:*	um ^hum
57	*Kendra:*	you- in^crease your *voice:* – *volume* a
58		lit.tle – inˏcrease your *pace* >a little< –
59		or *slow* it ˏ*down* >when (you have)< just *do* –
60		*something* ₁a little diffe ˏrent
61	*Kari:*	(that's) different⌉
62		₁oh that's a good ^idea
63	*Kendra:*	·hh *that* gives *them* – ⌉ because *they* get

64		*into – this* little *bit* of
65		*lethar*₍ₐ*gy* you ₐknow
66	*Kari:*	the ^sa:me] ₐthi:₍ng:
67	*Kendra:*	yeah' (0.4) *and*
68		>*pretty*< soo:n *they'r-* – and *they* were *doing*
69		– *s:o we*ₐ*ll*=
70	*Kari:*	=>ₐum ^hum<
71	*Kendra:*	so: – *sometimes* if the *tea*ₐ*cher chan*ₐ*ges* –
72		it *helps* – *them* refocus ₐa ₐ*little* ₐbit
73		₍(and)
74	*Kari:*	^*yea* '*h* – *that* makes *sen*ₐ*se*=
75	*Kendra:*	=·hh but- *you* ^*were* – >you know< *they* – ^*did*
76		– >*finally*< come ₐback=
77	*Kari:*	=um ₍hum um ₍hum-
78	*Kendra:*	mos'l|t of *them* – to ' (0.2) *being*
79		(0.2) *attentive* to the *discus*ₐ*sion*
80	*Kari:*	um hum
81	*Kendra:*	U:M – THIS IS ₐ*ONE* - I *wanted* to *ask* you
82		*a*^*bout* (0.2) >*this* young *man* now< ((Kari
83		clears throat)) – y- you *gave* him a
84		*warn*ₐ*ing:* (0.4) >you *told* him to move *up*
85		^*here:*< – ₍>about
86	*Kari:*	um hu'|m
87	*Kendra:*	*halfway* through the *discussion*< =
88	*Kari:*	=*right*=
90	*Kendra:*	=>and *he didn't* ₐmo₍*ve*<
91	*Kari:*	>I ' *knew* he ₐ*didn't*<
92		(0.4) and I *didn't* (0.2) *follow through* on
93		ₐ*that*
94	*Kendra:*	>*is that* because *you* were *real*ₐ*ly invol*ₐ*ved*
95		with your *discus*ₐ*sio*₍*n* and< – *concentr a*ₐ*ting*
96	*Kari:*	*ye*ₐ*ah* >it was-< '
97	*Kendra:*	on the *ques*₍^*tions?*
98	*Kari:*	*r*ₐ*ight*' (0.3) an₍d (0.6)
99	*Kendra:*	°u' hum°
100	*Kari:*	uh -e *stopped his* (0.1) ^*noise-ma*ₐ*king.*
101		(0.7) thought O^K well if you're *gon*^*na-* –
102		*it's* not *bothering* ₐ*me that's* ₐ*fine.*
103	*Kendra:*	y- I ₐ*see* >yeah< so you
104		*jus*₍*t* – let it ₐ*go* – and::
105	*Kari:*	>and when *he's* ta n ken a<
106		*stan:*'*ce* ₐon (0.3) I'm *not* participa ₐting um
107		*you* can't *make* ₐme. Um
108	*Kendra:*	>um hum<
109	*Kari:*	>you ^know?<

110	*Kendra:*	>um hum<
111	*Kari:*	*I'm tired* of *sending* him to the *of*fice.*
112	*Kendra:*	(Ed thinks)=
113	*Kari:*	=So=
114	*Kendra:*	=I *don't* blame ˰y˪ou
115	*Kari:*	>I'M NO˩T WASTING ANYmore<
116		˰time on ˰it.
117	*Kendra:*	I ˰don't blame ˰you – ˪(for ˪)
118	*Kari:*	so:˩ – u˩:m (1.3)
119		>SO – ˰THEN when he was *making* more ˰noise<
120		*then* it was just ˰like (0.6) >take the
121		^thing a˰way that ˰makes the ˰noise< go sit
122		some*where* ˰else. hhh
123	*Kendra:*	um ˰hum >um ^hum<
124		(1.2)
125	*Kari:*	so
126	*Kendra:*	·h *there* was ^one – ˰point I don't *know* you
127		*were-* – you were *bu˰sy*: – *atten^ding* to your
128		*stu^dents* but I *no˰ticed* – one – *point* ^he
129		*act^ually* got – *intere˰sted* in some˰thing
130		˪the kids *were* say˰ing, (0.5)
131	*Kari:*	^you're: *kid˰ding*˩
132	*Kendra:*	and *stopped* – for a *minute* (0.3) and *made* a
133		*comment* – like (0.4) >well *that* makes
134		*sen˰s:e*<
135	*Kari:*	um hu:m
136	*Kendra:*	and I *thought* – gosh is *this* kid *actually-*
137		but *then* that was ˪*it*
138	*Kari:*	um h˩um
139	*Kendra:*	hhh ((breathy laugh)) (that was it) lasted
140		about five seconds and it was gone hhh
141		((laughing))
142	*Kari:*	all right – o::h ˰dear
143	*Kendra:*	*and-* y- look how ^*long* how ^*long* the discus˰sion
144		^*went-* now *this* is ˰*my*˪: ^clock
145	*Kari:*	this is a lo:˩ng
146		ti˰m˪e:
147	*Kendra:*	^nine th˩ir^ty no n- I me:an (0.2)
148		*they* did ^well – *cl˪ear* up to: –
149	*Kari:*	yeah˩
150	*Kendra:*	ten fif^*teen*
151	*Kari:*	˰yeah
152	*Kendra:*	with *only* about – a *minute* (0.4)
153	*Kari:*	^*stretch*=
154	*Kendra:*	=^*here*=

155	*Kari*:	=uh huh=
156	*Kendra*:	=*this* is not – *actually* ^*right* you ʌwere=
157	*Kari*:	=um hum=
158	*Kendra*:	=*back* into *more* things ^*here*
159	*Kari*:	um ʌhum
160	*Kendra*:	u:m (1.3) °I *commented* on: u:m (0.3) y-
161		your – re^laxed ʌman^ner° (0.7) (ap)propriate
162		rein^*force*ʌ*ment* – you were *giving* (0.4)
163		*rea:lly appropriate* reinforcement to ʌsome
164		>you were *saying*< that's *interes*ʌ*ting* or I
165		*hadn't* – *th*ought about *that* before:
166	*Kari*:	°uh huh°
167	*Kendra*:	*good idea*:
168	*Kari*:	°uh hum:°=
169	*Kendra*:	=you *were* doing *a lot* of ʌ*that*.=
170	*Kari*:	=I'm *try*- I 'as *trying* to ^*follow* ʌup on
171		^ *their*
172	*Kendra*:	*yes* – yₗes-
173	*Kari*:	quesˈtion
174	*Kendra*:	an- an- and you- – you *always* have *really*
175		ʌgood *active* ^lisʌten^ing *skills*, ʌKari I
176		mean it's – *obvious* that you're *paying* (0.3)
177		*very* close ʌ*at*^*ten*ʌ*tion* – and *when* you got
178		ʌ*dis*^*trac*ʌ*ted* – you *said* ʌso.
179	*Kari*:	um ʌhum
180	*Kendra*:	((in raspy voice)) °you *said* – you know° –
181		could you re^*peat* ʌTHAT – *because* I was
182		ʌ*dis*^*trac*ʌ*ted* ((laugh in voice)) by the
183		*noi*^*ses* in the ^*back* ((laughs outright))
184	*Kari*:	^some ʌ*times* I *didn't* but – ^yeah
185	*Kendra*:	^any^way (0.3) u:h – OVER^ALL DID IT ʌGO THE
186		WAY YOU *WANTED* IT ^*TO*?
187	*Kari*:	^YEAH – *actual*ʌly it went *pretty* ^WELL (0.3)
188		um: – I *forgot* to ^*share* the ^*in*ʌ*forma*^*tion*
189		about the *number* of (0.3) ^*in*ʌ*terrup*^ *tions* –
190		and ʌ*con*^*tribu*ʌ*tors*.
191	*Kendra*:	·hh oh yeah – ʌrigh*t*
192	*Kari*:	Which is:=
193	*Kendra*:	=ran outta ʌ*time* for ^*that* y- y- you- c- *are*
194		you *gonna* do that ^*to*ʌ*mor*^*row*? or are you
195		*going* to *ski*ₗp ^*it* er-?
196	*Kari*:	yeahˡ *um*:: – I'm- I'll
197		*share* that ʌ*in*^*forma*ʌ*tion* tomorʌrow.
198	*Kendra*:	°>um hum<°
199	*Kari*:	=^so: – we have- (0.4) ʌ*twenty* ^six

200		∧inter^rup∧tions. *That's* some∧thing to
201		wo˻rk o n – °isn't ^it (0.2) *next* ∧year°
202	*Kendra:*	uhum˺
203	*Kendra:*	I *shared* with ∧Dun^can ((observer)) uh- I do
204		∧not – *think* those *kids* could've – *ever* had
205		a *dis^cus∧sion* ^like ∧*that* – ^*six* ∧*months*
206		a∧go. There's ^no ∧*way* >they would've been
207		able to *attend* – longer than about ∧*three*
208		*min˻utes<* at least –
209	*Kari:*	yeah ˺
210	*Kendra:*	*not* the *kids* that ^*I* ∧saw – and *these* are
211		the *same* ∧ki˻ds
212	*Kari:*	um˺ hum um hum
213	*Kendra:*	*NO:R* – *um*: I DON'T *THINK* THAT Y^OUR (0.2)
214		*behavio∧ral expecta∧tions* (0.3) w:ere
215		*near^ly* as ^*con∧sis^tent six months* ^a∧go as
216		they are ˻∧*now*
217	*Kari:*	yea˺h (0.4) that's ^true
218	*Kendra:*	>I mean you *have not-<* (0.3) >instead of< –
219		*relaxing* your ^*stan∧dards* at the ^*end* ∧of
220		the ^*year* – you've ^*actual∧ly* in^*creased*
221		∧*them*, *which* I *think* is- is – *admir∧able*.
222	*Kari:*	um hum
223	*Kendra:*	>It was *like<* just ^*be∧cause* there're only
224		∧*eight* ^*days* of school ∧*left:*
225	*Kari:*	∧um ^hum
226	*Kendra:*	I still *expect you* to ˻lis^ten ∧an-
227	*Kari:*	oh ^yeah˺ ^oh
228		^yeah WE'RE *PUS˻HING* TH IS ^*STORY* TO THE
229	*Kendra:*	attend ˺
230	*Kari:*	*LA:S˻:T:* ^ *WE:DNES:∧DAY:*
231	*Kendra:*	>YOU'RE GONNA GET< *THIS* WEDNES˻DAY?
232	*Kari:*	((laughs))
233		((student in background: Oh ∧No))
234	*Kendra:*	anyways I ^*was-* I ^*was* – >∧*pleased*< and
235		∧*your* – *level* of – ^*ques∧tion^ing* (0.4) was
236		∧*ex^cel∧lent* – some- ther-'as: there 'as
237		some ∧*big* ^*thing∧kin'* goin' on *in*
238		^*he˻re* ∧to ^*day*
239	*Kari:*	um ^um˺ um ∧hum – ∧o:h – ^yeah (0.6)
240		and ^*I find* ∧*that* if ∧I *ask ques∧tions* that
241		*I∧'m*: – ∧cur^ious a∧bo:ut (0.8) ^*that's* where
242		we *get* the ∧*best* – *dis^cus∧sion* – 'cause if
243		^*I'm* ∧in^*teres∧ted* – ^*some∧body* ^*else's* –
244		∧pro^*bably* ∧had a – >^*ques∧tion* about ^*it<* –

```
245                    ˄to˺o
246   Kendra:          um¹ ^hum um ^hum ^sure – ^g˺ood
247   Kari:                                       I dʲon't
248                    ˄know- I ^think ˄the – text˄book ques^tions
249                    are ˄just (0.6) ˄bo^gus hh
250                    ˺((la      ughs))
251   Kendra:          >yeah<¹
252   Kari:            I'm SOR^RY but – they don't- – they don't
253                    ^reach – ˄my in^te˄rest le^vel hh (0.4) so
254                    (1.1) >^yeah<
255   Kendra:          an- you're– tak– Duncan ^did˄chu wan^n:a –
256                    ask Kari ˄any^thing? or °^who ^knows°
257   Duncan:          u:m – may˄be at some ^o˄ther- ^la˄ter (   )
258   Kendra:          >not now< °OK°
259   Kari:            O^K (1.1) thanks for com^in'
260   Duncan:          thanks for in^vitin' ˄me
261                         .
262                         .
263                         .
```

Doug and Vern: 10 May 1989

```
1    Vern:       feel (0.2) about the various parts of the
2                lesson – there like the first part – where
3                you were doing: – what we call the modeling
4                part essentially, you wer- you were doing
5                the ˺(               ) in the modeling      and
6    Doug:           um hum                    um hum¹
7    Vern:       that (0.3) where wh- where are some things,
8                that you would like to make some changes?
9                (2.2)
10   Doug:       Uh – for (0.5) most parts I felt that this-
11               (0.6) they're (station) – because they've
12               been there a mu- kept there for awhile
13               an˺d so     and uh (1.3) ideally I sh:ifted
14   Vern:           um h¹um
15   Doug:       (0.6) because we: – remember at that time we
16               have more serious thing to do like uh (0.7)
17               math and thin˺g the re, so we go
18   Vern:                    right¹
19   Doug:       from – that serious thing and go over here
20               (0.5) it's kind of um (0.2) easier to: –
21               manage because uh- because of that I have to
22               stop several times – still. (0.8) uh:: Bring
```

166

23		their attentions ⌐back – so *that's* the *thing*
24		that *I* would *like* to cḥ⌐ange.
25	*Vern:*	*yeah*, (0.2) *one* a- *one* of the *things* that –
26		as I *watched* you
27	*Doug:*	um hum
28	*Vern:*	uh::m, *things* and I think we *practiced this*
29		one because *one* ((chuckle in voice)) of the
30		*things* ·hh that *I* was *going* to ·h *mention* –
31		in *watching* that *was* – wa:s (0.6) *I*: –
32		*might*'ve – *because* they *had been* on the
33		carpet *before*=
34	*Doug:*	=um hum=
35	*Vern:*	=*when* ·hh I *might've* – *felt* a *need* for
36		physical *change*. ·h and at – THAT *point* in
37		*time* your *only* option for *physical change* –
38		*would've* been to have 'em – re- – *go back* to
39		their *desks*, and *then* ·hh have 'em in their
40		*individual* seats – *while-* – *you* gave
41		*instructions*. ·hh I *think* that ·h >you know<
42		it has *been* – a – um: (0.4) *pattern* for –
43		*Lynne* of *course* and then for *you*:=
44	*Doug:*	=um hum=
45	*Vern:*	=to have *have followed* in ⌐*that* – deve^lop
46		*that*, that *normally* when you wanna *give that*
47		·h *that* um (0.7) *whole* group *type* of of of
48		*early* part of a *lesson*=
49	*Doug:*	=⌐um:
50	*Vern:*	where youʰre *doing* the *in put* as y-y-
51		*they* call *it* on an *ITIP* ⌐try ·h *input*
52	*Doug:*	um hum⌐
53	*Vern:*	modeling that you *gather them around* you, –
54		you *cluster* ·h *part* of *that* is their – their
55		*si::ze* – you ⌐know – the fact *that* they can
56		*fit* and everything *else* ·hh *but* – *remember*
57		when we *were* visiting the *night* at Mount
58		*Hood*?
59		(0.6)
60	*Doug:*	⌐umm *yeah*
61	*Vern:*	uhm:⌐ I *didn't* get a *sense* he *ever*
62		gathered *kids* on the *carpet*. – It *looked*
63		like he *always* – *did* what *teachers* tend to
64		*do* at the *higher* ^*grade* levels, – the *kids*
65		stayed *pretty* mu⌐ch in th eir *desk* ·h *And*
66	*Doug:*	um hum⌐
67	*Vern:*	*stuff* – um – I think *that* – what *you*: –

68		could *do* is is work *out* – the *best* of *both*
69		worlds – that is=
70	*Doug:*	=um hum
71	*Vern:*	*move* 'em *back* and *for*ˏ*th* ·h and *this*
72		would've *been* a *case* where *I* would've –
73		*prob*ˌably after *they're* on the *carpet* with
74		*Lynne* (0.3) *knowing* that it's a *change* in
75		their *routine* and *everything else,* es-
76		*establish* – the most (*settled*) – *pat*^*tern* –
77		the most (*settled*) pattern is to
78		﹙have 'em *seated*
79	*Doug:*	um hum ˌ
80	*Vern:*	*individually* at their own *desk* ·h um (0.7)
81		you *don't* have that *immediacy.* (0.5) *But* I
82		*don't* think *anything* you were *doing* that
83		(0.2) their *eyes* are *better* than ^*our eyes* –
84		normally around ((chuckle)) that *age.* ·h And
85		so I *don't* think *there* was *any* – *reason* that
86		*they* had to be *clustered* around you (0.3)
87		for – ﹙for *that.* So *that* might have been
88	*Doug:*	um﹚
89	*Vern:*	*something* that that *probably* ˙ um *I* would've
90		*done* in that *situation.* ·h *Because* – *during*
91		that part in *time,* there *weːre* that (0.8)
92		﹙( )
93	*Doug:*	>um hum﹚ um hum< *yeah*
94	*Vern:*	·h OR ANOTHER *THING THAT* YOU *MIGHT* HAVE
95		WANTED TO *CONSIDER* – ONCE Aˏ*GAIN,* (0.3) I
96		DREW IT – HERE. ((papers rustling)) *This* was
97		ESSENTIALLY – the *seating* pattern up *front* –
98		the *boys* were *all* in – a *row* in *front* of
99		*you,* – and the *girls* were *all* behind them.
100		(0.2) The *girls:* – on the *whole* – *there* was
101		– *oːnce* >in a *while*< there was a *girl*
102		﹙(in the re) but on *whole* it was the *boys*
103	*Doug:*	um hum﹚
104	*Vern:*	you *spoke* to ·h >*particularly*< you had *three*
105		boys *here,* – and *Tim right* here ·h and then
106		*Zack of course* was *doing* his *normal* (0.2)
107		*ballet* routine *around* the *room.* uːːM ((aside
108		to observer)) *Duncan,* for *your* benefit,
109		(0.4) *Zack* has some *very* (0.2) *special* –
110		*con*ˏ*cerns* >in fact *I* don't know *what*
111		they< *finally* – *decided* – he *is.* – But at
112		the *beginning* of the *year, they* were

113		*wondering* if *he* might *not* be – ·h *be* (0.5)
114		>I didn't *know*< *if* he could *be* this –
115		*borderline autistic,* – *he* wanders *in* and
116		*out* ·h >*what* they *have* found is *that he* has
117		a *genius* (0.3) *stat level.* I mean
118		[take and do *quad ratic* er- – *quations* in
119	*Doug:*	o h really. I can-]
120	*Vern:*	his ^head and- – and *he* was *one* of the *final*
121		competitors in the *spelling* bee and *things* –
122		*things* like *that* around *here* >I mean< *he's*
123		*just* (0.3) *bright* is *all.* ·h But *he's* (0.5)
124		*dis^connected.* – And he *wanders* – *in* and *out*
125		of *^ his* – an- or *^Lynne's, anybody* you watch
126		him (come over he'll know) the *group* so ·h
127		so *Zack* is a – SPECIAL *case* – as is um *Eric*
128		– *who* – *who* is the *kid* – *who* >*first* came
129		*back* and got a *pencil*< from ^ *me?*=
130	*Doug:*	=Right.
131	*Vern:*	·h and *he* – (*harangued*) at his *desk.* ·h well
132		*he* has some >*particularily*< intres- i-
133		*issues* in *dealing* w- doing *destructive* –
134		*things.* And *he* ^*lost* the *pen^cil* I *gave* him
135		he he he *just* (0.6) ^*eats* ^*up materials* –
136		*basically.* ·h But ((cough)) *there's* some
137		*kids* in *there* with *very special* ne˄eds, and
138		*that's* why I know their ^ *names* ((chuckle))
139		so *well* – because *there are* kids *with* that
140		*need.*
141	*Doug:*	um hum
142	*Vern:*	·h *um* – But – *once* ^again – if you were
143		*going* to *have* them *up* there, you *might've* –
144		>*taken* a more< *proactive role* in *seating*
145		them. (0.8) *I* don't *know* if y- a *boy* ^*girl*
146		*boy* ^*girl pat^tern*'ll be *better,* or the
147		*ones* who you *know* are going to interact
148		^*here* – ·h *you* do *that.* It's like a *seating*
149		˄chart=
150	*Doug:*	=um hum um [hum yeah
151	*Vern:*	you kn[ow? AN:D – u:m – u:m
152		(1.0) *I^: did it* with *ninth graders* – *so* the
153		*likelihood* that you'd *have* to do *it* with
154		*first graders* – *would* be *great.*
155	*Doug:*	um hum
156	*Vern:*	OK?
157	*Doug:*	*yeah* – *that* would be a *good* ^*idea* hhh

158	*Vern:*	*WHAT – WHATCHU NEE^::D* is to ˏ*expand* the
159		*repertoire – of skills – that you* can ^*use –*
160		*to – ensure classroom management.* And
161		₁whatchu *b ad going on: – up* ^*front –* was
162	*Doug:*	um hum ˥
163	*Vern:*	*less* than *productive* classroom *management –*
164		because there *were – a number* of *times –*
165		>you *had* to go< – *T:im* (0.8) >you know< –
166		*Zack: –* um: m-m-m >you know< *what*^*ever* the
167		*names* ˏ*were:: –* or wha- *whatever* u- w-
168		yo₁u *ba d* to go *o::n* with
169	*Doug:*	um: ˥
170	*Vern:*	*that –* a few *times* ·h *so that* w- would *be* of
171		*something –* you *really* need *to* focus *on.* h
172		the *second thing – that –* I would *mention*
173		*here* is is (3.0) °and *in* an art *lesson – I*
174		might *add* there- – there *isn't – an easy way*
175		of *doing* this, ·h – b:ut it's *something* for
176		you to *think* about.° (0.8) U::M (2.3) THE
177		*OL::D* >we've *talked* about *this* bef:ore< the
178		^*ol::d* (0.7) *never* give *more* than *three*
179		directions to k- *anybody* at *one time=*
180	*Doug:*	=um hum=
181	*Vern:*	=*bave* them *do* those *three* directions – and
182		then *mo:ve –* to the next *stage.*
183	*Doug:*	um hum=
184	*Vern:*	=*You*^*'ve bad* to – give a *number* of
185		*directions=*
186	*Doug:*	=um hum
187	*Vern:*	on *bow* to *cut* out a *butterfly –* an:d –
188		*whatchur* dealing *with* are *kids* where – *that*
189		– *paper cut –* is *still* a *real* (1.1)
190		*lear:*^*ning=*
191	*Doug:*	=um hum=
192	*Vern:*	=*skill.=*
193	*Doug:*	=um hum
194	*Vern:*	>I mean< *so* you'd *have* to *ta:lk* to *them*
195		about – *making* ^*su:re* thatchu – *fold* the
196		*paper* and *then* you – *cut* (0.4) on the –
197		*l:ine* where it's *folded, – not* on the *open*
198		*ends,* which fo- yo-u- – *they* were *fairly*
199		*successful – one kid* >you know<
200		₁before *that – did say – bey* look
201	*Doug:*	um hum hum˩
202	*Vern:*	at *this* ((claps)) you know *that* kind of

170

203		*stuff.* ·h um *You had to:* – um: – *talk*
204		about *how* to *poke* the *holes,* and *cut* those
205		*out,* – um *right down* to *how* to (0.2) *neatly*
206		*put* the glue *on* and everything *else.* ·h um-
207		– *You're under severe* time *constraints.*
208		(0.6) You as a- – you *wanted* the ditto- you
209		*wanta* ((claps)) have it *done,* you *wanted*
210		*them* to be *able* to go ((claps)) to *recess* –
211		*all* in a *period* of about a *half* hour or *so.*
212		·h *So the* – *longer* you take ^*time* to (0.3)
213		*give* – *two three* uh *directions,* – *have 'em*
214		do *it* and then *stop* them *all*=
215	*Doug:*	=um hum=
216	*Vern:*	and- *do* it *next*- (0.3) the *next* two or *three*
217		– *things* – it becomes *a problem.* – um *This*
218		*maybe* could've been a *two* day *art* lesson.
219		(0.7) *The* first ˏ*day* at their *desks,* *they*
220		cut the *butterfly* ˏout (0.4)
221		₁the *bla ck* part *out* – and *they* get
222	*Doug:*	um hum ˥
223	*Vern:*	it at their *desks.* you know. (0.2) *And* –
224		*step* by *step.* The second *day:* (0.4) *you* put
225		the – the *pa*₁*per* ˏou t, sort
226	*Doug:*	um hum˥
227	*Vern:*	of *thing.* OR *IT* COULD *ALL* HAVE BEEN *DONE* AT
228		*once* – but in *two pieces.* (0.4) ^*I'd* k- h *my*
229		*in*ˏstinct would *be* to *break* it in *two*
230		pieces, ·hh *and* – >you know< (0.2) *it was* –
231		*that* was *something* – *I*- – >*one* a the- *that*
232		was *one* uh the *big changes*< I *made* as a
233		*teacher* during my ˏ*years,* and *part* of *it* was
234		*through* – *through* – u::m – instructional
235		*skills* training of the *things* I *had* ·h – was
236		to (0.4) *do* things in smaller *pieces* with
237		the *kids.*
238	*Doug:*	um
239	*Vern:*	And I *always* (0.6) *said* – I always *did* it- –
240		ˏf:or – I always *joked* it *was:* – for the *lo*-
241		– uh – *worst* of *reasons,* *that* I'm *lazy* and I
242		*didn't* like to *repeat* myself or *have to* –
243		have *kids* – do it *over.* ·h *And* – *so* I found
244		that *if* I gave *fewer* – *things* at a *time* –
245		they *were* more *successful.* ·h Your *problem*
246		is *though* is the *brighter* kid, *where* you can
247		just *say* – *this* is the *butterfly,* – *you* do

248		*it* and *you* could *give* 'em *instructions* in –
249		*two* ⌄*seconds* (0.2) and *set* them *off* and
250		they *would* do it *right. Those* kids *get* a
251		little (0.5) *bored* – >BUT *ON* THE OTHER *HAND*<
252		IF YOU *NOTICED*, YOU *HAD* SOME KIDS *FINISHED* –
253		*BEFOREHAND* – *waiting* to go to re^*cess.* (0.3)
254		SO THEY *STILL:* – HAD A WAIT *TIme* – *it* was
255		jusᵢt *that* it was – *all* in a *lump,* – *versus*
256	*Doug:*	um hum⌐
257	*Vern:*	– at the *end* of *each* – *three steps* that you
258		would've *do*^*ne.* ·h You ⌄know >a- I *mean*<
259		*those* kids *would've* – *cut* ((claps hands))
260		*out* – if *you* would've *gone* – >okay<, *you're*
261		gonna *fold* the *paper,* (0.4) *had* 'em at the
262		*desks* – giving *instructions.* ·h *TODAY* –
263		we're gonna *do* – a *butterfly,* >the *first*
264		thing we *need to do*< is *fold* paper
265	*Doug:*	um hum
266	*Vern:*	*WATCH* as *I* fold *it* (1.0) ((claps hands))
267		(0.7) *hand* out *paper* to *everybody.* (1.0) um
268		(0.6) *Have* the *kids:* – then – >*hold* it up
269		^*again*< – >once *again* – I *folded* my *paper*
270		this ^*way*< (0.5) >*every*bod*y fold* your *paper*
271		– ((claps lightly)) (0.8) *now push* your
272		*paper* a⌄side. (0.8) *'Cause* you *don't* them
273		*holding* on to *it,* – you want *it*
274		ᵢaside:, and tha t's
275	*Doug:*	>um hum um hum<⌐
276	*Vern:*	the only *thing* they *need* on *their desks* –
277		except *right then* ·h *NOW* THE ^*NEXT* THING I
278		WANTCHU TO ⌄*DO* – IS *WATCH* ME: – *BECAUSE* >*I'm*
279		going to *take* this< *pat*^*tern* and *lay* it *on*
280		my *paper,* and *I'm* going to *put* it ^*here.*
281		(0.5) °OK° h you *might've had* enough
282		*patterns* – for *every* ⌄*kid. That* takes more
283		*work.* But ᵢthat *way* m- TH AT *ALSO* – *THERE*
284	*Doug:*	u m hum um hum⌐
285	*Vern:*	was – some *wait* time – >going *on* there< ·h
286		*and-* if ^*you* – if *you* sensed *it* to⌄day, as
287		the *kids* were *working:* – as *they* were *BACK*
288		at their *seats* and *they* were *doing* all of
289		*this,* – u::m – u:m (1.5) *THEY'RE* MORE MOVING
290		A^*ROUND* AND MORE *NOISY* AND *WHAT*^*EVER*, while
291		they're *waiting* to get *patterns.* >The
292		moment *everybody* had *gotten* their *pattern*<

293		and had *draw:n* – ₍*then* – *it* got *real* –
294	*Doug:*	um ˩
295	*Vern:*	^*quiet* for *awhile while* they *were* doing
296		*it.* >I *mean*< – *things* – *sort* of – got=
297	*Doug:*	=um hum
298	*Vern:*	THE *OLD*: (0.4) THE *BUSIER* KIDS *ARE* (0.4) the
299		fewer *management* problems – *kicks* in *there* –
300		>you know< so- th- um- *if* you can *HAVE* – if
301		you *can- could have* enough *pat*ₓ*terns*:, >you
302		know<
303	*Doug:*	um hum
304	*Vern:*	*do* it *that* way. U::M *Every kid* has a
305		*pat*ₓ*tern*, – *now*: – *let's* (0.5) cut *out* the
306		*butter*ₓ*fly.* – You ₓ*know* – *and*- you *model* ₓit
307		– then *you* hand *out* the *pattern*, – then *you*
308		have them *all* do that *piece* >uh- *draw*< –
309		₍*excuse* m e – >draw *it.*< ·h (0.6) *Stop* –
310	*Doug:*	u:m ˩
311	*Vern:*	have *them* put *it* aside. *Now* I'm going to
312		*show* you *how* to ₓ*cut*, – and you *cut* an- and
313		you *talk* about *how* if *you* were doing *it* and
314		the *modeling* is – *I*:: do *it* this *way* – *not*
315		*you* do *it* that *way*, *I*::: do *it* this *way*, *I* –
316		*I* ·h=
317	*Doug:*	=um hum=
318	*Vern:*	=*because*: they *might do* a *variation* on a
319		*the*ₓ*me*, but you're *showing* them the *ri:ght*
320		way, and *this* is the *way I*:: do *it*=
321	*Doug:*	=um h₍um
322	*Vern:*	th ˥*is* is *what* I'm – *th*::*inking* as *I'm*
323		doing ₓ*it.* – *I'm thinking* about *things* like
324		*this*, – *I m thinking* about t- *needing* to
325		have a *straight line*: (0.6) ^*I'm* ₓ*thinking*
326		about – *how*: I cut *this* center *part* out, –
327		*where* I *start here*, and *I'm* thinking *that*
328		it'd *probably* be *easiest* if I a – *sharp*
329		*scis*ₓsors, °*one* kid had *plastic* scissors and
330		it *didn't*° ₓwork ·h *I'm thinking* about °>you
331		know<° these *sorts* of *things* as
332		₍*I'm* doing *this.* ·h YOU'RE – MODELING
333	*Doug:*	um hum ˩
334	*Vern:*	WHATCHUR – *thinking* – *when* you're *doing that*
335		with *them.* ·h AND- then – THEY GET THAT PART
336		done. (0.6) ₓ*And:* – *then* the *next* piece is
337		yur- your – *tissue* paper on the ₍*back*: or

338	*Doug:*	um hum]
339	*Vern:*	your ^*holes* –°*where* it (*needs*) to be
340		*punched* in *first* >I don't *remember* which *way*
341		you're *going*<° ·h *and doing* those *sorts* of
342		˄*things*, ·h IT'S A *STEP* BY *STEP* – *THEY'RE* AT
343		THEIR ˄DESK, BUT YOU'RE ^*DOING* A *COUPLE* OF
344		*things* ˄*there*, – *TODAY* IT WAS AN *ART*
345		PROJECT, (0.4) *but* – if you- – *LOOK* WHAT *I*
346		HAVE JUST ˄*DONE* – *we* have *had* a *LES*^*SON* –
347		˄*in*: – u:m – *cut*˄*ting*: – we *have* had a
348		*lesson* in following *inSTRUC*^*TIONS*=
349	*Doug:*	=um hu[m
350	*Vern:*	y]ou know. ·h You *have* a – *number* of
351		*hidden things* going *on* in *that* art *lesson.*
352		(0.3) *I* mean *that's* what ^*art* is all ^*about*
353		– *it's where* the *kids* get to take *ALL* of
354		*this mas*^*sive STUFF* an- ·h your *goal* is *just*
355		to *have* it *done* – done ˄*well* – and *all*
356		cleaned ^*up* (0.2) *and* you're teaching *kids* a
357		*WHOLE* lot of – *basic classroom skills* there,
358		of just ·h a- *little* self *management* issues
359		going on [*there* an- ·h *and using* some of
360	*Doug:*	um hum]
361	*Vern:*	the other *s- other* ^*other* skills. >I mean<
362		*for* – a *first* grader *how* to *use* – a *scissors*
363		correctly – is – a *skill* they *need* to *learn*
364	*Doug:*	°right°
365	*Vern:*	*hopefully* with a *ninth* grader it's ^*not.*
366	*Doug:*	right
367	*Vern:*	With a *ninth* ^grader *it's* – tryin- – to
368		*convince* them that they're *not* going to *stab*
369		their *neigh*^*bor* with *it.*
370	*Doug:*	um hum=
371	*Vern:*	=U:M >You know< *it's* a different (0.2) *sort*
372		of *management* issue *there* but there're *still*
373		management issues the *moment* you *hand* out
374		*scissors* – the *moment* you *hand* out *paper*
375	*Doug:*	um
376	*Vern:*	°*and things*° (1.0) ·h SO there're (1.7) *there*
377		*are* – >*are some* things *there*< ·h NOW >ON THE
378		OTHER ˄HAND< (0.5) IF *I* WERE *YOU* – MY MIND
379		WOULD BE *going* (0.5) (oh) by the *time*
380		*re*^*cess* was *over* I had a (0.3) *butterfly*
381		from *everybody* and it *looked* pretty *good,*
382		^*right?* – I *mean* you *did.*

383	*Doug*:	um hum
384	*Vern*:	I *think* >h-h- you know< (0.5) i-i-if we *just*
385		take *it* from the *evaluative* end wh- what
386		didchu ^*want?* you wanted *butter-flies* that
387		looked a *certain* – like a *butterfly.* ·h
388		*Thatchu* could *put* ^*up* for par^*ent* night and
389		*you* wanted it *done* in a *quick* amount of
390		ˏ*time* – O^K?
391	*Doug*:	°yeah°
392	*Vern*:	*DIDCHU* HAVE *THAT* OCCUR? – *yes* you ˏ*did.*
393		(0.5) I mean=
394	*Doug*:	=um
395	*Vern*:	>You know< (1.3) you *said* from w-w- we
396		*should* be *there* from >twelve-*thirty* to one-
397		^*fifteen*< at one-*fifteen* – I think *basically*
398		we *walked* over ^*here* (0.4) *so* – th:ere: you
399		*met* your *objective.* (1.4) And – *there*
400		every*thing* was *fine:* ·h *but* – >you ˏknow< –
401		on the *other* ˏhand, – *were* there *wa:ys* –
402		*that* you could *deal* with *some* things *that*
403		you *noticed.* You- >you know< you *were:* –
404		*aware* of *the* – the *fact* that *they'd* been in
405		a *s-* – *down* on the ˏ*floor* too long, you *were*
406		*aware* that you *had* to say – *please don't* do
407		*this* enough- ·h >you know< *this* –
408		*frequently.* ah:m: I *don't* know ^*if* you *were*
409		aware of *that* part – *where* ·h *where some*
410		kids were *waiting* for par-*terns* th₍at *say*
411	*Doug*:	>um hum<˩
412	*Vern*:	were more – *behaviorally disruptive* then
413		on^*ce everybody* had – the – *cut* >and *they*
414		got
415		₍*quiet* – an- – *foCUS* (ED) – *LIKE* KIDS *DO:*
416	*Doug*:	u:m – right – right˩
417	*Vern*:	·h >and *stuff* like *that*< *SO* >you know< *what*
418		I'm *suggest*ˏing, *isn't* so much *that* – it'll
419		*help* ^*you* (0.4) ^*get* the end *pro*^*duct* (0.5)
420		*better, instead* ·h *it's:* (1.4) *w:*^*ill* – mean
421		– your *hair* won't – *turn* as- (0.2) *gr*ˏ*ey* as
422		*quickly* as ^*my* hair has
423		p₍*erhaps* – *that* type of *stuff* ·h
424	*Doug*:	((laughs)) h h h h ˩
425	*Vern*:	be*cause* – *you're* more at – >*you* can be *more*<
426		at *ease:* – °as you're going *through:* this
427		>you can *go*<° ·h *you* can *be* a- *a little* bit

428		*more – feel* like ^*Lynne* ˏdoes. °*You* can *go*
429		hh-oh ((chortle in voice)) isn't that-° I
430		*mean* you *have* more *time* for *the* – the *OH*
431		ISN'T THAT *NICE* KIND OF ˏ*STUFF* >instead of<
432		– >sort of< (0.2) *running* – °from *place* to
433		*place* and doing that ₁sorta thing° ·hh and
434	*Doug:*	um hum⌋
435	*Vern:*	so *THAT*'s (0.6) >*you* know *where* you're gonna
436		*go*< (0.4) >*one* of the *things* I just
437		*mentioned* to< *Lynne:* – is to *WORK* with *you* –
438		on *expanding* that *bag* of *refinement* and
439		*organizational* t- (0.7) *tr:icks:* – *or*
440		*tech*ˏ*niques*, ·h u-um you *used* toˏ*day*, a
441		*couple* of ˏ*times*, one of *moving* kids *back*, to
442		the *desk* ·h *and* ((cough)) (0.6) *one* thing
443		you did *well there:* – was – was ^*Tim:*. Tim
444		*didn't* wanna go *back* to his *desk*. – And *you*
445		said *it* – I- ((snaps fingers)) *he did* ^*it* –
446		*you* said *it* to *him* t- – *once* >and *he* didn't
447		go *back*, and I *thought* >is (Doug) going to
448		ignore *this* you said it *again* – he *didn't*
449		go *back* ·h and (finally-) th- you know – you
450		– *did it* again< and *you* got *Tim* to go *back*
451		to his *DESK. THERE'S* A *KID* WHO WAS BEING
452		*RESISTANT* but *you:* – WERE *PERSISTENT.* –
453		OK? ·h *THAT* WAS *GOOD* – you *did* not *choose*
454		to ig^nore ˏ*that, because* – >you know<
455		*sometimes* it's *easiest* to ignore *it* when
456		they *don'* ₁t do it >*sometimes*
457	*Doug:*	um hum⌋
458	*Vern:*	they *QUIT*< (0.5) *but* they don't- *in-* – >ya-
459		know< th- he *might* have *quit* – misbe*having*
460		₁ ·h *but* he *do esn't* ignore
461	*Doug:*	um hum ⌋
462	*Vern:*	^*it*. ·h *And* – *the* moment *he* ignores *one* of a
463		*com*^*mand, when* you make a *com*^*mand* at *that* –
464		*strength* and *that* commitment – ·h *other* kids
465		are *wa:tching.* (0.7)
466	*Doug:*	°yeah°
467	*Vern:*	If *TIM* doesn't have to do *it* in the long *run*
468		then *I* won't have to *do* ˏ*it,* – so *you*
469		*follou*(ed) through on *that,* ·h *you* gave *Zack*
470		the *choice* and the *second* time *arou:nd* you
471		*remembered* (0.2) *that* – Zack was *screwin'*
472		ˏaround – *he* needed to go *back* to his ^*desk*

473		and *you* had *him* go *back* to his ^*desk.* ·h
474		*ERIC*: (0.2) *chose* to stay at his ⌄*desk,*
475		(0.2) *my instinct* would *be* if *E- – Eric*
476		chooses to *stay* at his *desk* and he's *sitting*
477		in *it*, I would – *never* – °worry about *that*
478		with *Eric. – My* instinct *is* – *given* the
479		*problems that* kid *has* –
480	*Doug*:	u ⌊m
481	*Vern*:	⌈I⌉ *prefer* to *have* at his *desk* – than
482		⌊*anywhere* el se in
483	*Doug*:	um hum ⌉
484	*Vern*:	the *room. I* can *wa:tch* him *bet⌄ter – than*
485		when *he's* around *other* people.° ·h *SO – so* –
486		^*HE di:d* ⌄*that* >now *Eric* got a *little*< (0.5)
487		*TI⌄RED* – er- – >*sitting* or *whatever*< and he
488		started (1.2) do⌊ing his *li* tt*le* –
489	*Doug*:	hum ⌉
490	*Vern*:	*la:⌄y* on the *desk* – routine, ·h u::m – *and* –
491		and – of *course* – *Zack* – *can't* sit for more
492		^*than* – *two* seconds *it* seems *like*. >°You
493		know°< so – *there* – *there's* an *issue*. >With
494		*Tim* – *he'll* go *back* to his *desk*< so. ·h *SO*
495		*THOSE* WERE *GOOD* – *management* ⌄*things*, now
496		*whatchu* wanna *do* is *add* some *more* to *that*. –
497		*Just* sending kids *back* – to their ^*desk* –
498		*that's* one *step* – ·h *what* are other *steps*
499		you can ^*take*, – >°you know°<, *or* are *there*
500		preventative *things* from the *start*.
501	*Doug*:	um ⌊hum
502	*Vern*:	⌈Pre⌉ *ventative* things would've *been maybe*
503		to have 'em *sit* – *all* at their ⌄*desks* –
504		*because* – of – they'd *been* on the *floor* too
505		*long.* ah::m *Other things* – *if* you would've
506		*had them* (0.5) *SITTING* ^*THER:E* – is – is –
507		*versus* – u:m >y- you *know*< *sending* some *back*
508		to their *desks* as you *did.* – Another *option*
509		would *be* to *move* them with*in* the *group* (0.2)
510		*too* many *boys* together *too* many ⌄*girls*, as
511		*I've* mentioned. ·h u:m (1.0) ((coughs)) um
512		(1.2) *USING* SOME *MO:RE* – ^*POSITIVE* ^*NEGATIVE*
513		– *types* of – of *re:ward* point system, *yeah*
514		like ·h *OK* you're *being* too *noisy*, (0.2)
515		u:m *everybody's* going to *stay in* for *recess*
516		*ti:me* – *except* for *first graders* that's:: –
517		*a few* minutes *away* is *even* a *long* time *away*.

518		That *work* more *effectively* with ^older
519		k₍ids than it *does* with
520	*Doug:*	um hum ₐum hum ⌉
521	*Vern:*	*younger* kids. ·h U::M – U:M – you – might –
522		*have* – u::h – I- - I know *sometimes* and >I-
523		I- *I* didn't *really* look *around* the room
524		today,< *sometimes* you *have* the *thing* you –
525		*color* ₐin, >you know< they *get* so many
526		ₐ*points over* the *period* 'a *month* and *they*
527		get *that* >you know< ·h B- TEACHERS USE ALL
528		SORTS OF ₐTHINGS. *I listened* to a *teacher*
529		yesterday *talking* about *a* ·h (particularly)
530		he *chose* some uh *second* ^grade ^group an- –
531		·h *so she* went *on* a ^*pop*^*corn* party on
532		*Friday* routine you ^*know*, – I mean *sh-* –
533		*everybody* has their: *tricks,* they're
534		ₐcalled behavior *modi*₍*fi*^*cation* ^*tri cks* –
535	*Doug:*	um hum um hum⌉
536	*Vern:*	and Mister *O'Riley's* ₐnot ^*real* ^*big* ^*on*
537		^*them* but – you know if if – *that's* ^what's
538		gonna ^*work* – in *those* situations, *that* ^*is:*
539		– to *help* you *expand* that *bag* of *tricks.*
540	*Doug:*	um hum
541	*Vern:*	*Lynne* has a *very* small *bag* of *tricks* she
542		*uses* 'cause *she* doesn't *need* to *use* ^many.
543		·h *Newer* teachers – *have* to have a *bigger*
544		*bag* of *tricks,* – and *unfortunately* they
545		*often* don't *have* ₐit – and *Lynne's* the *one*
546		that ^*has* ₐ*it* but you *never* see ₐ*it.*
547	*Doug:*	um hum ₍um hum
548	*Vern:*	>*becaus*⌐e *she* doesn't *have* to *pull*
549		it *out*< ·h but the uh- >*newer* teachers *don't*
550		have *it* but *they're* the *ones* who *need* it
551		*because* y- you're *still*< (0.5) *trying* to
552		(0.5) *play* around and *get that* right *match*:
553		for ₐyou,
554	*Doug:*	°um hum°=
555	*Vern:*	=with the – *kids* – so that it *mo:ves* – as
556		*smoothly* and as *quickly* as it *does,* – as it
557		*would* when °you're a *seventh* or *tenth year*
558		teacher°=
559	*Doug:*	=uh huh – yeah (1.2) °um°
560	*Vern:*	I was *out* on-n *one* of my *lecture:* – ty- s-s-
561		*things,* (seems we) haven't *done* so much of a
562		*discussion.* Di- I- - you- are there

563		*anything?*
564		(1.7)
565	*Doug:*	₁uh I see *i t* as s-s- *yeah*, we've been *using*
566	*Vern:*	other- ˩
567	*Doug:*	them (0.6) some *kind* of *a- – left* it *off*
568		right *now* but *we've* been *using* the *a-*
569		*beanstalk – about Jack* and the *b*₁*eanstalk*
570	*Vern:*	OH, OK˩ I
571		*didn't –* I *didn't* see ₁that
572	*Doug:*	and *th*˩*ey –* are *there*
573		for the (0.3) *behavior.=*
574	*Vern:*	=uh huh
575	*Doug:*	And *it's* ^been – been ˅*working:* (0.6) ˅*kind*
576		of ^ *well –* I think *it's* the *last – week –*
577		*some* of them *had –* for *those who –* climb up
578		the *air* on the *castle –* ₁*they* ( )
579	*Vern:*	OH – I *DID – I*˩ did
580		*notice* that *last* time I was ˅*in,=*
581	*Doug:*	=uh huh yeah so *they* a- – *they – they* had
582		*lunch* with *me.* Also so *I – they* have *some –*
583		^ *cou*˅*pons – trading* for – *thing* and fo::r –
584		*good* things an- ·h ₁*and* they work *well,* but
585	*Vern:*	an- ˩
586	*Doug:*	*today* I didn't use *it* much
587		ye₁ah right *not* a s *much* as I-
588	*Vern:*	hh yeah I ^see˩ SO – *THERE*
589		WAS ^A ·h *THERE* ₁WAS A ^*TRI CKT –*you *had* in
590	*Doug:*	I thought ˩
591	*Vern:*	your ˅*bag –* that you *didn't* pull *ou:t.*
592	*Doug:*	₁uh huh
593	*Vern:*	*Maybe* ˩ you *could've –* at *times.*
594	*Doug:*	uh huh
595	*Vern:*	*You did* towards the *en::d – once –* ˅*quiet*
596		them ˅*dow:n,* and *say: –* >you know< –
597		*something* >you *looked* at the *clock*< you
598		^ *looked* impatient, I mean you ^*looked –*
599		*frustrated,* and then ·h >you know< you *said*
600		– a- *made* some *comment* that *we* weren't- –
601		*you* weren't *going* to mo- ^go ^*anyplace* 'til
602		they *had don::e this,* so- *I don't* know *how*
603		you *put it* but ·h *but* >you know< and *then*
604		that *quiet*₁*ed* 'em for a *second.* ·h AND
605	*Doug:*	°um hum°˩
606	*Vern:*	*YOU* ALSO *dismissed* 'em *back- –* by ^*rows*
607		again. (0.2) *to*˅*day –* >you know< you w-were

608		*working* on *things* like m-m- *smoother*
609		^ *move-ment* °from one *place* to *another*
610		so₁: *those* were *so me*°
611	*Doug:*	um hum um hum‌ˡ
612		(1.8)
613	*Doug:*	yeah – *basically* they – ^they ^*do* – tend to
614		*responds-* uh – *respond* to *me* – *more* (0.9)
615		°kind of uh – *immediately* an-°
616	*Vern:*	um hum
617	*Doug:*	*more* effectively than *before* – °*because* of
618		uh they just *before* sometime *just-* – *they*
619		*just keep-°* – *kept talking* an-
620	*Vern:*	yeah
621	*Doug:*	°while I was-° – ·h *but now* when they're
622		*asked* for their *attention* (t- it the-) – um-
623		*most* of *them* will give *it* right – just
624		like *that.* (0.7) So *I* can see *that* – or I
625		can *pro:ve* that. *I'm still* working on *it.*
626		hhh ((laughs)) You *see* it *again.* I don't
627		know ^*how* -*well* – I try to s:*ee* how *well*
628		they can – *hear me* – *back there* (0.3) just
629		because *they-* – *they* chose *not* to *respond* or
630		*because* they didn't *hear me* – °very well –
631		(most impor₁tant to my-)°
632	*Vern:*	now you're‌ˡ *talking* about back
633		*where?*
634	*Doug:*	I mean *whenever* I say (0.5) in *their:* – *at*
635		their *chair* – at their *seat* or (0.8)
636	*Vern:*	·h ₁THEY COULD- ^*TH: EY* CAN HEAR -YOU.
637	*Doug:*	on the (counter) ‌ˡ
638		(0.5)
639	*Vern:*	°₁yeah° ·h *I* don't *think* – *hear*ing's:
640	*Doug:*	yeah ‌ˡ like
641		that hh – yeah
642	*Vern:*	an *issue. Unless* there's- – would (*it*) be *a*
643		*lot* of *other* -*noise* around=
644	*Doug:*	=um hum
645	*Vern:*	*um::* (1.1) >you know< *so* – *so::* – *having*
646		them ^*at* their *desks* – when *you* give
647		*instructions,* I do₁*n't* think *hear*ing
648	*Doug:*	um hum‌ˡ
649	*Vern:*	°would be *difficult.*°
650	*Doug:*	YEAH I *SAW* THE *POINT* THAT *YOU:* – UH GAVE
651		EARLIER AB- ABOUT *BREAKING* – THEM *DOWN* BY
652		S:*MALL* STEPS?

653	*Vern:*	um hum
654	*Doug:*	AND WHAT I *DID* WITH *A* (0.8) *WINDSOCK* – I
655		*think* that *one* we did (*it*) in *three days:.*
656	*Vern:*	yeah=
657	*Doug:*	=*They* did – *good jobs* of just – the first
658		*day* – they just (*colored*) *that,*
659	*Vern:*	>um hum< =
660	*Doug:*	=*second* day they *put together* and then *put*
661		the tails ^*on.* (1.4) And the *la:st* day *they*
662		put *the:* – *the strings* on.
663	*Vern:*	yeah
664	*Doug:*	Yeah YEAH *I* TRIED *THAT.* AND *IT'S*- – *WORKS*
665		AND U::H (1.2) *I* also *tried* to give *out* –
666		*some* kind of (0.3) *di^rection* that- at their
667		*s:eat.* (0.6) ·h u:h *but* right *now* its- – at
668		their- – *this* stage *if* I do *it* – *there* it's
669		*gon*- take
670		(0.5)
671	*Vern:*	much *LONGER* yeah hhh YEAH IT
672		⌊DOES: – it doe⌊s
673	*Doug:*	yeah ⌋ y⌋eah
674	*Vern:*	I I'm aware of *that.*
675	*Doug:*	um hum
676	*Vern:*	u:m (0.2) *But* >you know< *it's* the *old* idea
677		of *active participa˰tion,* – ^*where* you can
678		have the *kids in˰volved:*=
679	*Doug:*	=um hum=
680	*Vern:*	=⌊*obviously* ·h *and so:* – *when* you *have* a:
681	*Doug:*	that's true⌋
682	*Vern:*	series of ^*instruc˰tions,* if you – >*break* it
683		in *pieces*< *then* you *have active*
684		participation in *between those* pieces, –
685		*there's* two ^*ways* of getting *kids* actively
686		*in*VOL⌊VED >*one* 's to< ·h *be* – *fore*
687	*Doug:*	uh huh ⌋
688	*Vern:*	((sound of paper rustling)) *all* discussion,
689		*turn* to your *neigh˰bor share* with your
690		*neigh˰bor,* – *say* it in *unison.* ·h >*that* type
691		of *thing.*< *The other* is *that* –
692		*manipula⌊tive* part °*so*°
693	*Doug:*	uh huh g⌋ood uh huh
694		(2.7)
695	*Doug:*	^O˰K – *is* the⌊re *anyth*⌊*ing?* (0.9)
696	*Vern:*	°OK?° ⌋ I ^*don't*
697		think ˰*SO.* I- *I* ·h *I* know *that* – um – ^*I:*

698		just *having* a: – *little* bit of a *discussion*
699		the other ˏ*day*: – *with He*ˏ*len*: – and *Lyn*ˏ*ne*:
700		– an::d – ˏ*Molly* – an:d ^*KE:N* – *all met*
701		(0.3) and I *think* what *they* – *ta:lked* about
702		and *arranged* was *fer*: – between *now* and the
703		– *end* o' the ^*year*: – and – *I* – think – that
704		>*Lynne* probably< *shared* with *you* (0.2) *what*-
705		– *they're* going to *do* is – >*she's* coming in
706		*NOW*< to teach the *LOGO* part,
707	*Doug*:	uh huh
708	*Vern*:	*then* >*for the* remainder of the *year*< –
709		>*she'll be*< – *arou:nd* – *more* ^*than*- – >*I*
710		mean< the *firs*- – those ^*three* ˏ*weeks*, we
711		*told* her >not *even* to walk in the *room*
712		because we *wanted* to make *sure* that< the
713		*kids* weren't *turning* to ˏ*her*,
714	*Doug*:	uh huh
715	*Vern*:	*now* I think s- (they) – w-s- – >IF *SHE'S* in
716		the *room*-< they're *always* going to *turn* to
717		some- – *they* turned to ^*me* today. When
718		there's another *adult* >in the *room*< ·h you
719		know th- the ₍^*kids*:
720	*Doug*:	um hum]
721		(0.4)
722	*Vern*:	*ALL* OF 'EM want *attention* – *so* they'll *turn*
723		to the *clo*₍*sest adu lt* f₍or the *atten tion* ·h
724	*Doug*:	uh huh] uh huh]
725	*Vern*:	but the *goal* is *fer*: – *her* to just – *be* –
726		more °an *assistant* for you *most* of the *time*,
727		and for ^*you* – to: – then – *do* – the *primary*
728		instruction. >I think *you* had the *discussion*
729		– probably – with *her* on ˏ*tha:t*? er-°=
730	*Doug*:	=yeah (she's ₍sure)
731	*Vern*:	OK]
732	*Doug*:	°OK yeah°
733	*Vern*:	°*so*: – *that'll* keep you *busy* being
734		o₍ut of° *trouble*
735	*Doug*:	OK]
736	*Vern*:	be₍tween *now* and the *end* of the ˏ*year*.
737	*Doug*:	hh ((laughs))] OK.
738		(1.0)
739	*Vern*:	·h *One* of ₍the *th ings*: – that we- – *you* and
740	*Doug*:	( )]
741	*Vern*:	I need to *arrange* a *ti:me* to do, ·h ^*probably*
742		after ˏ*schoo:l*, when we *could* maybe *meet* for

743		ˏ*coffee* or *something*, ·h *is a* (1.4) *period*
744		of *ti::* *me* – uh – for *us* to d- – *just discuss*
745		you ˏknow – *where* to go and ^*what's* ˏ*next.* –
746		You know after this – ˏ*year.* – u::m – *and*
747		u:h – '*course* you have an *interview* in a
748		little *whi::le* for ₍pa- PRACTI CE
749	*Doug:*	yeah yeah ⌋
750	*Vern:*	in *that* ₍ˏ*area* – ^*right?*
751	*Doug:*	uh huh⌋ *yes::.*
752	*Vern:*	and *so* (1.2) (you're gonna) it's –
753		*PARTIALLY pointing* you in °*those* directions°
754	*Doug:*	OK
755	*Vern:*	OK?
756	*Doug:*	and ˏso *jus:t* let me ˏ*know* – whenever you –
757		*have* time and *then* I'll see – if we could
758		(*fix*)=
759	*Vern:*	=*BRINGING* THAT ^*UP* – did *you, when* you were
760		at the ((*university name*)) an- – and you
761		*registered* for classes this *term,* did you
762		*register* for an *additional* two *credits* of
763		some sort?
764	*Doug:*	(yeah)
765	*Vern:*	that's gonna putchu *be^hind* in credits ˏ*then*
766	*Doug:*	*no* – but I *talked* to u::h=
767	*Vern:*	=*Quincy?*
768	*Doug:*	yeah >bu- bu- bu-< because I have a: *six* –
769		*credits* to: *trans*ˏ*fer*
770	*Vern:*	°um ₍'K°
771	*Doug:*	unless I⌋ get *OK* for those
772		thre₍e – *those*
773	*Vern:*	NO (W) I'M NOT⌋
774	*Doug:*	TWO ARE: (0.8) uh:=
775	*Vern:*	=no ₍I- (huh)
776	*Doug:*	pass/no-⌋ pass=
777	*Vern:*	=OH and- they're *pass/no-pas*₍s any way, *OK*
778	*Doug:*	sure ⌋
779	*Vern:*	so *it* all comes *out* ₍in the *wash* then
780	*Doug:*	*it's* – for *sure* ⌋
781	*Vern:*	good – ˏ*good* because we *did* the *other* ones
782		*graded*=
783	*Doug:*	=uh h₍uh – yeah ₍yeah
784	*Vern:*	(uh:)⌋ th at's ⌋ °all right°
785	*Doug:*	I *checked* with *them* and I jus- (0.9) I: just
786		take *regular* – *load* hhh ((laughs)) again.
787		(1.1) °*So* I *don't* have very – *cheery* term

788		this
789		(2.4)
790	*Vern:*	O^K
791	*Doug:*	*because* I *took – six* here from um – RSU
792		(1.0) °so I have *enough* to *trans*⌐*fer* it's
793		*jus:t-°* (0.7) *up* to *fifteen* ⌐right but I
794		have *six* and jus- you know ((laughs)) AND A-
795		(1.6) this aside hhh (some way I get-) *I*
796		have *bumped* inta ^*Ernie* ^*Quinn* – I heard
797		from *Ed:* ((another teacher intern)) and u:h
798		– *Laura* ((another intern)) about the –
799		*registration – pre – registration* ⌐there
800	*Vern:*	*oh* forget abo⌐ut it
801	*Doug:*	*it's* ⌐ not *allowed* for –
802		res⌐ident
803	*Vern:*	I would⌐ – *forget* about *it* (0.6) I'd
804		(talk to) *Quincy.* Don't *worry* about *it.*
805	*Doug:*	but *do* we have *to:* uh *preregister?*
906		(1.3)
807	*Vern:*	*I: don't know – you- – we – on Satur*⌐*day:* –
808		*you* could ask *Quincy* what – >*needs* to go on
809		for *summer* registration< I *don't* know *that.*
810	*Doug:*	uh huh
811		((background noise of children passing in
812		the hall))
813	*Vern:*	*I- I* WOULD *IMAGINE* – TH – you know if
814		there're *CLASSES* you're *taking outside* the
815		*basic – required* ones
816	*Doug:*	um hum=
817	*Vern:*	=you know – if you *can* preregister for
818		⌐*classes, it's* sorta *nice* because it *ensures*
819		you a *position.*
820	*Doug:*	um hum=
821	*Vern:*	=Some *class*^*ses* – it *depends* whatchu wanta
822		⌐*take* >you know< ·h *some* classes get *real*
823		competitive *others* ⌐don't for (0.2) *slots* –
824		in the *summer*⌐*time,* – *any* university.
825	*Doug:*	°umkay° (0.7) so *hopefully* we *can* uh – *we'll*
826		be able to *find* out *this* Saturday:
827	*Vern:*	°yeah°
828	*Doug:*	or *just* have to send *it* ⌐*there,* if they
829		*don't* let *it – they* just *reject* it hh
830		((chuckle))
831	*Vern:*	°yeah°
832	*Doug:*	*we* just have to *take* care of *later* ( )

833		(1.0) *yeah* because *I* want to (*pay* just late)
834		for that (one so) – *because* it's *different.*
835		(0.9) °*because* it's°
836	*Vern:*	°OK°
837	*Doug:*	*other* than *that* – that's *all*: are we *going*
838		uh – *to* meet *with* you at *all* – *this* evening?
839	*Vern:*	*This* evening? OH – I *WILL BE* – there. *Come*
840		to *the* – >I *forgot* to *tell* people ˏ*that* <
841		(0.2) if you *see* ^peoˏple (0.2) n- n- c- –
842		be *THERE* by around *four* ^*thirty* >is *that*
843		what *Helen* told ^*you?*<
844	*Doug:*	°*no* I didn't hear *anything* from°=
845	*Vern:*	=So you *didn't* hear *anything* from-?
846	*Doug:*	₁( )
847	*Vern:*	OK ¹=
848	*Doug:*	=I'm *scheduled* for four: – *fifteen* to *four*
849		forty *five* but ₁( )
850	*Vern:*	*yes*¹ we can *meet* every –
851		*body* – between *four* thirty and *four* ^*fifteen*
852		– in the LO:^*BBY* – of the *personnel* office.
853	*Doug:*	um hum
854		(0.5)
855	*Vern:*	OK?
856	*Doug:*	>yeah OK<
857	*Vern:*	·h I have been *SO:* – beˏ*hind* lately *that* I'm
858		*muddled* over when I'm (*correcting*) ((sound
859		of paper rustling)) I – *keep forgetting* to –
860		send out ( ) efficient *mem*₁os and tear
861	*Doug:*	(sure:)¹
862	*Vern:*	those *things*
863	*Doug:*	so: are ^*you* ((to observer)) – want to: uh
864		*talk* with *me* ah?
865	*Duncan:*	um – *maybe* today *wouldn't* be a *good* time. I
866		was *thinking* if we come on *Fri:*ˏ*day*, or – *we*
867		can have some *time* on *Friday* or *Saturday* to
868		talk.
869	*Doug:*	OK. So: it's *up* to *you* I'll *be* –
870		₁>what it *is* you want
871	*Vern:*	( )¹
872	*Doug:*	*say*< OK I'll jus:: – uh *if* I have *any* I'll
873		jus- uh- (know 'bout) you hhh ((laugh in
874		voice)) OK?
875	*Duncan:*	Or maybe *what* you *could* do *also* is: – you
876		*could* – um – if y:ou – *feel* like *it* (0.3)
877		*jot down* some re^*actions* to: – the

878		*conference.*
879	*Doug:*	um hum=
880	*Duncan:*	=And *then* you *could* – give *that* to *me* or
881		bring *that* and *use that* to re^*fresh* yourself
882		when we – we talk=
883	*Doug:*	=OK=
884	*Duncan:*	=on *Friday* or *Saturday* ₍(
885	*Doug:*	( )¹ *particularly*
886		or:=
887	*Duncan:*	=yeah
888	*Doug:*	OK
889	*Vern:*	may you u- *probably* also – in *general* about
890		the ₌*year*:=
891	*Duncan:*	uh huh=
892	*Vern:*	=too=
893	*Duncan:*	=*that* too. u:m – *If* you can *separate* those
894		*two,* that might *not* be *able* to be *separated*
895	*Doug:*	hh ((chuckle))
896	*Vern:*	w- we PROBABLY are *going* to come *in* on –
897		Fr:i₌*day* and do *this* again: um – *Duncan's*
898		going to *be here* – so: – if *you* >you'll *be*<
899		– *primarily* instucting on Fri₌*day* ^*too* like
900		we've ₍been (doing)
901	*Doug:*	Fri^*day* – uh¹ *morning* or – *afternoon?*
902	*Vern:*	WE:LL – >I'm not *certain* what *time* Duncan
903		*plans* to get *here* I- I-< I *nee:d* to *start*
904		with the *other* students at eight *thirty* so
905		I'll be *dropping* the *students* who're
906		*visiting* here *off* around – ^*nine* ₌*thirty* ·h
907		and *so* – you know, *I* don't *know* but – I *know*
908		– *If* we *don't* get *here* – *prior* to ele^*ven* –
909		then *it's* after ₌*noon* – because you've: got
910		*lunch* pretty *much* from *eleven* to *what* –
911		^*twelve?*
912	*Doug:*	uh huh *yes*
913	*Vern:*	yeah
914	*Doug:*	to: – ·h eleven *thirty.* And *then* we'll *have*
915		– just *kind* of uh – *sharing* and – *more story*
916		and tic-₌toe
917	*Vern:*	OK
918	*Doug:*	and from *there* we'll *have*
919	*Vern:*	and I'm – *assuming* is: – she: doing *Logo*
920		about the *same time* she did ^*it:*=
921	*Doug:*	=um ₍ hum um ₍hum
922	*Vern:*	*now*¹ from¹ *twelve::* – to *about* (0.2)

923		*what* >*twelve* forty ^*five?*<
924	*Doug:*	uh: – *twelve* – *thirty*: (1.2) from – *twelve*
925		to twelve ˰*thirty* – or – *thirty* – *five*
926	*Vern:*	O˰K. ·h *So* if we *came* in i-it – *would*
927		*either* need to *be* – *aBOUT* the *time* we came
928		in *to˰day*, – or we ₁need to ge t
929	*Doug:*	um hum ⌐
930	*Vern:*	*here* before *eleven*. – *One* of the *two*.
931	*Doug:*	um hum
932	*Vern:*	OK
933		(1.4)
934	*Doug:*	OK
935	*Vern:*	'*cause* it – we're *NOT* (1.1) >you know<
936		((outside noise)) – we could *HAVE* – *our*
937		discussion on *anything*, and *today* it's on
938		^*art*: – you know *another* day *it's* – on
939		˰*reading*, it does- *that* doesn't make – *a*
940		*diffe*^*rence*, I just ((drum noise))
941		(interested in)
942		(3.0)
943	*Doug:*	OK thank you for- =
944	*Vern:*	=all ˰*right* well thank ^*you*:
945	*Doug:*	((laugh))
946	*Vern:*	thank *you* very *much*, *Doug* for – helping *me*
947		with *this*
948	*Doug:*	OK hhh
949	*Vern:*	it was *good* seeing you *teaching*. I-
950		((noises from hall enter as door opens))
951	*Doug:*	( )

Ed and Vern: 10 May 1989

1	*Vern:*	The ^*first* ˰*thing* *before* we do *any* of ˰*this*
2		– I probably should get ˰*him* the *fo*˰*rm*. hh
3	*Duncan:*	((observer)) You don't want to *scare* ^him
4	*Vern:*	°I don't *want* to *scare* him°=
5	*Ed:*	=oh is *this* the ^*con*˰*fidentia*^*lity* ˰form?
6	*Vern:*	yeah ( )
7	*Ed:*	I'd ₁^*love*: to ˰see::
8	*Duncan:*	you're *familiar* with *what* I'm *do*⌐ing
9		^*right*?
10	*Vern:*	he- he- can he can ˰*Duncan* can *explain* it to
11		˰you.
12	*Duncan:*	·h *Basically* what I'm ^*do*˰*ing* is I'm ^*do*˰*ing*

13		a um: (0.6) a *study* of ^su˄per^vi˄sion.
14	*Ed:*	O˄K:
15	*Duncan:*	so I'm ^ l:ook˄ing ^more ˄at – how (0.2) *Vern*
16		inter˄acts with ˄you in the ^*role* of a
17		^*su˄per^vi˄sor* than >I'm not I- I wou- sh-
18		probably should *explain* that be^*fore*< so
19		that I *didn't* make you ₍^*nerv˄o us*
20	*Ed:*	^oh ˄no]
21	*Duncan:*	₍hh *I'm* not *writing* stuff ˄do wn on ˄*your:*
22	*Ed:*	it *didn't* even (occur to) *me*]
23	*Duncan:*	^*in˄struc^tion* as *much* as I ˄*am* on ˄may^be
24		what *Vern's* °attempting to – so I'm-°
25		>*you're not*< the ^*fo˄cus*
26	*Ed:*	*he's* ₍the ^fo:^cus:
27	*Duncan:*	*you're* just *kind*] of *a* – ˄*foil* or a
28		^*ve˄hi^cle* >for *me*< *to* ^try to ˄*get* – an
29		^*i˄dea what* it *is* s- that he's *do˄in'*
30	*Ed:*	um
31	*Duncan:*	um and ^*all* ˄this a- con^*sent* ˄*form* is
32		^*say˄ing that* basical^ly (0.3) you ˄*con^sent*
33		to *be* ^*in˄volved* ^*in-* in- in *that* ˄*role*
34		(0.4) °in the stu˄dy, um but- that – if ^I
35		˄*need* to ^*men˄tion* ^you at *all* or *things*
36		that ^you ˄say, I'll *protect* your *anonym˄ity*
37		– and ^*con˄fiden^tia*₍*l˄ity*°
38	*Ed:*	>OK<]
39		₍*I trus:t* – ˄*you*
40	*Vern:*	un^less you make] *mo˄ney* off of ˄*it* – and
41		then ˄*he'll*=
42	*Ed:*	=then hhh ((laughs)) *then* we ^*get* to ˄*be*=
43	*Vern:*	=there's *not* a lot of *mon˄ey* to split ^ *it*=
44	*Ed:*	YES:
45	*Vern:*	yes
46	*Ed:*	I *trust* ˄you ((sound of pen on paper)) there
47		you ˄go
48	*Vern:*	thank you – does *that* go to *you* ^then?
49	*Duncan:*	yeah
50		(2.3) ((sound of paper rustling))
51	*Vern:*	let me um:
52	*Ed:*	>COME ˄ON ^DAN˄NY ^FO˄CUS YOUR ATTEN˄TION< –
53		˄PLEASE ((to student)) FO˄CUS YOUR
54		˄AT^TEN˄TION ON *SCI˄ENCE*:
55	*Vern:*	°*how's* – she do^ing?°
56		(0.6)
57	*Ed:*	°you know ^Dede ˄Smith?°

58 *Vern*: (that gonna end-?) (0.7) ^spring�time

59 *Ed*: aₗnd ^(con⸌do)

60 *Vern*: uh¹   ((laughs))

61 *Ed*: and Dave Lendle

62 *Vern*: ((laughs)) u:m: (0.7) *cou:ld* – could *be* that

63 ⸌*he's* – getting *rea*^*dy* to *lea*⸌*ve* – ^too

64 (0.6) >^*that's* (where) the ⸌peo^ple< –

65 ⸌*distance* ^*them*⸌*selves* ·h *and* what they ⸌*do*

66 in their *distan*^*cing pro*⸌*cess* when they've

67 been *clo*∧*se* ₗto ^some⸌one

68 *Ed*:   ^is   to   de⸌ta¹ch:=

69 *Vern*: = ·h ^is to *de*⸌*tach* and go ^*back* – ^*re vert*

70 to – *what they we*⸌*re*: (1.0) ⸌be^fore – >they

71 *worked* with *that* ^per⸌son<

72 *Ed*: °^um ⸌hum°

73 *Vern*: an:*d* ⸌uh:=

74 *Ed*: =^sur⸌vi^val too ⸌eh?

75 *Vern*: °yeah – yeah° >and< – >you know< *some* of

76 your ⸌con^ver⸌sa^tions with ⸌*him* – *might* –

77 ⸌*fo*^*cus* a⸌bou:t uh- >around< *some* of *tho*^*se*

78 -^is⸌sues about – ·h ^a⸌bout ^*that* – or ⸌*you*:

79 >you ⸌*know*< ⸌*re*^ *in*⸌*force* ^the ⸌group, all of

80 ⸌us ^*here* and *these* are *things* I *know* you

81 can *do* on your ⸌*own* without ^*ha*⸌*ving* ^*mis*⸌*ter*

82 *Thomas* ^al⸌ways ^*there* –

83 ₗto   ·h >^da⸌da ^da⸌da ^⸌dada ^⸌dada

84 *Ed*: ^uh¹ ⸌huh

85 *Vern*: ^da⸌o:< and ^*see* i*f* – ⸌*he* – >you know<

86 ⸌*may*^*be*: – >*you* can ⸌*start*< – mov⸌ing into

87 ^*that* ⸌*phase* so *he* – *can de*⸌*tach* with

88 ^*growth* – ^*ver*⸌*sus* – I mean – *w:hat* we ^*see*

89 ⸌*are* ^*a* ⸌*lot* ^*of* ⸌*kids* who ^*it's* be⸌cause

90 it's ^*per*⸌*son*^ *nel* you're ⸌*in* ·h *they they* ·h

91 (the adults) ^*are* ⸌*here* – >they⸌*shoot* ^*up*

92 with the< ^*tea*⸌*cher* >and then the *moment*

93 the< ^*tea*⸌*cher leaves* ⸌'em then they'll

94 ^*shoot* ⸌*down* to the (   ) – ⸌*drop*

95 ^back ⸌*down* and then g- back ^*up* –

96 ^*hope*⸌*ful*^*ly* they always ⸌*end* ^up a little

97 ^*hi*ₗ*gh*⸌*er*

98 *Ed*:   >right<¹ and the ^*go:al* ⸌*is* to make *sure*

99 they *putz*

100 *Vern*: um ₗhum

101 *Ed*:   the ¹ ⸌goal – ^*i*⸌*deal* is for

102 ₗ^*them* to stay ₗ^*up*:

103	*Vern*:	yeah⌉ yea⌉h >th^ough< ˄though *like*
104		with it's *mo˄re* like *they're* going ˄uh=
105	*Ed*:	=°OK°=
106	*Vern*:	=˄*down* ˄*here* then – then
107		˄*u⌊p* th ere (0.5) °*things like*
108	*Ed*:	OK ⌉
109	*Vern*:	˄*that* ( )° – ·hh U:M (0.4) *you're going*
110		to ˄*Bon*^*ne*˄*ville* on *Tues*^*day*?
111	*Ed*:	>˄yeah *you* wanna ^*come*?<
112	*Vern*:	·h *unfortuantely* it's ˄*our* – Ore˄gon ca˄reer
113		*fair* ˄*day* ((student interrupts with
114		request))
115	*Ed*:	YES MA'^AM:
116	*Vern*:	um: *it's* our or- >*last*< – re˄cruiting ^*fair*
117		but it's *here* in *Rock*˄*land* so I don't have
118		to *tra*˄*vel* ⌊ex cept to the *Holiday*
119	*Ed*:	u m:⌉
120	*Vern*:	˄*I*⌊*nn*
121	*Ed*:	we're go˄i⌉ng to *Trojan Nu*^*clear* on *June*
122		˄*ninth* – *Fri*^*day* – *if* you wanna
123		co⌊me with us ˄*that day*
124	*Vern*:	^ooo- – ˄glow day – ⌉ ^huh? we're gonna
125		go ˄ou⌊t-
126	*Ed*:	co⌉me on ((laughter in voice)) *s:top*
127		˄*it* ^that's what the ˄*kids* say
128		^*too*: ((both laugh)) *but*
129	*Vern*:	c⌊ho-
130	*Ed*:	ty⌉˄ing in *all of* th˄*ese* – ^*field trips*
131		(1.1) ˄*with this* – ·h and ^that's ˄*one good*
132		*thing* about ^*it* being *here* in the ^*Rock*˄*land*
133		area – having ⌊all of ^these ^*re*˄*sources*.
134	*Vern*:	uhum⌉
135		(1.1)
136	*Vern*:	y- you're going to ^*Tro*˄*jan that* ^da:y?
137	*Ed*:	>yup< shou⌊ld co˄me:
138	*Vern*:	I'm *just*⌉ gonna n- *put* a –
139		*ques*˄*tion* mark – I've ^*al*˄*ways wanted* to go
140		on a >*field trip*< to >^*see* what's-< –
141		*obvious*˄*ly* I'm – *empty* ˄*then* but – ·h °it
142		would- ˄de^*pends* ˄*what* comes ^*up*°
143	*Ed*:	^*this* ˄*one* is the *field* ^ *trip* ˄*I'm* plan^ning
144		to ^*Bon*˄*ne*^*ville* ˄*dam* – °*so*°
145	*Vern*:	·hh *right* ˄*now* >*what* I *have* on my ˄*desk*< is a
146		^*stack* of ˄*un*^returned ˄*phone calls* and
147		>^*little* th˄*ings*< – ^*like* ˄*that* s:o ((Ed

148		chuckles)) so as ˏyou ˆguys get
149		ˆ*hys*ˏ*te*ˆ*ri*ˏ*cal* about your – ˆ*pa*ˏ*per* and
150		ˆ*stu*₁*ff* you know
151	*Ed:*	ˏoh – I got¹ta – do ˏ*mine* ₁I'm wri ˏting
152	*Vern:*	and- *be*¹
153		be *appreci:a*ˏ*tive* ˆof ˏ*that* ·hh u:m: (1.3)
154		>*obviously* a little ˏ*late*< *here* >so we
155		*didn't* get *in*< to the – >*beginning* of the<
156		ˆ*les*ˏ*son:* an: – *I* came ˏ*in* ˆand *star*ˏ*ted* –
157		ˆ*just a*ˏ*bout* eˏleven, taking some ˆ*notes*
158		ˏ*here* °on° – ˆ*re*ˏgards – u:m ·h – to ˏ*that.* –
159		u:m You're >*talk*ˏ*ing*< and you're- – were –
160		aˏbou:t um: >*the* ˆ*first thing*< I had ˏ*down*
161		from ˏ*you* is *how* do ˏ*tur*ˆ*bines* – ˆ*run: when*
162		the water's ˆ*still. You* had them ˆ*think*
163		about ˏ*it.*
164	*Ed:*	um ˏhum
165	*Vern:*	·hh You – *one* thing you did ˏ*there* that-
166		was- r- *good* ˆ*wait* ˏ*ti:me* – ˆ*think about* ˏ*it*
167		and *you wait*ˏ*ed* (0.7) ·h and then *O*ˏ*k*
168		ˆ*share* ˏ*it with* ˆ*neigh*ˏ*bors* – an- an- – then
169		*you* asked for – for – *one's* child *Brent* –
170		to: g₁o on ·h °one *thing*
171	*Ed:*	um hum¹
172	*Vern:*	you *might've* – *wanted* to uh- be *do*ˆ*ing*
173		ˏ*there*° – is Brent did ˆ*not* give ˏ*you* the
174		*cor*ˆ*rect* ˏ*re*ˏ*spons:e* – if you ˆ*re*ˏcall – *he*
175		– ·h was c- he gave a *con:*ˏ*fuse*₁*d* resp ond
176	*Ed:*	*different*¹
177		respon₁se
178	*Vern:*	an-¹ an- and- – ˆit *took* more *prob*ˏ*ing*
179		·h u:m (1.2) >and you ˏ*said* – uh- ˆ*some*ˏ*thing*
180		to the ˆ*ef*ˏ*fect* – like ˏ*O*ˆ*K*< *how* does a
181		ˏ*still* – *ap*ˆ*pear*ˏ*ing wa*ˏ*ter* – ˏturn – >ˆ*you*
182		ˏknow< the ˏ*turbines* you ˏhad to ∧*re*ˏ*phrase*
183		ˏthat ₁·hh and ˏthen – you as k ˆ*Ber*ˏ*nice*
184	*Ed:*	ˆ*re*ˏ*phrase the ques*ˏ*tion*¹
185	*Vern:*	ˆ*some*ˏ*thing* an- you- it ˆ*looks* – ˏ*still* but
186		– >you know< y- (0.4) but- it's: ˏ*still:* ·h
187		you ˏknow and- and- and ˆ*what's* the ˏ*word*
188		and ˆ*then* ˏ*they came up* with the w-word
189		ˆ*cur*ˏ*rents:*
190	*Ed:*	um '₁K
191	*Vern:*	or¹ s- ˆ*they came* up with the ˏ*wor:d* and
192		>*look* at these ˆ*cur*ˏ*rents* and< ·hh and you

193		˄said *oh* ˄*good* >their ˄vo^cabulary ˄word
194		there's ^*cur*˄*rents*< *then* you went ˄*on* and- –
195		– you – you ˄got ^*throu:gh* ˄that ^*part* – ·h
196		°*one* of the ˄*things* you ^*might* wanna've
197		˄*done*° – >*when* you were do˄ing ˄*that* ^*ac*˄*tive*
198		˄*par*^*ticipa*˄*tion piece*< was *to* have ·h –
199		˄*mo:ved arou:nd* – and ^*lis*˄*tened to* – ˄*what*
200		they ˄were *talk*^*ing* a˄bout ·h '*cause* you
201		^*would've* ˄heard it ˄*ra:nge* >every˄thing<
202		from *these* ˄two – >°over here< who *didn't*
203		˄know so *they* ˄were – >^they were< –
204		>*polite*< but *they* were *si*˄*lent* –
205		^*lis*˄*ten*^*ing* to° ^*these* ˄two over ˄*here* – he
206		*po*- he ˄*pro*^*bab*˄*ly* ˄knew
207	*Ed:*	uh huh=
208	*Vern:*	= >is ^*his* name ˄*Ed?*<
209	*Ed:*	^Ed˄win
210	*Vern:*	>^*Ed*˄*win* Ed˄win< ·h °ok° (1.1) be˄cau:se –
211		um – ^he ˄*seems* to ˄*be* ^*pret*˄*ty* ^tuned ˄*into*
212		˄some of tha₍t *st* ((cough)) *to*
213	*Ed:*	um₎
214	*Vern:*	the ˄*range* of ^*o*˄*ther* – ˄re^spon˄ses which
215		˄*va*^*ried* >and *that* ˄way< ·h you ˄could –
216		°per˄haps – *call on*° – >so^me ˄body
217		(according to the method)< °who'd ^*an*˄*swer*
218		more ˄like you *wan*˄*ted*°
219	*Ed:*	^O˄₍K:₍
220	*Vern:*	˄y₎ou ˄were: – ^*risk* ˄*tak*^*ing* ˄*there*
221		and the ˄*risk* didn't turn ˄out
222		₍·h ini tial˄ly ·hh ^and – ^things
223	*Ed:*	>OK<₎
224	*Vern:*	·h ^*and* what˄chu wanna *be* – *very* °^*care*˄*ful*
225		about of cour^se *is* – ·h *is* as you *well*
226		˄know: – the *mo*˄*ment* – the ˄*incor*^*rect*
227		˄*an*^swer is – ˄ *first hea:rd* ·h *it* ˄might –
228		*car*˄*ry* – *throu:gh* – >^*some* ˄kids might< *pick*
229		*that* ^*up*°=
230	*Ed:*	=pick *that* – u:*p*=
231	*Vern:*	=and they're ^*ad*˄*ded* – there's ˄*con*^*fu*˄*sion* –
232		'*cause* he ^*ga*˄*ve this* ˄*re*^spon˄se – >but
233		there're< ˄*re*^*spon*˄*ses* over ˄*here* – ^so ˄*now*
234		·h >^*ra*˄*ther* than just< *hav*˄ing – ˄*one*
235		^*cor*˄*rect re*^*spon*˄*se* – they ha^ve ˄*to* sort
236		˄*out* the ^*incor*˄*rect* – °*from* the
237		*cor*˄*rec*₍*t*°

238	*Ed:*	>t⌐he *cor⌐rect*< ·hh >and in< *st⌐ill:*
239		^mak⌐ing *sure* that the ^*lear⌐ner* – ⌐feels
240		that *they've* >⌐con^tribu⌐ted<
241		an⌐d *not*
242	*Vern:*	(>you accept⌐ him<) °yeah° it's-⌐hh
243	*Ed:*	>so⌐
244		^ma⌐king *those* ⌐tw⌐o< °considera⌐°tion°
245	*Vern:*	*an-*⌐ an- *but in*⌐
246		– but ⌐when he ^*did* do ⌐*that* you ⌐*did not* say
247		oh ⌐no nona- >you ⌐know< ·hh you you (0.3)
248		you ⌐*did* move – grace:ful⌐ly to lo- – bu-
249		⌐you ⌐re^*phrased* the *ques⌐tion* >ra⌐ther than
250		^*say⌐ing no*< ·h but *ho:w* ⌐*does* the *st*^*ill*
251		appear⌐ing wa⌐ter – °*turn* the ⌐tur^bine you°
252		said ^you're *talk⌐ing* about some⌐thing a
253		lit^tle *diffe⌐rent* so you- ·h you *did* ⌐*that*
254		*part* – ⌐though ⌐*very*
255	*Ed:*	°OK°⌐
256	*Vern:*	^*well* with ^*him* – so that ^wa- ·hh >I
257		⌐think< ·h *ONE OF THE* ⌐*THINGS* that ^*I'll* just
258		*mention* ^*here* – that's a *cou*^*ple pla⌐ces* ·h
259		*both* with the ^*cu:r⌐rents* ((sound of paper
260		rustling)) and then: ^*la⌐ter* ⌐*on::* ((more
261		paper sounds)) ⌐I *know* ^I *have* ⌐*it* (1.9) ⌐you
262		^*used* – uh- ^*la⌐ter on* you- use- the word
263		*simpli*^*fi:ed* and ^then – you ⌐used
264		^*com⌐plex* >an- in *each*< *case* you ·h you – uh
265		>⌐*made sure* they ⌐*un*^*der⌐stood* the ⌐*word*< and
266		^you – >*pointed* ⌐out< *that* was *good* use of
267		*vo⌐cabulary* words, so you were ^*bring⌐ing* ⌐*in*
268		another – ^*a⌐rea* – from your *lan⌐guage* ^*arts*
269		a⌐r⌐ea is-
270	*Ed:*	^O⌐K⌐
271	*Vern:*	of your *vocab⌐ula⌐ry* and >then the lesson ·h<
272	*Ed:*	is ⌐that ^O⌐K to ⌐do – ⌐s
273		*what* I was *gonna* to ^*ask* ⌐⌐*you*
274	*Vern:*	*that*⌐*s:* -
275		⌐*ex*^*ce⌐llent* – to ⌐*do* – ^*be:*>⌐*cause*< ·hh *those*
276		*words* as- as – as (2.0) ^I *think* I've ⌐*told*
277		you *this* ⌐story be⌐fore but as as our >⌐*dear*
278		old< *friend* Madeline *Hun⌐ter* always ⌐said ·hh
279		^*says* a⌐bout *this* stuff – ⌐*she* uses the
280		sto^ry °about the ⌐*kid* – in um: – w- th- the
281		^*tea⌐cher's* teaching ⌐*them*° (0.7) *want*^*ing*
282		⌐them *to:* – >*have*< – *vocab*^*ula⌐ry* in their

283		daily ˏ*life – because* it's always ˏ*taught –*
284		^ *iso*ˏ*lated*=
285	*Ed:*	=um hum=
286	*Vern:*	=(and >more or less some) ˏ*kids* couldn't
287		ˏun^derˏstand ˏ*it*< so the ^*tea*ˏ*cher* ·hh has
288		ˏ*kids* come ^*in* and >put ^up< – *what* they
289		wanted to – ˏ*tell* – >*what* a word ˏ*is*<
290		*they've learn*ˏ*ed* and a ˏ*kid* ^hears his
291		*parents* ^fightˏing and they're – using the
292		ˏ*word* ·hh – the – >*fa*ˏ*ther's* (yelling at) the
293		*mo*ˏ*ther*< that she's nev- – ˏ*fru*^*gal* eˏnough –
294		and so – the ˏ*kid* picks *up* (hears) this
295		ˏ*word* he *doesn't* ˏ*know* ·h what *does* it
296		ˏ*mea:n* (0.3) u:m to ˏ*dad* – and *dad* just *goes*
297		– it *means* – to ˏ*save*- so the ˏ*kid comes* ˏ*in*
298		and ˏ*he* – >they're *supposed* to draw a
299		^*pic*ˏ*ture*< °you ˏknow° of a voˏcabu^lary-
300		₍w- wi th *pic*^*tures?*
301	*Ed:*	um hum⌋
302	*Vern:*	·hhh so *what* ^he has ˏ*drawn* is a *pic*ˏ*ture* of
303		a ^*per*ˏ*son* – *who* has *fal*ˏ*len off* of a –
304		ˏ*boa:t* (0.6) and *he* is ^*scream*ˏ*ing* – to the
305		*peo*ˏ*ple* on the ˏ*deck* – *frugal* ˏ*me* – *frugal*
306		ˏ*me.*
307	*Ed:*	((lau₍ghs))
308	*Vern:*	and (1.1)⌋ the *pro*ˏ*blem* is is we –
309		*oft*ˏ*en* ˏ*teach* voˏcabu^lary in *isola*ˏ*tion* and
310		*we* don't *use* the – ˏ*con:text*=
311	*Ed:*	=um ˏ'K₍ – °I see°
312	*Vern:*	>so ˏwhat^chur *do*ˏ*ing* ^*is*< u⌋sing ˏ*it*
313		in ˏ*co:ntext* ·hh to your *sub*ˏ*ject* mat^ter –
314		you're ^*inter*ˏ*grating* – *cur*^*ricu*ˏ*lum*=
315	*Ed:*	=O₍K
316	*Vern:*	>*whi*⌋*ch* is of ˏ*course*< what we ·hh *scream*
317		aˏbout but we *ne*ˏ*ver:* – we- wo- we won- we
318		wan- pay ^*lipser*ˏ*vice* ((sounds of paper
319		rustling)) to ˏ*it* than
320		act₍ualˏl y *doing* ˏ*it.*=
321	*Ed:*	OK ⌋
322		=>because ^*see* ^I *do that* all the *time* – I
323		*keep* wonderˏing if I'm addˏing< – ˏ*more* –
324		*harm* than – ˏ*good* – to – *what* I'm do₍ˏin g
325	*Vern:*	*no*⌋ *no*
326		I *think* (1.4) hh I *sup*^*pose* if a ^*co:m*ˏ*plec*-
327		uh co- (0.5) >^*con*ˏ*cept* you're *dealing*

328 ╷with< is – *high^ly* com:╷plex – in ·h >you're
329 *tryin'* to *break* ╷it into< ╷*real small pie*╷*ces*
330 an- on^ly *fo*╷*cus* on ╷*that* ·h to *sudden^ly*
331 ^keep (0.2) *throw*╷*ing* ╷in >*a*╷*lot* of
332 vo╷*cabula*╷ry< ╷*words* – *that* they're
333 *unac^customed* ╷to – to – *ex^plain* ╷*it* ·h and
334 *have* them >try to *remember* ╷*those* on ^top *of*
335 *every*╷*thing else* could b╷e *real*
336 Ed: *then th'at's* not a
337   ╷*good* strate╷gy=
338 Vern: = >strate╷gy.< ·hh I *don't* ╷*think* – >you know
339   *to*╷*day*< *it* was somewhat ╷*com^plex*: (0.2)
340   i:╷*dea* for *some* of *these* ╷kids but ·h I *don't*
341   – *th*ink that ╷*you* – *did* ╷it – *enough* – that
342   it °was:°
343 Ed: *was*: – *ob^tru*╷*si*╷ve to *their* lea rn╷i╷ng
344 Vern: yes: – yeah ╵   ye╵ah
345 Ed: OK
346 Vern: yeah – so *no* – uh ^*NO* ╷*BIG* – *deal* with
347   ╷*that* >*in fact* I *think* it was a< ╷*good* ╷*thing*
348   to °have ╷*done* rather ╷*than*° ·h to *not* ((sound
349   of paper rustling)) ^*have* done ╷*it*. UM:
350   (1.6) ·h *THERE WERE* a *COU^PLE TIMES* ╷*HERE*
351   AS YOU WERE *TALK*╷*ing* about ^*ques*╷*tions* an-
352   >an- *this* is ^*one* of those< *situation*╷*al*
353   (0.4) ╷*things* where ·h you *can't* (0.3) °uh-°
354   ╷*like* in *this* first ╷*case* I- uh- >*we* talked
355   *about*< where you *had* to *ad^just* your
356   *ques*╷*tions*, u:m ·h u:m (0.5) *for* the ╷*kids* to
357   *try* to *get* just *that* – ╷*right way* >outta
358   them.< ·h I *don't know* if – if – hav╷ing
359   *may*╷*be* ((sound of electric pencil
360   sharpener)) (1.3) >^*writ*╷*ten*< – *were* they
361   ╷*from* the *b^oo:k?* – Or were ^*they* – ╷*things*
362   you were *just* do╷ing as you were
363   *ta:lk*╷╷*ing*:? Or
364 Ed: *no*:   we╵'ve ta╷ken *notes* – from them
365   ╷be╷fo re. ·h >So it's *more* or ╷*less*< (0.2) °I
366 Vern: O^K ╵
367 Ed: *wanted* ╷*them* to get *familiar* with the
368   *mate*╷*rial* – *being* ╷that I *know sci*╷*ence* is
369   one of ^*hard a*╷*reas*. ·h I'm having ╷them >go
370   *through*< do ^*all* the *vocabu*╷*lary*,° – >*in*
371   *fact*< they're ^*prepar*╷*ing* – for my *next*
372   *lec*╷╷*ture*   is what –

373   *Vern:*   >um hum<╵

374   *Ed:*   ˏ*that's* all *aˏbout.* Sₗo

375   *Vern:*   O╵K

376   *Ed:*   ^*it-* – *beˏcomes* more *tangiˏble* and

377   *manageˏable* – to ˏ*them*=

378   *Vern:*   =°>'K<° ·h *so* w- w-ˏ*what* you were *havˏing*

379   ˏ*here* – *more:* >rather than< – *actual^ly* –

380   >all the ^*quesˏtion*/^*anˏswer*< is a *diaˏlogue.*

381   *Ed:*   y::es:

382   *Vern:*   I *mean* – you were *tryˏing* to ·h to ^*point*

383   some *things* ˏ*out* >by asking some *quesˏtions*

384   – getting ˏ*kids* to ˏ*talk* about *them*< – in –

385   a ^ *diaˏlogue* kiₗnda ˏ*thing* >OK<

386   *Ed:*   YES::   ╵

387   *Vern:*   ((sound of paper rustling)) *BE* – ˏ*CAUSE*

388   SOME^*TIMES there* was some – *questionˏin:g:*

389   - *a*^*da:pˏting* >going on ˏ*there,*< *which* –

390   w:as >ˏ*good* on your ^*part*< that you *kept*

391   *adaptˏing* >the *question* – when they *didn't*

392   get ˏ*the*< (0.2) ·h ˏ*right* ^ *reˏsponse* –

393   *initialˏly* ·h but ^I didn't ˏ*know:* if ^*mayˏbe*

394   you *needed* ˏ*to* (0.2) have – *writˏten*

395   *questions* ˏ*out* in a more – ˏ*fo*^*cused* manˏner

396   – *initial^ly* – because *there* was ˏ*some* – ˏ*un*

397   *clariˏty*

398   *Ed:*   >OK< I *guess* it's to *clariˏfy* ^any

399   questions *they* may *have* – once ˏthey've

400   (0.2) >*interacted* with the *material* on their

401   ˏown.<

402   *Vern:*   OK ·hh UM

403   *Ed:*   ˏyeah – *that's* my *purpose:*

404   *Vern:*   >A ^*REAL INTERESTˏING*< – ˏ*THING HAP^PENED*

405   (0.4) A ˏ*BOUT* – *eleven* oh ˏ*six.*

406   *Ed:*   ((whispers))°Edwin over here°

407   *Vern:*   °(is he gonna talk) – because he ^*hears* ˏ*us*°

408   ·hh *he* h- you *said* do you have a ^*quesˏtion*

409   ^*Edˏwin.* An- he said – *no* – I – *think* I got

410   ˏ*it* – and he *explain:ˏed*=

411   *Ed:*   =°(thank you)°

412   *Vern:*   the ^*thing* to ˏ*you* ·hh and ˏthen *sud^denˏly*

413   (0.9) u::m >oh you ˏ*said*< see how things

414   ˏ*wo:rk* you know they're ˏ*for-* – they're

415   ˏ*forcing* in an opposite ˏ*wa:y,* ·h and ^*then*

416   you ^had *an^other* ˏ*quesˏtion,* an- then ·h um

417   about the a- *p- photo* in ˏ*there* >°it was

418		*something* about< – *France*°
419		₁an- then- – – *then you* ˌsaid
420	*Ed:*	OK
421	*Vern:*	*Dan^ny* ·h um *your* ^mom *went* ˌthere – could
422		^you *check* that ˌout for ^ *us?* ·h and *then*
423		*Ken*ˌ*dra* started talking about *Board*ˌ*man*
424		((sound of paper rustling)) an:d – *you* ˌhad
425		– a *number* of – *other* ˌkids >who *suddenly*
426		starˌted< – *asking ques*ˌ*tions* or *talk*ˌ*ing*
427		about ˌ*things* ·h or whatever, ·h and
428		^*sud^den*ˌ*ly* it ˌ*went* from *be:*ˌ*ing* – *the*
429		*tea:*ˌ*cher* – being the ˌ*one* – >having to
430		^*a:sk*< the ^*ques*ˌ*tions* – >and *bringing*
431		it *a*ˌ*long*< to ^*KIDS* (0.3) ·h getting the ˌda-
432		– *going* for the *dialo*ˌ*gue*.=
433	*Ed:*	=°um hum:°=
434	*Vern:*	=An:d – *that's* one of ˌ*those those those* –
435		*sh:^ifts* – that ˌ*you* – *you* >abmp< I *mean*
436		((sound of paper)) >I *don't* know ^*why* – I
437		*suddenly* noˌted tha*t*- ^*I* guess *I* was *just*
438		notˌing ˌ*time* (and ha₁d to i̠ t) aˌbout what
439	*Ed:*	um hum₁
440	*Vern:*	he ˌ*did* that- *I* guess *I* had< *tim:e* to do
441		ˌ*it*, and *if* – (even) write ^his *ques*ˌ*tion*
442		ˌ*down*. ((paper rustling)) ·h And *that* –
443		*suddenly* ˌit *took* ^*off* – and *that's* sort of
444		*what* you wanna have a *les*ˌ*son* suddenˌly
445		₁^*do* >re*member*
446	*Ed:*	um hum₁
447	*Vern:*	with ^*kids*< – *they're* asking
448		ques₁tions ·hh
449	*Ed:*	doing thi₁ngs
450		and *they'r:e in:ter:ested* and *they're* going
451		*al-* – ˌ*long* in- in=
452		=*their ownership* – in the *les*ˌ*son*=
453	*Vern:*	=yeah=
454	*Ed:*	=*too*=
455	*Vern:*	=yˌeah *an-* ·h so – ˌ*that* was *real^ly* ˌ*good* –
456		*there* ·hh *the* ^one *thing* >I would *point* ˌ*out*
457		about ˌ*that*< – ˌ*though* – ˌ*that I found* that
458		was >°*really*° *interest*ˌ*ing*< – >and I *did^n't*<
459		(0.2) ˌ*start* the ˌ*count* – *right a^way* – >I
460		didn't *think* about ˌ*it* until I ˌ*got*<
461		somewhere ˌ*down* in ˌ*here* >so I °*can't*< give
462		ˌyou – a° – ˌ*cou:nt*=

463	*Ed:*	=°um ˄K:°
464	*Vern:*	·hh *as* the ˄*discus*^*sion* went °a˄long – ·h –
465		during the *discussion* ˄time – there were
466		*on*˄*ly* (1.3) there was – *one girl.* – more
467		*involv*˄*ed* (0.2) *than* any *others* – and then
468		*there* was a *secondary* ˄*one.*° The ˄*one* who was
469		^*involv*˄*ed* was *the* girl from *Board*˄*man.*
470		>*Ken*^*dra?*<
471	*Ed:*	uh huh
472	*Vern:*	·h °And then *Ber*˄*nice*° – *finally* gave – *a*
473		*co:*˄*mment, but* when she ^*gave* the *co*˄*mment,*
474		she *tied* Kendra *to* ^*it.* ˄*She* and *Kendra* ˄*had*
475		to go to the *beach.* ·hh=
476	*Ed:*	=um ˄hum:
477	*Vern:*	*The REST* – of the *ques*˄*tions* – and –
478		*co*˄*mments* during that ˄*time* – *all* came from
479		˄*boys.*
480	*Ed:*	uh ₗhuh
481	*Vern:*	°Not¹ *one* – ˄*girl* – said a ˄*word* – *except*
482		for those *two* during *that* period of ˄*time*°
483		·hh *when* – *you then* – *went* an- I – *so* I had
484		*writ-* th- >*written* this ˄*thing*< *girls*
485		Kendra only *girl* who *volun*˄*teers,*
486		ₗ*Be rnice:* >you know<
487	*Ed:*	OK¹
488	*Vern:*	*just* a: – ^*ques*˄*tion* how 'bout >you know<
489		we- other ˄*ways* that – we can *strategize* to
490		get the ˄*girls* ((sound of paper rustling))
491		to do more ^*talk*˄*ing* because – ·h >*what*chur
492		*see*˄*ing is not* – >*you*< – you're *seeing* a
493		*ve*˄*ry tradition*˄*al* (quorum) going ˄*on* –
494		ₗ˄*that* – *hap*^*pens* – >*natural*˄*ly*< ·hh
495	*Ed:*	u h huhᴵ
496	*Vern:*	((sound of paper)) *yet*
497		– ₗ*then* – yet – *when* you'd
498	*Ed:*	(°that's when you get-°)ᴵ
499	*Vern:*	˄*got* – to *asking* ^*ques*˄*tions*
500	*Ed:*	uh huh
501	*Vern:*	>you know< the *work*˄*sheets* – *listen* – >to
502		this< *In*˄*grid* – *Carl* – *Ken*˄*dra* – *Steve* –
503		*McKen*˄*zie* – °is that a girl (who's name-)?°
504	*Ed:*	um hum: – little ˄*girl*
505	*Vern:*	˄*Lynn Kendra* – *Edwin* – *Vic* was a ˄*girl*=
506	*Ed:*	=um hₗum:
507	*Vern:*	a bⁱ*oy* – then *Ken* then *Ber*˄*nice* – *boy* –

508		*girl* >I *didn't get* some of these ⌐names< I
509		⌐jus t
510	*Ed*:	O K˩
511	*Vern*:	put *b* or ⌐g: ·hh U:M – *there* you ⌐had –
512		ac^*tual*⌐*ly* – >a *pre^ponder*⌐*ance*< of your
513		*ques*⌐*tions* – go⌐ing ·h (0.3) uh- *just* a⌐bout
514		*six*⌐*ty for*⌐*ty* I'd (caught) if *I* did
515		*thi*⌐s rough ly – *split*
516	*Ed*:	um hum˩
517	*Vern*:	·h >*going towards* the *girls*< °so you *did not*
518		– *ignore* the ⌐*girls* – ⌐th⌐ere
519	*Ed*:	OK˩
520	*Vern*:	·h >when it was< – what I'm *say*⌐*ing* is –
521		>when *it was* a< *na::tural*⌐*ly* – *generat*⌐*ed* –
522		*discus*⌐*sion* wer-° (0.5) ·h where – h (0.5)
523		*which* ^*is* whatchu ⌐*wa:nt* (0.3) th- *this* is
524		*where* you're in a ⌐real *Catch* ⌐2^2:
525		(0.2) ·h *is* there a ⌐*way:* you can *non-*
526		*obtrusive*^*ly* >without tak⌐ing< *control*
527		*a*⌐*gain* (0.3) >°you know of a-°< a *natural*
528		discus⌐sion >a way< ·h *get* – *that* – *group*
529	*Ed*:	uh huh˩
530	*Vern*:	(0.2) in *this case:* >it happened to be
531		⌐*girls*< =
532	*Ed*:	= >um hum< =
533	*Vern*:	=some*how invol*⌐*ved*=
534	*Ed*:	=um:
535	*Vern*:	·h YOU ⌐were- a- eh- you ^*did* ⌐*it* (0.5) as
536		it- >⌐when you ⌐*were* directed as *tea*^*cher*,<
537		when it's *ques*⌐*tion an*⌐*swer* you *did*
538		⌐a *very* ^*fine job* of ⌐it.
539	*Ed*:	s:ee – I >noticed< that –˩ I *notic*⌐*ed*
540	*Vern*:	⌐yeah
541	*Ed*:	that *too* >you know its- it was-s-s in the
542		^*back* of my ⌐*mind* but I *didn't* – ·h *pick* it
543		^*up* but I no⌐ticed< (0.2) °for some ^*rea*⌐*son*
544		the° *flags* went ^*up* and said – ⌐*call* ⌐*girls* –
545		pre ⌐*dominate*⌐*ly* ⌐du r^ing
546	*Vern*:	((cough))˩ ye ah˩
547	*Ed*:	>*thi*⌐s ti me< to *balance*
548	*Vern*:	yeah˩
549	*Ed*:	o⌐n my *cl ass participa*⌐*tion*
550	*Vern*:	·hhhh ˩·h >*and the thing*
551		^*a*⌐*bout* ^*it* that's was *interest*^*ing* ⌐*is*< –
552		*is* ex^cept °when *one girl* who *didn't do* the

553		∧*right* (0.3) *an:swers apparently* over
554		₁∧*the* re ·hh *I* think *all* of *the* ∧*girls*⌐
555	*Ed:*	um hum⌐
556	*Vern:*	*did* respond *appropriately* to your *ques*∧*tions*
557		>as did< *most* of the ∧*boys* – *too*. ·h That –
558		it *doesn't* mean *that* – they – *don't* – *know*
559		∧*it*° (0.5) but they ^*se::em* ∧*to:* – *know* ∧*it* –
560		on – *what* I would *ca:*ll ·hh ((h)) *the*
561		*academic* or *book* ∧*le*^*vel*. ^*They* are *not*
562		showing their °*natural curiosi*∧*ty* – um – at
563		*this* ^point – *except* for *Ken*∧*dra* >an-
564		*Bernice*.< ·hh have both- p- are *Kendra* and
565		*Ber*^*nice* being re-booked by Carl *Egan?*°
566	*Ed:*	oh yeah=
567	*Vern:*	=good *students?*=
568	*Ed:*	= >yeah< – ·h and Kendra's ∧*dad* came in
569		*yester*∧*day* – who's – an *energy engineer*
570		>wh₁o ^*work ed* at
571	*Vern:*	uh huh ⌐
572	*Ed:*	∧*Bon*^*ne*∧*ville* – who ^*worked* at *Board*∧*man*
573		who ^*worked* at *Tro*∧*jan*,< ·h
574		₁s o *she* – has a – °*active vested*
575	*Vern:*	s o⌐
576	*Ed:*	*involveme*₁*nt* in *this* as we ll°
577	*Vern:*	yeah yeah °yeah°⌐ and – *then* – do
578		she and- *Kendr-* uh:: >*Bernice*< must be
579		*friends:* – of *some* sort °*too*°
580	*Ed:*	°um° *not* anymore h₁hh ((chuckles))
581	*Vern:*	no – but *they were* at
582	*Ed:*	((continues chuckle))
583	*Vern:*	one *ti*^*me:*, so there was a- – it's kinda –⌐
584		it is – *spring ti*∧*me*
585		and ₁they're in *fifth* ∧*grade* and *this'll-*
586	*Ed:*	*yes:* ⌐
587	*Vern:*	(0.2) between ∧*now* and (0.5) >the *time*
588		they *graduate*
589		fr₁om high ^*school* 'll be< *thou sands* of
590	*Ed:*	they're in *ruins:* ⌐
591	*Vern:*	*fri*∧*ends*
592	*Ed:*	*yes::*
593	*Vern:*	°OK° (0.3) so – um (1.0) but – ((clears
594		throat)) >you know< (0.5) that that that was
595		the- the *one thing* that – I *think* we've
596		*talked* a little bit *before* about *that* – *this*
597		∧*year* – about – are *there* ·hh those *things*

598		an- ·hh and I *think* I've- >a couple times<
599		*quoted* um *Carol Gilligan* the *woman* from
600		Har:vard, ⌈who –
601	*Ed:*	I don't *think*⌋ *I've heard* of –
602		her=
603	*Vern:*	=er- uh- well *she* – *she* has *done* a lot of
604		*research* ⌃on (0.2) *girls* – and uh w- e- and
605		– um partic- more ˆ*teen*⌃*age* ⌃*girls* ·hh and
606		it's >particularly in the areas< of *math* and
607		*science* and *why* – they *fall* – *be*⌃*hind*:
608		(0.2) in *math* and *science* ·hh and what uh-
609		two >two reasons< – *one* – *math* and- *science*
610		are generally ⌃done in what you might *call*
611		for (0.6) >*quick* summary *purpose*< – *l::inear*
612		*way*⌈:s
613	*Ed:*	>linear *m*⌋odalitie⌈s<
614	*Vern:*	*modal*⌋*i-ties* and *boy:s*
615		– tend to *learn*: -*that* – *way* – *better* by the
616		time *they* – you know – *they* always *claim*
617		that ·h that boys're right *brained* – to – to
618		*left* brain. They're *right* brain when they're
619		*supposed* to be learning *reading* and- that's
620		why *they* fall *be*⌃*hind*, because it's a *left*
621		brain *activity* ⌈the *ba sic learning* process
622	*Ed:*	u h huh⌋
623	*Vern:*	in – ((papers rustling)) in *girls* is *fine*.
624		*Girls* then *shift*- and are *left*- (0.3) the
625		*opposite* – *left* brain *right* brain, ·hh so by
626		the *time* we start teaching *what* – *some* would
627		*call* the *left* – *brain* – subject *matters* of
628		of ˆ*science* and ˆ*math*, *girls* are moving
629		toward ·hh a more *right* (0.2) *brai:n* (0.5)
630		u:m (1.4) *mode* o⌈f *lear*- – pu-
631	*Ed:*	*mode* of *think*⌋*ing*
632	*Vern:*	*thinking* of ˆ*lear*⌃*ning*. ·hh um: uh She's
633		taken *that* I *think* in – a *deeper* ⌃*vein* and
634		*what* she's looked *at* – are – the *issues* of
635		the ⌃*way* ·hh *women*: – are – b- still brought
636		ˆ*up* in our – *cul:*⌃*ture*. And the *way* women
637		are *still* brought up in our *cul*⌃*ture* – is is
638		a very *sexist way*. ·hh They – *help* –
639		m ⌈om
640	*Ed:*	just a⌋ second – *SAM* – *BRENT*
641		(4.1)
642	*Vern:*	they help *m*⌃*om* (0.2) they – °they° – they

643		make *sure* (0.3) *dad˄dy's* taken care of and
644		their *brother's* taken care of and they're
645		°*taking care of.* ·h So what *happens* is – ·h
646		is *math* and *science* are taught in a *linear*
647		fashion (0.3) ·h u:m you *get* into a
648		*discussion* like *this°*. ·h and the *gir˄ls* –
649		pull ˄*back.*
650		(0.5)
651	*Vern:*	[Girls a re *good* when *qui˄et* and *po˄lite,*
652	*Ed:*	(is it)]
653	*Vern:*	·h *yet they* – *academical˄ly* – *these* are
654		bright *kids* – that academically can do *it*
655		·hh the *boy:s* – are just *really* (into)
656		*discussion,* – it's – *v:ery traditional* and
657		whatchur going to go *through* is the *worst*
658		period of *time* from *fifth:* – to *ninth* –
659		*grade* – ·h *where* that occurs. (0.4) You know
660		*I* – >I *have* mentioned be˄fore< the reason we
661		don't have *tag programs* at the –
662		*intermediate* schools but have en˄*riched*
663		*programs* is because *girls* refuse to go into
664		*tag,* ·h because – *they felt* – that *they* –
665		were *isolating* themselves from the *potential*
666		o-of having – ˄*boyfriends* – because they
667		were *brighte[r* than the *b oys*
668	*Ed:*	°um – hum°]
669	*Vern:*	and – *they* – you're *not* supposed to *do* ˄*that*
670		– ˄*culturally.* ·h so >you had to go to< to
671		en˄*riched* classes which – *f:orce* the *girls*
672		into 'em – I mean *they didn't* have a *choice*
673		– they were placed in en˄*riched* English –
674		they were *track:ed* – into their *tracking*
675		˄*group,* ·h and *then* – they were tracked
676		*there,* ·h °*well* – *that* – is – going to *begin*
677		to hap˄pen ·h I mean – for *these girls* to sit
678		˄here – ·h they are *potentially* (0.6) in
679		the ˄ *mi:nds* of other ˄*gir:ls* – *particular˄ly*
680		and in *some* of the *b˄oys'* maybe become – ·h
681		*those* girls who are – *egg head* (0.3) who
682		(are all those) – you know – *intellec:tual*
683		or whate[ver
684	*Ed:*	um h]um
685	*Vern:*	·h in the *stereo˄ty˄ping* – by – *talking* too
686		much about *science* or °*excelling* too much in
687		*math.°* (0.4) ·h um *It has* changed

688		₍somewhat from *twenty years* a go
689	*Ed*:	°lis ten can you turn that ( )° ₎
690	*Vern*:	– that's –have *changed* – *somewhat* but you're
691		*still* seeing the ^*signs* of *it*. In a
692		*situation* – *like* this ·h and *that's*
693		something to *think* about ·h because *what she*
694		*claims* in her book- >*her work*< – on *Harvard*
695		·h is *that* – *girls* – *actually* – *do* – *learn*
696		better because of their need *to* – make sure
697		*other* people are feeling *comfortable* – *other*
698		people are brought *a*ₓ*long* – *other* people –
699		are – *inclu*ₓ*ded* – and *they* – step *back*=
700	*Ed*:	=um hum=
701	*Vern*:	=she argues *that what* – >you *really* need
702		*then*< *i:s to cooperative* – *lear:ning* because
703		*that* is the best *way* for *women* – to
704		*learn*, ·h=
705	*Ed*:	=um hum=
706	*Vern*:	=at *that* point in *ti:me*, ·h because
707		it *a*^*llow:s* them *both* to – to – *listen* and *to*
708		*partici*ₓ*pate* – to make *sure* that *everybody*
709		in a *group*< is- is feeling a *pa:rt* – of a
710		*group* – ·h to *take care* of their *nee:ds* –
711		but *also* for them to *then* be *part*, –
712		>because *everybody* has a *responsibility*-< to
713		*that* group – *everybody* is – *requ:ired* to
714		learn a *piece* – everybody is – *requ:ired* to
715		speak.
716		·hh ₍*everybody* is *required* °to-°
717	*Ed*:	what's *her* name? – I can put *this*₎ in my
718		*resea*₍*rch* ((laughter in voice))
719	*Vern*:	*her* name i₎s >Carol *Gilligan*< *I* have a
720		*bo*₍*ok* –
721	*Ed*:	O'K₎
722	*Vern*:	at *home* ₍that – I'll rem- >I *haven't*
723	*Ed*:	can I *borrow* it?₎
724	*Vern*:	bothered to *read*, < I bought *it when* I was
725		at *Harvard* er- a month *ago* an- I'll- >I'll
726		*have* to *bring it* – to ₓ*you*< ·hh an- tj-
727		*where* she *talks* about *these* very *issues*=
728	*Ed*:	=°um – I mean *cooperative learning* to *me*°
729		and *I'm* doing it on the *math* ₓ*test*=
730	*Vern*:	=yeah=
731	*Ed*:	=so I *need* ·h (0.3) to l₍ike get o ver that
732	*Vern*:	you don't₎

733		sh- *I* don't think *she – she* is – I I – I
734		*have* (0.2) *read* only uh-n *article* or *two* but
735		I haven't read the book *yet* =
736	*Ed:*	= >um hum<
737	*Vern:*	·h *an-* – *she* talked about *cooperative*
738		*techniques* – I don't know – *how much* – *she* –
739		herself – *knows* and ^*uses* cooperative
740		*lear:ning* but she *talks* about ther- –
741		₁more coop- – *co llegial*
742	*Ed:*	*the nee::d* ₁
743	*Vern:*	cooperative tech₁niques
744	*Ed:*	the *ne*¹:*ed* to do that=
745	*Vern:*	=·h and for *science* and *math* teachers – to
746		*foster that*, ·h and she said the *danger's*
747		gonna *be* is that (0.5) the people who will
748		become *math* and *science* teachers in here
749		are the *boys* (0.4) if they become *teachers*
750		at all, – and the *girls* will *ten:d* to *still*
751		become the *English* (0.2) *teachers* those who
752		are currently- >'cause if you *look* at *how*
753		language *arts* is done< (1.4) you know what
754		goes on
755	*Ed:*	°um hum°
756	*Vern:*	you know it's it's a ₁(her-)
757	*Ed:*	more holi¹stic
758	*Vern:*	and it's *more* sensory *more* appealing. More-
759		·h °like – you know- a (phenomena) – type of
760		*thing*° ·hh so it was – e- *this* panned out
761		that way=
762	*Ed:*	=um=
763	*Vern:*	=that *the* lesson – *did that* – an'
764		it probably
765		wa₁s good because of that uh issues
766	*Ed:*	(it) was – *good that* you noticed *th*¹*at*
767		((paper rustling))
768	*Vern:*	((slight cough)) °that came up°
769	*Ed:*	because *yesterday* when we had Kendra's *dad* –
770		('n all) of my *boys* (0.2) I mean °(the
771		quality) of the questions I was impressed
772		with° it was just getting- hh they *impressed*
773		me with their – uh – *statements* and-
774	*Vern:*	>I think< – >you know< – *that's* (0.4) where
775		(0.3) you know *that's* where the *schools* uh
776		da- – for a long time *failed* because *science*
777		was hardly covered at *all*, ·h=

778 *Ed:*   =um hum=
779 *Vern:*   =and *that's* where *this* district had to *begin*
780   to *force* to *te-* – *teachers* to *teach* science,
781   we *finally* began to *mandate* that there're *x*
782   – *units* ·h that *had* to *happen*, and this was
783   in the *seventies*=
784 *Ed:*   =°um hum°=
785 *Vern:*   =·h and *I* had a friend *who* – who *admitted*
786   one of the reasons she's *transferred* to the
787   – *junior* ^high so *she* could teach *English.*
788   ·h Was *Because* – she was teaching – >*fifth*
789   and *sixth* graders, she was supposed to
790   teach< *certain* science *units* – she *didn't* do
791   it. ·hh She would *rumple* up the *materials,*
792   you know you *get* some of those *kits* you've
793   now have *books* but in *those* days *they* had
794   these *kits* ·h and *you're* supposed to use
795   *this stuff* so she'd *take* the *stuff* they're
796   supposed to have *used* – *consume* and *throw* it
797   in the *garbage* room >rumple *everything else*
798   up< and *send* it *back* after *tw*₁o wee ks
799   ·hh   ⌉
800 *Vern:*   ·hh and said *yeah* I *did* the science *unit.*
801   (1.1) *Because* that's *was her* comfort *level*
802   °with *science*° (0.7) *in*stead they did more
803   *art* – and more *whatever.* (0.4) And *things*
804   like that >well what happened was< *she* had
805   *kids* who went – *science illiterate* into the
806   *inter*^*mediate* schools (0.3) you know they
807   were already *be*˻*hi:nd* (0.2) um:: – uh
808   *further* behind than their *colleagues* who at
809   ^lea*st* – got the *little* science that was=
810 *Ed:*   =um hum=
811 *Vern:*   =·hh so *there's* been a big *fo*˻*cus* in *this*
812   district – *just* on *that* – *issue,* ·h tryin'
813   to make ^*tea*˻*chers* feel more
814   *com*₁*fortable* in *that* area so that *our* –
815 *Ed:*   um hum⌋
816 *Vern:*   *kids* as they get ^*in* to the *intermediate*
817   schools have ·h – *some science* – *literacy.*
818   (0.5) And uh (0.3) so – it – >you know< so –
819   ·h uh the important *is*˻*sue* ·h and you ^*see*
820   how your *goals* lie ^*up* in that area.
821   (0.6)
822 *Vern:*   ₁And s o *that's* important for

823	*Ed:*	(yes:)¹
824	*Vern:*	th₍em *too* you sh- they
825	*Ed:*	(°and I go in°)¹
826	*Vern:*	shouldn't – *that* – *should* not be *stopped.*
827	*Ed:*	I kn₍ow – *I* try – to ben:d
828	*Vern:*	The *goal* is to get the¹ *GIRLS* into
829		that same ₍kind of a-
830	*Ed:*	IN THAT *PIC*¹*TURE* too and it's
831		just (0.4) h::ow – >you know what I mean<
832		it's just so *hard* – because
833		(0.4)
834	*Vern:*	it's (hard on) a lot of
835		ki₍ds hhh ((laugh ter))
836	*Ed:*	but it's like ¹ more or less – when I
837		try to – ^*think* of *myself* or call *myself* as
838		a *non*-sexist person you know ·hh *more* so
839		that I *don't*
840		(0.9)
841	*Vern:*	·h ·hh *you're* fighting – *cultural* things –
842		*certain* things that *you can't* even *begin* –
843		to *deal* with, ·h um – or *don't* know *how* to
844		*deal* with because *how* do you *reshape* that –
845		*how* – do you get *girls* who by – *the fifth*
846		*grade* are *already* taking care of their
847		little *brothers* and little *sisters,* ·hh and
848		have *mommy* sending 'em *in* to see if – *daddy*
849		₋you know da da da ₋da=
850	*Ed:*	=um hu₍m
851	*Vern:*	y¹ou know (and) *this* or *that* ·hh *how* –
852		do you – you overcome *that* type of *stuff* ·h
853		to get them – *not to* – pull back. *Ho:w* do
854		you *get* them *to* – ·h be – (feminine) or h- –
855		by *just* lookin' at *colors I* was *about* to *say*
856		– use that *terrible* (0.4) >that film title<
857		*how* do you get them to *be* ((Ed sneezes))
858		*pretty* – in – *pink* – and – *cute* – an- ·hh
859		an- *appear* to be=
860	*Ed:*	=°I don't know°=
861	*Vern:*	=*plus* so that *boys* – who are *beginning* to
862		*lear:n* – you know that *girls* are supposed to
863		*be* a *certain* ₋way. *How* do you – you know –
864		how do you *integrate* all that stuff –
865		because what you're *fighting* is – is
866		*centuries* of ·h of *acculturation* ((Ed
867		sneezes)) in: – *trying*

868		t|o get *them* to – *change* it
869	*Ed:*	it *still* goes on in the *ho*me – *too*. And
870		*still* making *sure* that we *va:lue what* goes
871		on in the *home* and *supporting* them, ·h but
872		*yet* (0.8) *shape the* – *this* to *me* is kind of
873		*high* level *stuff* – that *I* think *is* gonna
874		*happen* over *time,*
875		|you really need – to *think* about
876	*Vern:*	oh yeah – it can – take – forev|er
877	*Ed:*	to think |more – °about it°
878	*Vern:*	I mean – you'l- y-| *thirty* years
879		into your *career* (0.5) h *if* you y- y- *you*
880		*might* – *you* might *see* more changes than –
881		*we've* seen largely because – there're more –
882		*girls* whose – who – who come from the *single*
883		parent ˏfam^lies – whose mothers are out
884		*there* – ·hh in that – *dog* eat *dog world* as
885		we like to *call* it and *that* kinda *stuff.*
886		·hh So you *might* just *naturally* see some
887		*changes* ·h the *FAct* that you're *seeing* the
888		*girls* respo:nd when they're – *asked* the
889		questions °directly (when they're)° we're
890		seeing them *respo:nd* ·h with an academic
891		*kno:w*^*ledge* of the *subject* area. It's prob-
892		might – be better – I've no *statistics* on
893		ˏthis, than it would have been a *generation*
894		ago then it would've been °oh I don't
895		remember seeing this stuff° (0.4) (on input)
896		– and – um (1.0) and – so – >you know< – an-
897		I *interviewed* this *morning* a very *bright*
898		^*wo*ˏ*man* – who *wants* to be an intermediate
899		ˏ*school* – ^*sci*ˏence *tea*ˏ*cher* – *for* – *that* –
900		very *reason* – that she feels a *woman* needs
901		to be a *role* model – ·h in that – *profession*
902		where we a|re seeing more o f
903	*Ed:*	°just a second°	
904	*Vern:*	*that* occurring
905	*Ed:*	CAN *YOUR TEAM* HELP YOU – *NICOLE*? (0.4) OK
906		– *thank you*
907	*Vern:*	and- this- *so* – so – anyway it it's jus::t
908		(0.2) uh an *is*ˏ*sue* ((Ed coughs)) that um –
909		um is an *important* one an- -and- *I* think it
910		(0.4) it was (0.2) *you* did – r:*ight* – by
911		*adjusting* for it in *questio*ˏ*nings* – >but
912		it's just *interesting* to see *it*< (0.8)

913		>*comes* ^up< – *all* over *the* place
914	*Ed:*	go ahead – *yeah* I just *notice* I'm just – um
915		*hum* – *hum* I'm (into the fra) ((Vern coughs))
916		I don't know *what's* so except my *signals*
917		just said ((Vern sniffles)) – I'm *off* –
918		bal:ance=
919	*Vern:*	=yeah=
920	*Ed:*	=you know it just – *that* – brings *scales* –
921		back into *tip* (1.6) >but other than *that*<
922		the *questioning* strategy- – am I mak- am –
923		*my* question to *you* then would be – am
924		I – *s:till* – *dignifying* the *learner*, –
925		*that's* been one of my –
926		·h *bigg*₁*est* – thoughts
927	*Vern:*	yeah – no – I di¹dn't (0.4) they're –
928		n- – no that wa- uh s- (0.2) *I:* – did *not* –
929		have – *flags* – raised -there ((sound of
930		paper rustling)) um – and- the few *times* – I
931		don't *think* you *ever* – said uh *now* – ·h
932		there was *one* – *time* (0.8) ·h *sometimes* it's
933		the *little* stuff *that* – we don't even *think*
934		about ·h °*Edwin* responded to your *question*.
935		*He* did it *right*. ·h And *you* said ·h you said
936		– *yes::*° (0.8) *that* was- – u:m – *that* was *an*
937		(1.4) and you said *that* was – an *easy one*
938		>or *you* said *something* like *that*< ·hh *you* –
939		*you* meant to say – ˄*say::* – you know *that*
940		was – a *good* answer: or it was an *easy* one
941		to come out with ₁or *som* e-
942	*Ed:*	u h huh¹
943	*Vern:*	*thing* – like *that* ·h instead *it* might have
944		*sounded* to him like – *well* >OF *COURSE* YOU
945		SHOULD'VE GOTTEN IT *RIGHT*,< – it was simple
946		₁>I me an< ·h *that* – *ther*- – *that* it –
947	*Ed:*	˄O :::H ¹
948	*Vern:*	*the way* you said *it* – uh *you* meant it *one*
949		way – but it was *one* of *those* two *edged*=
950	*Ed:*	=could've been *taken*:=
951	*Vern:*	=*taken* a different ˄way. ·h um The *girl* who
952		– who – had her *things* lost, there was no
953		((Ed coughs)) *easy* way to do *that* except to
954		*look* and you went – *huh?* (0.4) 'cause *she*
955		gave you such a – *weird* – an:^swer.=
956	*Ed:*	=hh=
957	*Vern:*	=that you knew it wasn't *com:pletely*

958		(incongruent), you went along
959		⌐raised your
960	*Ed:*	h hh ((coughs⌐))
961	*Vern:*	*eyes* – and *you* sort of *went* – °uh° – like
962		*that* and – you know *some* of the other *kids*
963		quickly *responded* and – ·hh *all* you could
964		*say* is – go *back* and *check* it ⌐out, there
965		was *no way* you could *handle* (0.7) that
966		⌐°in any other way.°
967	*Ed:*	°OK° ⌐
968	*Vern:*	( ) for th⌐e most *part* –
969	*Ed:*	°that they could understan⌐d°
970	*Vern:*	·h um I think that – that – *that* was – °not°
971		– >*something* that I *saw* as a *concern* here<
972		(0.6) 'K=
973	*Ed:*	=huh
974	*Vern:*	OK?
975	*Ed:*	was it *an* OK ^*les*⌐*son* then?
976	*Vern:*	*I* thought *it* was a *very* – *fine* lesson. ·h um
977		And – the *only* thing I *think* that *you* have
978		to look at *it* as being *a* – *that* lesson *that*
979		was – was – *you* were – ·h *you* were the (*old*)
980		person *there* trying to *light* ^the ^*logs*?
981	*Ed:*	uh huh
982	*Vern:*	and – *if* they *don't* light – and that's when
983		((laughter in voice)) you get *concerned* –
984		but *suddenly* you had that *dis:CUSSion*
985		suddenly go *off* on its *own*. ·h And *it* – *it*
986		was – you know °*some* people call *that* the
987		*teachable* moment° – whatever ·hh you *had*
988		that *take* ^off – and *it* went *on* (0.2) ·h and
989		then – you know – *part* of this – *lesson* was
990		a *meat* and *potatoes* lesson, – you – had
991		*certain* issues to *talk* – and then you *needed*
992		to get back to *work*. ·h >Were the *answers*
993		predominantly *right* on the *work* as *they* gave
994		'em to you?< *yes* they ⌐*were*.
995	*Ed:*	yes::⌐:
996	*Vern:*	*That* would *indicate* to *me*. – that >you know<
997		– the *instruc*⌐*tion* an- – >an- *it* was< –
998		*Ed:* makes sense⌐
999	*Vern:*	being *successful* that – ·h the *evaluation*,
1000		*which* would be those *questions* part?=
1001	*Ed:*	=(um hum)=
1002	*Vern:*	=Were ⌐good. (0.4) You know – *that* type of

1003		*thing,* so (0.7) *yes:*
1004		(1.3)
1005	*Ed:*	that – and – *oh* 'K ((to observer)) you can
1006		*turn* it *off,* if you *want.* But can this
1007		((recorder turned off))
1008		.
1009		.
1010		.
1011	*Vern:*	he – he ((laughter in voice)) starts taping
1012		again
1013	*Ed:*	oh OK, – hi hhh
1014	*Vern:*	that *last* ˏfall this: – *thing* – put you *off*
1015		– a *whole* lot ((laughter in voice))
1016		₁*more* than *it* does right *now*
1017	*Ed:*	yeah ¹ *now* it doesn't
1018		even *faze* me ˏanymore ((to observer)) *you*
1019		have any *questions* that you wanna ^*ask?* >I
1020		mean just< – I *guess* it comes – with
1021		*looking* at *cultural* – *backgrounds* too
1022		*especially,* ·h looking at *Vern* as an
1023		ˏ*authority,* and *each* time *he* comes *in* it's
1024		like being=
1025	*Duncan:*	=um hum=
1026	*Ed:*	=*him* being the *principal.* ·h Or *him* –
1027		*especially* working ˏin *personnel,* you know
1028		·h what are *my* – *what* I- do I *perceive*
1029		him ˏto *be.* ·h An- – *somebody* that's in
1030		– you know – a *lot* of ˏ*power,* have a
1031		*lot* of responsibilities- *somebody* that
1032		can *really* – help *sh:ape* – or *break*
1033		my *future*-hhh ((laughter in
1034		₁voice)) hhhh ((out right laughter))
1035	*Vern:*	I have *no* power but¹ ((both laugh))
1036	*Duncan:*	I *did* notice how the – how the *conversation*
1037		ended *up* talking about – what kinda ^*jobs* –
1038		*positions.* ₁y ou it's- was kind
1039	*Vern:*	yea h¹
1040	*Duncan:*	of – you *can* kinda look at the *things*
1041		that're at the *beginning* of might – you know
1042		*things* that're at the *beginning* of the
1043		*conversation* >and at the *end*< are probably
1044		the more *important* things.
1045	*Vern:*	Oh wh₁en you were talking- ₁yeah
1046	*Duncan:*	(like) *that* – was im¹por tant ¹ but *also*
1047		the *teaching* was (a point at the end but not

```
1048                    the reason that                )
1049    Vern:          it – uh::m – yeah – well I imagine – Melanie
1050                   ((the principal)) might- did a lot – (in)
1051                   that with you this year, she's extremely
1052                   comfortable to be comfortable with
1053                      ⌈even though she is a principal
1054    Ed:            ye: s::   ⌉
1055    Vern:          when she walks in to observe, so
1056    Ed:            and when my lesson flopped on my formal
1057                   observation and she made me re-do it again,
1058                   ·hh that was the best thing that could've
1059                   happened- and now it's just (0.6) I've
1060                   learned that I don't have to over plan
1061                   anymore. (0.3) ·h An- I can just do: what I
1062                   need to ⌈do
1063    Vern:                  Ed⌉ – is – HYPERperfectionist
1064    Ed:            hhhh
1065    Vern:          and – and you do: – I mean you – really
1066                   (0.2) I remember when you first came in last
1067                   ˄August, last fall – or (when it stopped)
1068                   everything – you know – it – was just-
1069                   s⌈hh shh
1070    Ed:             ⌊just   i¹t ((laughs))
1071    Vern:          and we would – then say – mellow – ^OUT –
1072                   ˄Ed.
1073    Ed:            hhhh but I'm still like that – but not
1074                   ⌈as::
1075    Vern:          ⌊yeah⌋
1076                   (1.8)
1077    Vern:          well you prob- I think you have a lot of the
1078                   good quality and so that those things which
1079                   keep you – ·h um trying to do different
1080                   things
1081    Ed:            sh⌈:^:::::::::::::::::::::::::::::::::   ::
1082    Vern:            ⌊different sorts of activities and⌋
1083                   stuff and so – um you know that's
1084                   im^portant. Some of ˄that. (You know) some
1085                   of the best teachers have some of those
1086                   qualities (0.8) °they shut it out° – that's
1087                   why they' ⌈re really-
1088    Duncan:                  ⌊it's   level⌋ of concern, right?
1089    Vern:          yeah – and- that's why you keep – you're
1090                   willing to keep coming back here (when)
1091                   you're not working with kids: – because you
1092                   (0.6) you know – always have another way of
```

1093		*doing* it – you know – there's
1094		al₁*ways* another *chall enge*
1095	*Ed:*	s:ometimes I actua-] I just – *change*
1096		my whole *lesson* plan >you know I mean I
1097		*start*< on some way – then like – I *notice* at
1098		one *point* in *time* ·h the *kids* were headed
1099		some⌃*where* – and I sort of *needed* to
1100		>readapt< like ·h >*Kenny* I think it *was*< –
1101		*he* had *this* idea that – t- the *dams* create
1102		*tides* – and I went – *oh* – *OK* >you know
1103		*what* I *mean?* I'm *making*
1104		₁*sure* I'm *being* an *active*< listener
1105	*Vern:*	y eah] °yeah°
1106	*Ed:*	to *what* their (0.4) *statements* are and
1107		it's just – *ding* and the *light finally* (0.5)
1108		°went *on* – so *that* was *good*° ·hh what *else*
1109		was I *going* to ⌃*ask* ⌃*you?* – *oh I* know. ·h um
1110		(0.8) *That letter* that we *got* – about *saying*
1111		that we haven't been in *graduate* schoo₁l
1112	*Vern:*	I] –
1113		*sent* it to ⌃*Sean* – and *just* said what *is*
1114		*this* and *he* called me *yesterday* and said
1115		(0.3) *WHERE'D* YOU GET *THAT* ⌃FROM, and *I* said
1116		– ·h *all* of *my* candidates got *it* they just
1117		i- (0.4) *ignored* it and *he* s:::aid – *I* said
1118		– *did* the *other* scho- ie- *I* don't *know*, >*I*
1119		said *something* why don't we *check* with the
1120		*other* schools< and *see* if *they* ⌃got ⌃it.
1121		(0.3) ·h *He* was – *upset that* it had been
1122		*sent* o:ut – to *you guys.* ₁*ignore* *it*
1123	*Ed:*	°OK°] *ignore*
1124		*the letter* ₁*enti rely*
1125	*Vern:*	yeah] *y*- – *you* don't know
1126		what we're *talking* about – ·hh *is* that=
1127	*Duncan:*	=it wasn't signed from ⌃*our* office?=
1128	*Vern:*	=*no*
1129	*Ed:*	the *graduate* school
1130	*Vern:*	*that* that *since* they hadn't been *students* –
1131		there at the *university* for a *long* time –
1132		*they* needed to *reapply* for admission.
1133	*Ed:*	hh and *I'm* going – *just* a *second here*, I
1134		s:*wore*
1135		(₁)
1136	*Vern:*	But – *I* – *think* one of the *prob*₁*lems* is:
1137		you're *currently* registered in *continuing*

1138		education
1139	*Ed:*	um 'K
1140	*Vern:*	versus the *regular* – um *program* – and *so* –
1141		*what* happened – *was* – *they* just looked at
1142		*your* letter an- – *didn't* search far enough
1143		to find your *name* – in *another* – fₗile
1144	*Ed:*	anoᐟther
1145		file
1146	*Vern:*	yeah=
1147	*Ed:*	=*so* – *Sean's* taking care of
1148		iₗt then
1149	*Vern:*	*yeah he* just saᐟid – you know don't wor-
1150		*that's* – *not* an *issue.*
1151	*Ed:*	*I* don't want *my*
1152		paₗcket *not* to be *there* on that *day*
1153	*Vern:*	*Besides* – *normally* in *summer* schoolsᐟ
1154		we *don't* have to *register* –
1155	*Ed:*	*I* know *isn't* that sₗtupid
1156	*Vern:*	ᐟfor yeah but I don't
1157		know.
1158	*Ed:*	>*oh* and I *got* my *program* all *typed* out.<
1159	*Vern:*	OK ₗta-
1160	*Ed:*	>*An-*ᐟ I *gotta* get a *letter*< to *Doctor*
1161		*Loman* too (0.4) *she'll still* be there *this*
1162		summer? Right *I* knₗow *she* and
1163	*Duncan:*	um humᐟ
1164	*Ed:*	*Sean* aren't *getting* along – so
1165	*Vern:*	I *guess* you got *those* at the *seminar* when *I*
1166		wasn't *there* right?
1167	*Ed:*	y:ₗ::::::::::::::::::es::::::::::
1168	*Vern:*	And you *were told* to do sᐟomething
1169		ₗwith them OK good
1170	*Ed:*	*yes* and *we* need tᐟo *turn* it *into* ˰you
1171	*Vern:*	oh OK – *because* I haven't asked
1172		anyₗbody yet. *I-* w-
1173	*Ed:*	an- we need toᐟ
1174	*Vern:*	*surprised Erica* didn't have it *back* to *me*
1175		like *that* unless *she* gave it to *Helen*
1176	*Ed:*	*no* – *you* want *me* to tell *you why* h- you
1177		didn't get it *back because* ·h the *day* that –
1178		*I said* – *I know* we *registered* for *these*
1179		classes *last* term – and *that's* why we
1180		coulₗdn't turn *it* in – and *we're* all *huffy*
1181	*Vern:*	ah (yeah)ᐟ
1182	*Ed:*	about *that* so hhhhhhh

```
1183   Duncan:   mmmmmm ((all enjoy a chuckle))
1184   Vern:     hhhhhh
1185   Ed:       hhh so I finally got it done last night s-=
1186   Vern:     =yeah – Ok
1187   Duncan:   you missed the-?
1188   Vern:     yeah – well Helen told me about it
1189   Ed:       hh °I was (1.0) ⌐^up⌐set
1190   Vern:                       awright⌋ (1.2) no:w >we're
1191             gonna move on 'cause we're gonna go see<
1192             Doug now
1193   Ed:       ·h if you wanna come back – I'm doing
1194             glasser circle at twelve fifty? – to one oh
1195             ⌐five.
1196   Vern:     well:: we have Doug at twelve thirty to one
1197             fifteen=
1198   Ed:       =OK=
1199   Vern:     =so – sorry about that.
1200   Ed:       (I think I'll make it)
1201   Duncan:   Aren't people coming up Friday, they're
1202             gonna come in to see you? on Friday?=
1203   Vern:     =um he has one=
1204   Ed:       =just one
1205   Vern:     one person – so are you coming up here
1206             Friday?
1207   Duncan:   (I think for some)
1208   Vern:     OK – so – if you wanna come back and see –
1209             y- I I might not be: – y- well – I'll try
1210             to- - ·h you know get – maybe if you're
1211             coming up Friday – then I'll try to arrange
1212             to come see Ed again, so that
1213             w⌐e can – get him on  a
1214   Ed:          oh – good I can get⌋
1215   Vern:     (videocassette)=
1216   Ed:       =two for one. h⌐hhhhhhhhhhhhhhhhhhhhh hhhhh
1217   Vern:                  Two for one in one week⌋
1218             make up for all the weeks I haven't been
1219             around
1220   Duncan:   thanks for letting me in
1221   Ed:       no no problem – I'm assuming that things are
1222             not alarm-
1223             ((end tape))
```

References

ABRELL, R. and HANNA, C. (1978) 'Symbolic interactionism and supervisor–teacher relationships', *Clearing House*, **51** (9), pp. 439–43.

ACHESON, K. and GALL, M. D. (1992) *Techniques in the Clinical Supervision of Teachers: Preservice and Inservice Applications*, 3rd edn, New York: Longman.

AGAR, M. H. (1980) *The Professional Stranger: An Informal Introduction to Ethnography*, New York: Academic Press.

AGAR, M. H. (1986) *Speaking of Ethnography*, Beverly Hills, CA: Sage.

ALFONSO, R. (1986) 'The Unseen Supervisor: Organization and Culture as Determinants of Teacher Behavior', paper presented at the annual meeting of the American Educational Research Association, San Francisco, CA, April.

ALFONSO, R. J., FIRTH, G. and NEVILLE, R. (1984) 'The supervisory skill mix', *Educational Leadership*, **41**, pp. 16–18.

APPLE, M. (1986) *Teachers and Text*, New York: Routledge and Kegan Paul.

BAKHTIN, M. M. (1968) *Rabelais and His World* (H. Iswolsky, trans.) Cambridge, MA: MIT Press.

BAKHTIN, M. M. (1973) *Problems of Dostoyevsky's Poetics* (W. W. Rostel, trans.) Ann Arbor, MI: Ardis.

BAKHTIN, M. M. (1981a) 'Discourse in the Novel', in M. HOLQUIST (Ed.) *The Dialogic Imagination* (C. Emerson and M. Holquist, trans.) Austin, TX: University of Texas Press, pp. 259–422.

BAKHTIN, M. M. (1981b) *The Dialogic Imagination*, M. HOLQUIST (Ed.) (C. Emerson and M. Holquist, trans.) Austin, TX: University of Texas Press.

BARSKY, R. F. and HOLQUIST, M. (Eds) (1990) 'Bakhtin and otherness', *Social Discourse*, **3** (1, 2), pp. vii–371.

BATESON, G. (1972) *Steps to an Ecology of Mind*, New York: Ballantine Books.

BAUMAN, Z. (1988/89) 'Strangers: The social construction of universality and particularity', *Telos*, **78**, pp. 7–42.

BENHABIB, S. (1990) 'Epistemologies of postmodernism: A rejoinder to Jean-François Lyotard', in NICHOLSON, L. J. (Ed.) *Feminism/Postmodernism*, New York: Routledge, pp. 107–30.

BENHABIB, S. (1992) *Situating the Self*, New York: Routledge.

BLASE, J. (1986) 'Socialization as humanization: One side of becoming a teacher', *Sociology of Education*, **59** (2), pp. 100–13.

BLASE, J. (1993) 'Micropolitics of effective school-based leadership: Teachers' perspectives', *Educational Administration Quarterly*, **29** (2), pp. 142–63.

BLOOMFIELD, L. (1933) *Language*, New York: Holt, Rinehart and Winston.

BLUMBERG, A. (1970) 'Supervisor–Teacher relationships: A look at the supervisory conference', *Administrator's Notebook*, **19** (1), pp. 1–4.

BLUMBERG, A. (1980) *Supervisors and Teachers: A Private Cold War*, 2nd edn, Berkeley, CA: McCutchan.

BLUMBERG, A. and AMIDON, E. (1965) 'Teacher perceptions of supervisor–teacher interactions', *Administrator's Notebook*, **19**, pp. 1–4.

BLUMBERG, A. and JONAS, R. S. (1987) 'Permitting access: Teacher's control over supervision', *Educational Leadership*, **44**, pp. 58–62.

BLUMER, H. (1972) 'Symbolic interaction', in SPRADLEY, J. P. (Ed.) *Culture and Cognition: Rules, Maps, and Plans*, San Francisco, CA: Chandler, pp. 65–68.

BODEN, D. and ZIMMERMAN, D. H. (Eds) (1991) *Talk and Social Structure: Studies in Ethnomethodology and Conversation Analysis*, Berkeley, CA: University of California Press.

BOLIN, F. S. and PANARITIS, P. (1992) 'Searching for a common purpose: A perspective on the history of supervision', in GLICKMAN, C. D. (Ed.) *Supervision in Transition*, Alexandria, VA: Association for Supervision and Curriculum Development, pp. 30–43.

BOURDIEU, P. (1977a) *Outline of a Theory of Practice* (R. Nice, trans.) Cambridge: Cambridge University Press.

BOURDIEU, P. (1977b) 'The economics of linguistic exchanges', *Social Science Information*, **16** (6), pp. 645–68.

BOURDIEU, P. (1986) 'The forms of capital', in RICHARDSON, J. G. (Ed.) *Handbook of Theory and Research for the Sociology of Education*, New York: Greenwood Press, pp. 241–58.

BOWERS, C. A. (1982) 'The reproduction of technological consciousness: Locating the ideological foundations of a radical pedagogy', *Teachers College Record*, **83**, pp. 529–57.

BOWERS, C. A. and FLINDERS, D. J. (1991) *Culturally Responsive Supervision: A Handbook for Staff Development*, New York: Teachers College Press.

BRANDT, R. (1993a) 'On restructuring roles and relationships: A conversation with Phil Schlechty', *Educational Leadership*, **51** (2), pp. 8–11.

BRANDT, R. (1993b) 'On teaching for understanding: A conversation with Howard Gardner', *Educational Leadership*, **50** (7), pp. 4–7.

BREHM, S. S. and KASSIN, S. M. (1990) *Social Psychology*, Boston, MA: Houghton Mifflin.

BREMME, D. W. and ERICKSON, F. (1977) 'Relationships among verbal and nonverbal classroom behaviors', *Theory into Practice*, **16** (3), pp. 153–61.

BRIGGS, C. L. (1986) *Learning How to Ask: A Sociolinguistic Appraisal of the Role of the Interview in Social Science Research*, Cambridge: Cambridge University Press.

BROWN, P. and LEVINSON, S. C. (1978) 'Universals in language usage: Politeness phenomena', in GOODY, E. N. (Ed.) *Questions and Politeness: Strategies in Social Interaction*, London: Cambridge University Press, pp. 56–310.

BROWN, R. and GILMAN, A. (1972) 'The pronouns of power and solidarity', in GIGLIOLI, P. (Ed.) *Language and Social Context*, Baltimore, MD: Penguin, pp. 252–82.

BRUNER, J. (1985) 'Narrative and paradigmatic modes of thought', in EISNER, E. (Ed.) *Learning and Teaching the Ways of Knowing*, Eighty-fourth Yearbook of the National Society for the Study of Education, Part II, Chicago, IL: National Society for the Study of Education, pp. 97–115.

BURBULES, N. C. (1986) 'A theory of power in education', *Educational Theory*, **36** (2), pp. 95–114.

BURBULES, N. C. (1992) 'Forms of ideology-critique: A pedagogical perspective', *Qualitative Studies in Education*, **5**, pp. 7–17.

BURBULES, N. C. and RICE, S. (1991) 'Dialogue across differences: Continuing the conversation', *Harvard Educational Review*, **61**, pp. 393–416.

CAZDEN, C. B. (1976) 'How knowledge about language helps the classroom teacher – or does it: A personal account', *Urban Review*, **9–10**, pp. 74–90.

CENTRE FOR EDUCATIONAL RESEARCH AND INNOVATION (1993) *Education at a Glance*, Paris, Organization for Economic Co-Operation and Development.

CICOUREL, A. V. (1974) *Theory and Method in a Study of Argentine Fertility*, New York: Wiley Interscience.

CICOUREL, A. V. (1992) 'The interpenetration of communicative contexts: Examples from medical encounters', in DURANTI, A. and GOODWIN, C. (Eds) *Rethinking Context: Language as an Interactive Phenomenon*, Cambridge: Cambridge University Press, pp. 291–310.

CLANDININ, D. J. (1985) 'Personal practical knowledge: A study of teachers' classroom images', *Curriculum Inquiry*, **15**, pp. 361–85.

COGAN, M. L. (1973) *Clinical Supervision*, Boston, MA: Houghton Mifflin.

COOK-GUMPERZ, J. and GUMPERZ, J. (1976) *Papers on Language and Context*, Working paper no. 46, Berkeley, CA: Language Behavior Research Laboratory, University of California.

CORNBLETH, C. (1990) *Curriculum in Context*, London: Falmer Press.

DANNEFER, D. and PERLMUTTER, M. (1990) 'Development as a multidimensional process: Individual and social constituents', *Human Development*, **33**, pp. 108–37.

DAVIS, H. E. (1992) 'The tyranny of resistance, or, the compulsion to be a "good feminist"', *Philosophy of Education, 1991*, Proceedings of the Forty-seventh annual meeting of the Philosophy of Education Society, Normal, IL: Philosophy of Education Society, pp. 76–86.

DE CERTEAU, M. (1986) *Heterologies: Discourse on the Other* (B. Massumi, trans.) Minneapolis, MN: University of Minnesota Press.

DEFORGE, Y. (1979) 'Systems of knowledge production and acquisition', *Prospects*, **9** (1), pp. 3–21.

DORR-BREMME, D. W. (1990) 'Contextualization cues in the classroom: Discourse regulation and social control functions', *Language in Society*, **19** (3), pp. 379–402.

DUNLAP, D. M. and GOLDMAN, P. (1991) 'Rethinking power in schools', *Educational Administration Quarterly*, **27** (1), pp. 5–29.

DURANTI, A. and GOODWIN, C. (Eds) (1992) *Rethinking Context: Language as an Interactive Phenomenon*, Cambridge: Cambridge University Press.

EDGAR, D. E. and WARREN, R. L. (1969) 'Power and autonomy in teacher socialization', *Sociology of Education*, **42**, pp. 386–99.

EISNER, E. W. (1991) 'What really counts in schools', *Educational Leadership*, **48**, pp. 10–17.

ELLIOTT, J. (1990) 'Teachers as researchers: Implications for supervision and for teacher education', *Teaching and Teacher Education*, **6** (1), pp. 1–26.

ELLSWORTH, E. (1989) 'Why doesn't this feel empowering? Working through the repressive myths of critical pedagogy', *Harvard Educational Review*, **59**, pp. 297–324.

EMERSON, C. (1993) 'Revolutionary Dissident against the Russian Idea: Mikhail Bakhtin in the Perspective of American Pragmatism', paper delivered to the University of Georgia Humanities Center, Athens, GA, October.

ERICKSON, F. (1975) 'Gatekeeping and the melting pot: Interaction in counseling encounters', *Harvard Educational Review*, **45**, pp. 44–70.

ERICKSON, F. (1986a) 'Qualitative methods in research on teaching', in WITTROCK, M. C. (Ed.) *Handbook of Research on Teaching*, 3rd edn, New York: Macmillan, pp. 119–61.

ERICKSON, F. (1986b) 'Tasks in times: Objects of study in a natural history of teaching', in ZUMWALT, K. (Ed.) *Improving Teaching*, Alexandria, VA: Association for Supervision and Curriculum Development, pp. 131–47.

ERICKSON, F. (1992) 'Ethnographic microanalysis of interaction', in LECOMPTE, M. D., MILLROY, L. and PREISSLE, J. (Eds) *The Handbook of Qualitative Research in Education*, San Diego, CA: Academic Press, pp. 201–25.

ERICKSON, F. and SHULTZ, J. J. (1981) *Talking to 'the Man': Organization of Communication in School Counseling Interviews*, New York: Academic Press.

ETHERIDGE, C. P. (1989) 'Acquiring the teaching culture: How beginners embrace practices different from university teachings', *Qualitative Studies in Education*, **2**, pp. 299–313.

ETZIONI, A. (1993) *The Spirit of Community*, New York: Crown Publishers.

FAIRCLOUGH, N. (1989) *Language and Power*, London: Longman.

FAY, B. (1977) 'How people change themselves: The relationship between critical theory and its audience', in BALL, T. (Ed.) *Political Theory and Praxis: New Perspectives*, Minneapolis, MN: University of Minnesota Press, pp. 200–33.

FAY, B. (1987) *Critical Social Science: Liberation and Its Limits*, Ithaca, NY: Cornell University Press.

FEIMAN-NEMSER, S. and FLODEN, R. (1986) 'The cultures of teaching', in WITTROCK, M. (Ed.) *Handbook of Research on Teaching*, (3rd edn) New York: Macmillan Publishing Company.

FIRESTONE, W. A. (1993) 'Alternative arguments for generalizing from data as applied to qualitative research', *Educational Researcher*, **22**, pp. 16–23.

FLINDERS, D. J. (1991) 'Supervision as cultural inquiry', *Journal of Curriculum and Supervision*, **6** (2), pp. 87–106.

FOUCAULT, M. (1981) 'The order of discourse', in YOUNG, R. (Ed.) *Untying the Text: A Post-Structuralist Reader*, Boston, MA: Routledge & Kegan Paul, pp. 48–78.

FRIEDRICH, P. (1989) 'Language, ideology, and political economy', *American Anthropologist*, **91**, pp. 295–312.

FULLAN, M. (1992) 'Visions that blind', *Educational Leadership*, **49**, pp. 19–20.

GARDINER, M. G. (1992) *The Dialogics of Critique*, London: Routledge.

GARDNER, H. (1983) *Frames of Mind*, New York: Basic Books.

GARDNER, H. (1991) *The Unschooled Mind: How Children Think and How Schools Should Teach*, New York: Basic Books.

GARFINKEL, H. (1967) *Studies in Ethnomethodology*, Englewood Cliffs, NJ: Prentice-Hall.

GARMAN, N. (1990) 'Theories embedded in the events of clinical supervision: A hermeneutic approach', *Journal of Curriculum and Supervision*, **5**, pp. 201–13.

GEARING, F. O. and HUGHES, W. (1975) *On Observing Well: Self-Instruction in Ethnographic Observation for Teachers, Principals, and Supervisors*, Amherst, NY: The Center for Studies in Cultural Transmission.

GEERTZ, C. (1983) *Local Knowledge: Further Essays in Interpretive Anthropology*, New York: Basic Books.

GIDDENS, A. (1984) *The Constitution of Society*, Berkeley, CA: The University of California Press.

GIDDENS, A. (1990) *The Consequences of Modernity*, Stanford, CA: Stanford University Press.

GILBERT, D. T., PELHAM, B. W. and KRULL, D. S. (1988) 'On cognitive busyness: When person perceivers meet persons perceived', *Journal of Personality and Social Psychology*, **54**, pp. 733–40.

GIROUX, H. A. (1981) 'Hegemony, resistance, and the paradox of educational reform', *Interchange*, **12** (2–3), pp. 3–26.

GIROUX, H. A. (1983) 'Theories of reproduction and resistance in the new sociology of education: A critical analysis', *Harvard Educational Review*, **53** (3), pp. 257–93.

GIROUX, H. A. (1992) 'Educational leadership and the crisis of democratic government', *Educational Researcher*, **21** (4), pp. 4–11.

GLATTHORN, A. (1983) *Differentiated Supervision*, Alexandria, VA: Association for Supervision and Curriculum Development.

GLICKMAN, C. D. (1990) *Supervision of Instruction: A Developmental Approach*, (2nd edn) Boston, MA: Allyn & Bacon.

GLICKMAN, C. D. (1993) *Renewing America's Schools*, San Francisco, CA: Jossey-Bass.

GODZICH, W. (1986) 'Foreword: The further possibility of knowledge', in DE CERTEAU, M. *Heterologies: Discourse on the Other* (B. Massumi, trans.) Minneapolis, MN: University of Minnesota Press, pp. vii–xxi.

GOFFMAN, E. (1959) *The Presentation of Self in Everyday Life*, Harmondsworth: Penguin.

GOFFMAN, E. (1967) *Interaction Ritual: Essays in Face to Face Behavior*, Garden City, NY: Doubleday.

GOLDHAMMER, R. (1969) *Clinical Supervision: Special Methods for the Supervision of Teachers*, New York: Holt, Rinehart & Winston.

GOODMAN, J. (1988) 'The disenfranchisement of elementary teachers and strategies for resistance', *Journal of Curriculum and Supervision*, **3** (3), pp. 201–20.

GOODWIN, C. and HERITAGE, J. (1990) 'Conversation analysis', in SIEGEL, B. J. (Ed.) *Annual Review of Anthropology*, Vol. 19, Palo Alto, CA: Annual Reviews Inc., pp. 283–307.

GREEN, J. L. and WALLAT, C. (Eds) (1981) *Ethnography and Language in Educational Settings*, Vol. 5, in FREEDLE, R. O. (Ed.) *Advances in Discourse Processes*, Norwood, NJ: Ablex Publishing.

GRICE, H. P. (1975) 'Logic and conversation', in COLE, P. and MORGAN, J. L. (Eds) *Syntax and Semantics: Volume 3, Speech Acts*, New York: Academic Press, pp. 41–58.

GRIMMETT, P. P. and HOUSEGO, I. E. (1983) 'Interpersonal relationships in the clinical supervision conference', *The Canadian Administrator*, **22**, pp. 1–6.

GRIMMETT, P. P., ROSTAD, O. P. and FORD, B. (1992) 'The transformation of supervision', in GLICKMAN, C. D. (Ed.) *Supervision in Transition*, Alexandria, VA: Association for Supervision and Curriculum Development, pp. 185–202.

GUBA, E. G. (1991) 'Introducing "Qualitative" Research: Concepts and Issues', Presession of the Qualitative Research in Education Annual Conference, Athens, GA, January.

GUBA, E. G. and LINCOLN, Y. S. (1989) *Fourth Generation Evaluation*, Newbury Park, CA: Sage.

GUMPERZ, J. J. (1992) 'Contextualization and understanding', in DURANTI, A. and GOODWIN, C. (Eds) *Rethinking Context: Language as an Interactive Phenomenon*, Cambridge: Cambridge University Press, pp. 229–52.

HABERMAS, J. (1976) *Legitimation Crisis* (T. MacCarthy, trans.), London: Heinemann.

HALL, B. (1984) 'Research, commitment and action: The role of participatory research', *International Review of Education*, **30**, pp. 289–99.

HALL, E. T. (1959) *The Silent Language*. Greenwich, CT: Fawcett Publications.

HALL, E. T. (1983) *The Dance of Life*, New York: Anchor Books.

HALL, J. K. (in press) '(Re) Creating our worlds with words: A Sociohistorical perspective of face-to-face interaction', *Applied Linguistics*.

HARDING, S. (1990) 'Feminism, science, and the anti-Enlightment critiques', in NICHOLSON, L. J. (Ed.) *Feminism/Postmodernism*, New York: Routledge, pp. 83–106.

HARDING, S. (1993) 'After Eurocentrism: New Directions in Social Studies of Science', Paper presented to the annual meeting of the American Educational Research Association, Atlanta, GA, April.

HARGREAVES, A. (1984) 'Experience counts, theory doesn't: How teachers talk about their work', *Sociology of Education*, **57**, pp. 244–54.

HARGREAVES, A. (1990) 'Teachers' work and the politics of time and space', *Qualitative Studies in Education*, **3** (4), pp. 303–20.

HARGREAVES, A. (1991) 'Prepare to Meet Thy Mood?: Teacher Preparation Time and the Intensification Thesis', paper presented to the annual meeting of the American Educational Research Association, Chicago, IL, April.

HARGREAVES, A. (1993) 'Dissonant Voices, Dissipated Lives: Teachers and the Multiple Realities of Restructuring', paper delivered at the Sixth International Conference of the International Study Association of Teacher Thinking, University of Gothenburg, Sweden, August.

HARGREAVES, A. (1994) *Changing Teachers, Changing Times*, New York: Teachers College Press.

HARGREAVES, A. and DAWE, R. (1990) 'Paths of professional development: Contrived collegiality, collaborative culture, and the case of peer coaching', *Teaching and Teacher Education*, **6** (3), pp. 227–41.

HARGREAVES, A. and MACMILLAN, R. (1992) 'Balkanized Secondary Schools and the Malaise of Modernity', paper presented to the annual meeting of the American Educational Research Association, San Francisco, CA, April.

HEAD, F. A. (1992) 'Student teaching as initiation into the teaching profession', *Anthropology and Education Quarterly*, **23**, pp. 89–107.

HENRY, J. (1972) *On Education*, New York: Vintage Books.

HERSEY, P. and BLANCHARD, K. H. (1982) *Management of Organizational Behavior: Utilizing Human Resources*, 4th edn, Englewood Cliffs, NJ: Prentice-Hall.

HIRSCHKOP, K. (1986) 'Bakhtin, discourse and democracy', *New Left Review*, **160**, pp. 92–113.

HIRSCHKOP, K. and SHEPHERD, D. (Eds) (1989) *Bakhtin and Cultural Theory*, Manchester: Manchester University Press.

HOLLAND, P. E. (1989) 'Implicit assumptions about the supervisory conference: A review and analysis of literature', *Journal of Curriculum and Supervision*, **4**, pp. 362–79.

HOLLAND, P. E. (1990) 'Stories of Supervision: Tutorials in the Transformative Power of Supervision', paper presented at the annual meeting of the Council of Professors of Instructional Supervision, Athens, GA, November.

HOLLAND, P. E., CLIFT, R., VEAL, M. L., JOHNSON, M. and MCCARTHY, J. (1992) 'Linking preservice and inservice supervision through professional inquiry', in GLICKMAN, C. D. (Ed.) *Supervision in Transition*, Alexandria, VA: Association for Supervision and Curriculum Development, pp. 169–82.

HOLLAND, P. E., VEAL, M. L., CLIFT, R. and JOHNSON, M. (1991) 'A Structural Analysis of Supervision', paper presented at the annual meeting of the American Educational Research Association, Chicago, IL, April.

HOLLOWAY, E. L. (1982) 'Interactional structure of the supervisory interview', *Journal of Counseling Psychology*, **29** (3), pp. 309–17

HOLQUIST, M. (1990) *Dialogism*, London: Routledge.

HOOKS, B. (1990) 'marginality as a site of resistance', in FERGUSON, R., GEVER, M., MINH-HA, T. T. and WEST, C. (Eds) *Out There: Marginalization and Contemporary Cultures*, Cambridge, MA: MIT Press, pp. 341–43.

HOY, W. K. and REES, R. (1977) 'The bureaucratic socialization of student teachers', *Journal of Teacher Education*, **28** (1), pp. 23–26.

HUNTER, M. (1973) 'Appraising teacher performance: One approach', *The National Elementary Principal*, **52**, pp. 62–63.

HUNTER, M. (1980) 'Six types of supervisory conferences', *Educational Leadership*, **37**, pp. 408–12.

HUNTER, M. (1983) 'Script taping: An essential supervisory tool', *Educational Leadership*, **41** (3), p. 43.

HYMES, D. (1972) 'Introduction', in CAZDEN, C. B., JOHN, V. P. and HYMES, D. (Eds) *Functions of Language in the Classroom*, New York: Teachers College Press, pp. xi–lvii.

HYMES, D. (1980) *Language in Education: Ethnolinguistic Essays*, Washington, DC: Center for Applied Linguistics.

HYMES, D. (1981) 'Ethnographic monitoring', in TRUEBA, H. T., GUTHRIE, G. P. and AU, K. H. (Eds) *Culture and the Bilingual Classroom: Studies in Classroom Ethnography*, Rowley, MA: Newbury House, pp. 56–68.

HYMES, D. (1982) *The Ethnolinguistic Study of Classroom Discourse*, Washington, DC: National Institute of Education. (ERIC Document Reproduction Service No. ED 217 710)

INGVARSON, L. (1986) 'With critical friends, who needs enemies?' in FENSHAM, P., POWER, C., KEMMIS, S. and TRIPP, D. (Eds) *Alienation from Schooling*, London: Routledge & Kegan Paul, pp. 344–50.

JOHNSON, D. W. and JOHNSON, F. P. (1991) *Joining Together: Group Theory and Group Skills*, 4th Edn, Englewood Cliffs, NJ: Prentice Hall.

JUSKA, J. (1991) 'Observations', *Phi Delta Kappan*, **72**, pp. 468–70.

KANPOL, B. (1988) 'Teacher work tasks as forms of resistance and accommodation to structural factors of schooling', *Urban Education*, **23** (2), pp. 173–87.

KANPOL, B. (1991) 'Teacher group formation as emancipatory critique: Necessary conditions for teacher resistance', *The Journal of Educational Thought*, **25** (2), pp. 134–49.

KARIER, C. (1982) 'Supervision in historic perspective', in SERGIOVANNI, T. J. (Ed.) *Supervision of Teaching*, Alexandria, VA: Association for Supervision and Curriculum Development, pp. 2–15.

KILBOURN, B. (1982) 'Linda: A case study in clinical supervision', *Canadian Journal of Education*, **7** (3), pp. 1–24.

KILBOURN, B. (1984) 'Ethnographic research and the improvement of teaching', in MUNBY, H., ORPWOOD, G. and RUSSELL, T. (Eds) *Seeing Curriculum in a New Light: Essays from Science Education*, New York: University Press of America.

KILBOURN, B. (1991) 'Self-Monitoring in teaching', *American Educational Research Journal*, **28**, pp. 721–36.

KYTE, G. C. (1971) 'The supervisor–teacher conference: A case study', *Education*, **92**, pp. 17–25.

LACEY, C. (1977) *The Socialization of Teachers*, London: Methuen.

LATAPÍ, P. (1988) 'Participatory research: A new research paradigm?' *The Alberta Journal of Educational Research*, **34**, pp. 310–19.

LATHER, P. (1991) 'Deconstructing/Deconstructive inquiry: The politics of knowing and being known', *Educational Theory*, **41** (2), pp. 153–73.

LINDSTROM, L. (1992) 'Context contests: Debatable truth statements on Tanna (Vanuatu)', in DURANTI, A. and GOODWIN, C. (Eds) *Rethinking Context: Language as an Interactive Phenomenon*, Cambridge, UK: Cambridge University Press, pp. 101–24.

LISTON, D. P. and ZEICHNER, K. M. (1990) 'Teacher education and the social context of schooling: Issues for curriculum development', *American Educational Research Journal*, **27** (4), pp. 610–36.

LITTLE, J. W. (1990) 'The persistence of privacy: Autonomy and initiative in teachers' professional relations', *Teachers College Record*, **91** (4), pp. 509–36.

LORTIE, D. (1975) *Schoolteacher*, Chicago: University of Chicago Press.

LUCIO, W. and McNEIL, J. (1959) *Supervision: A Synthesis of Thought and Action*, New York: McGraw-Hill.

LYOTARD, J. (1985) *The Post-modern Condition*, Minneapolis, MN: University of Minnesota Press.

LYOTARD, J. (1993) 'The other's rights: An approach to the question of human rights', lecture sponsored by the University of Georgia Humanities Center, Athens, GA, March.

McCOOMBE, M. (1984) 'Clinical supervision from the inside', in SMYTH, W. J. (Ed.) *Case Studies in Clinical Supervision*, Victoria, Australia: Deakin University Press, pp. 45–57.

McCUTCHEON, G. and JUNG, B. (1990) 'Alternative perspectives on action research', *Theory into Practice*, **29** (3), pp. 144–51.

McDERMOTT, R. P. (1976) 'Kids Make Sense: An Ethnographic Account of the Interactional Management of Success and Failure in One First-Grade Classroom, doctoral dissertation, Stanford University, *Dissertation Abstracts International*, **38**, 1505A.

McDERMOTT, R. P. (1977) 'Social relations as contexts for learning in school', *Harvard Educational Review*, **47** (2), pp. 198–213.

McDERMOTT, R. P. and CHURCH, J. (1976) 'Making sense and feeling good: The ethnography of communication and identity work, *Communication*, **2**, pp. 121–42.

McDERMOTT, R. P. and GOLDMAN, S. V. (1983) 'Teaching in multicultural settings', in BERG-ELDERING, L. v. d., DE RIJCKE, F. J. M. and ZUCK, L. V. (Eds) *Multicultural Education: A Challenge for Teachers*, Dordrecht, Holland: Foris, pp. 145–63.

McDERMOTT, R. P., GOSPODINOFF, K. and ARON, J. (1978) 'Criteria for an ethnographically adequate description of concerted activities and their contexts', *Semiotica*, **24** (3/4), pp. 245–75.

McDermott, R. P. and Tylbor, H. (1983) 'On the necessity of collusion in conversation', *Text*, **3** (3), pp. 277–97.

McHoul, A. W. (1990) 'The organization of repair in classroom talk', *Language in Society*, **19**, pp. 349–77.

McLaren, P. (1985) 'The ritual dimensions of resistance: Clowning and symbolic inversion', *Journal of Education*, **167** (2), pp. 84–97.

McTaggart, R. (1991a) 'Community Movements and School Reform: A New Coalition for Action Research', keynote address presented at the Biennial Conference of the Australian Curriculum Studies Association, Adelaide, South Australia, July.

McTaggart, R. (1991b) 'Reflection on Teaching: Creating an Enquiry Culture in Education', address presented as Lansdowne Visitor at the University of Victoria, British Columbia, March.

Mehan, H. (1979) *Learning Lessons: Social Organization in the Classroom*, Cambridge, MA: Harvard University Press.

Mehan, H. (1980) 'The competent student', *Anthropology and Education Quarterly*, **11**, pp. 131–52.

Migra, E. (1976) 'The Transition from Theory into Practice: A Microethnography of Student Teaching as a Cultural Experience', doctoral dissertation, Kent State University, *Dissertation Abstracts International*, **37**, 6247-A.

Mills, S. (1992) 'Discourse competence: Or how to theorize strong women speakers', *Hypatia*, **7** (2), pp. 4–17.

Minh-ha, T. T. (1986/87) 'Introduction', *Discourse*, **8**, pp. 3–9.

Moerman, M. (1988) *Talking Culture*, Philadelphia, PA: University of Pennsylvania Press.

Munro, P. M. (1991) 'Supervision: What's imposition got to do with it?', *Journal of Curriculum and Supervision*, **7** (1), p. 77–89.

Noddings, N. (1984) *Caring*, Berkeley, CA: University of California Press.

Nolan, J. and Francis, P. (1992) 'Changing perspectives in curriculum and instruction', in Glickman, C. D. (Ed.) *Supervision in Transition*, Alexandria, VA: Association for Supervision and Curriculum Development, pp. 44–60.

Odum, E. (1994) 'Solving Problems in Global Change: The Challenge to the Ecological Sciences', panel discussion, The Human Dimensions of Global Ecological Change, sponsored by The University of Georgia Anthropology Association, Athens, GA, April.

Oja, S. N. and Smulyan, L. (1989) *Collaborative Action Research: A Developmental Approach*, London: Falmer Press.

Oliva, P. F. (1989) *Supervision for Today's Schools*, 3rd edn, New York: Longman.

Ovando, M. (1993) 'The post-observation conference from the teacher's perspective: A collaborative process', *Wingspan*, **9** (1), pp. 8–14.

Pajak, E. (1989) *The Central Office Supervisor of Curriculum and Instruction: Setting the Stage for Success*, Boston, MA: Allyn & Bacon.

Pajak, E. F. (1992) 'A view from the central office', in Glickman, C. D. (Ed.) *Supervision in Transition*, Alexandria, VA: Association for Supervision and Curriculum Development, pp. 126–38.

Pajak, E. and Glickman, C. (1989) 'Informational and controlling language in simulated supervisory conferences', *American Educational Research Journal*, **26** (1), pp. 93–106.

Pajak, E. and Seyfarth, J. T. (1983) 'Authentic supervision reconciles the irreconcilables', *Educational Leadership*, **40** (8), pp. 20–23.

Palmer, R. (1969) *Hermeneutics: Interpretation Theory in Schleiermacher, Dilthey, Heidegger, and Gadamer*, Evanston, IL: Northwestern University Press.

Phillips, S. U. (1972) 'Participant structures and communicative competence', in Cazden, C., John, V. and Hymes, D. (Eds) *Functions of Language in the Classroom*, New York: Teachers College Press, pp. 370–94.

PIKE, K. L. (1965) *Language in Relation to a Unified Theory of the Structure of Human Behavior*, The Hague: Mouton.

QUIGLEY, P. (1992) 'Rethinking resistance: Environmentalism, literature, and poststructural theory', *Environmental Ethics*, **14**, pp. 291–306.

RETALLICK, J. A. (1986) 'Clinical supervision: Technical, collaborative and critical approaches', in SMYTH, W. J. (Ed.) *Learning about Teaching through Clinical Supervision*, London: Croom Helm, pp. 85–110.

RETALLICK, J. (1990) 'Clinical Supervision and the Structure of Communication', paper presented at the annual meeting of the American Educational Research Association, Boston, MA: April.

RIVERS, J. (1989) 'Is this peer coaching: Conversation analysis of a teacher conference', paper presented at the annual meeting of the American Educational Research Association, San Francisco, CA, MARCH.

ROGERS, C. R. (1971) 'Can schools grow persons?' *Educational Leadership*, **29**, pp. 215–17.

ROSS, L. (1977) 'The intuitive psychologist and his shortcomings: Distortions in the attribution process', in BERKOWITZ, L. (Ed.) *Advances in experimental social psychology*, Vol. 10, New York: Academic Press, pp. 173–220.

RYAN, M. (1982) *Marxism and Deconstruction*, Baltimore, MD: John Hopkins University Press.

SACKS, H., SCHEGLOFF, E. and JEFFERSON, G. (1978) 'A simplest systematics for the organization of turn taking for conversation', in SCHENKEIN, J. N. (Ed.) *Studies in the Organization of Conversational Interaction*, New York: Academic Press, pp. 7–55.

ST MAURICE, H. (1987) 'Clinical supervision and power: Regimes of instructional management', in POPKEWITZ, T. S. (Ed.) *Critical Studies in Teacher Education: Its Folklore, Theory and Practice*, London: Falmer Press, pp. 242–64.

SALE, K. (1990) *The Conquest of Paradise*, New York: Alfred A. Knopf.

SARASON, S. B. (1990) *The Predictable Failure of Educational Reform*, San Francisco, CA: Jossey-Bass.

SCHEFLEN, A. (1973) *How Behavior Means*, New York: Gordon & Breach.

SCHENKEIN, J. (1978) 'Explanation of transcript notation', in SCHENKEIN, J. (Ed.) *Studies in the Organization of Conversational Interaction*, New York: Academic Press, pp. xi–xvi.

SCHMUCK, R. A. and RUNKEL, P. J. (1985) *The Handbook of Organizational Development in Schools* (3rd edn), Palo Alto, CA: Mayfield Publishing.

SCOLLON, R. (1981a) *Human Knowledge and the Institution's Knowledge*, Final Report on the National Institute of Education Grant No. G-80–0185. Washington, DC.

SCOLLON, R. (1981b) *Tempo, Density, and Silence: Rhythms in Ordinary Talk*, Fairbanks, AK: Center for Cross-Cultural Studies, University of Alaska.

SCOLLON, R. and SCOLLON, S. (1981) *Narrative, Literacy and Face in Interethnic Communication*, Norwood, NJ: Ablex.

SCOLLON, R. and SCOLLON, S. (1986) *Responsive Communication: Patterns for Making Sense*, Haines, AK: Black Current Press.

SERGIOVANNI, T. J. (1985) 'Landscapes, mindscapes, and reflective practice in supervision', *Journal of Curriculum and Supervision.* **1** (1), pp. 5–17.

SERGIOVANNI, T. J. (1991) The Dark Side of Professionalism in Educational Administration, Phi Delta Kappan, **72** (7), pp. 521–26.

SERGIOVANNI, T. J. (1992) 'Why we should seek substitutes for leadership', *Educational Leadership*, **49** (5), pp. 41–45.

SERGIOVANNI, T. J. and STARRATT, R. J. (1988) *Supervision: Human Perspectives*, 4th edn, New York: McGraw-Hill.

SHILLING, C. (1991) 'Educating the body: Physical capital and the production of social inequalities', *Sociology*, **25** (4), pp. 653–72.

SHUTZ, A. (1962) *Collected Papers*, Vol. 1, The Hague: Martinus Nijhoff.

SHUTZ, A. (1964) *Collected Papers*, Vol. 2, The Hague: Martinus Nijhoff.

SMITH, N. S. and ACHESON, K. A. (1991) 'Peer consultation: An analysis of several types of programs', *OSSC Bulletin*, **34** (6), Eugene, OR: Oregon School Study Council.

SMYTH, W. J. (Ed.) (1984) *Case Studies in Clinical Supervision*, Victoria, Australia: Deakin University Press.

SMYTH, J. (1985) 'Developing a critical practice of clinical supervision', *Journal of Curriculum Studies*, **17** (1), pp. 1–15.

SMYTH, J. (1991a) 'Instructional supervision and the re-definition of who does it in schools', *Journal of Curriculum and Supervision*, **7** (1), pp. 90–99.

SMYTH, J. (1991b) 'Problematising teaching through a "critical" approach to clinical supervision', *Curriculum Inquiry*, **21**, pp. 321–52.

SMYTH, J. (1991c) *Teachers as Collaborative Learners: Challenging Dominant Forms of Supervision*, Milton Keynes: Open University Press.

SMYTH, J. (1992) 'Teachers' work and the politics of reflection', *American Educational Research Journal*, **29** (2), pp. 267–300.

STERNBERG, R. J., OKAGAKI, L. and JACKSON, A. S. (1990) 'Practical intelligence for success in school', *Educational Leadership*, **48** (1), pp. 35–39.

TABACHNICK, B., POPKEWITZ, T. and ZEICHNER, K. (1979/80) 'Teacher education and the professional perspectives of student teachers', *Interchange*, **10**, pp. 12–29.

TERDIMAN, R. (1985) *Discourse/Counter-Discourse: The Theory and Practice of Symbolic Resistance in Nineteenth-Century France*, Ithaca, NY: Cornell University Press.

TODOROV, T. (1984) *Mikhail Bakhtin: The Dialogic Principle*, Minneapolis, MN: The University of Minnesota Press.

WAITE, D. (1989) 'The Supervisor's Role in Intern Teachers' Socialization: An Ethnography of Communication of Supervisory Conferences', paper presented to the annual meeting of the American Anthropological Association, Washington, DC, November.

WAITE, D. (1990/91) 'Behind the other set of eyes: An ethnographic study of instructional supervision', doctoral dissertation, University of Oregon, *Dissertation Abstracts International*, **51**, 3708A.

WAITE, D. (1992a) 'Instructional supervision from a situational perspective', *Teaching and Teacher Education*, **8**, pp. 319–32.

WAITE, D. (1992b) 'Supervisors' talk: Making sense of conferences from an anthropological linguistic perspective', *Journal of Curriculum and Supervision*, **7**, pp. 349–71.

WAITE, D. (1992c) 'The instructional supervisor as a cultural guide', *Urban Education*, **26** (4), pp. 423–40.

WAITE, D. (1993) 'Teachers in conference: A qualitative study of teacher–supervisor face-to-face interactions', *American Educational Research Journal*, **30** (4), pp. 675–702.

WAITE, D. (1994a) 'Ethnography's Demise: What's Next for Narrative?', paper presented to the American Educational Research Association annual meeting, New Orleans, LA, April.

WAITE, D. (in press) 'Teacher resistance in a supervision conference', in CORSON, D. (Ed.) *Discourse and Power in Educational Organizations*, Cresskill, NJ: Hampton Press.

WAITE, D. (1994b) 'Understanding supervision: An exploration of aspiring supervisors' definitions', *Journal of Curriculum and Supervision*, **10** (1), pp. 60–76.

WALKER, J. C. (1985) 'Rebels with our applause? A critique of resistance theory in Paul Willis's ethnography of schooling', *Journal of Education*, **167** (2), pp. 63–83.

WAX, R. H. (1971) *Doing Fieldwork: Warnings and Advice*, Chicago, IL: University of Chicago Press.

WELLER, R. H. (1971) *Verbal Communication in Instructional Supervision*, New York: Teachers College Press.

WENTWORTH, W. (1980) *Context and Understanding: An Inquiry into Socialization Theory,* New York: Elsevier.

WEST, C. (1990) 'The new cultural politics of difference', in FERGUSON, R., GEVER, M., MINH-HA, T. T. and WEST, C. (Eds) *Out There: Marginalization and Contemporary Cultures,* Cambridge, MA: MIT Press, pp. 19–36.

WHITE, A. (1984) 'Bakhtin, sociolinguistics and deconstruction', in GLOVERSMITH, F. (Ed.) *The Theory of Reading,* Brighton, Sussex: The Harvester Press Ltd, pp. 123–46.

WHITE, J. (1989) 'Student teaching as a rite of passage', *Anthropology and Education Quarterly,* **20** (3), pp. 177–95.

WILES, K. (1950) *Supervision for Better Schools,* Englewood Cliffs, NJ: Prentice-Hall.

WILLIAMS, R. (1977) *Marxism and Literature,* Oxford: Oxford University Press.

WILSON, T. P. (1991) 'Social structure and the sequential organization of interaction', in BODEN, D. and ZIMMERMAN, D. H. (Eds) *Talk and Social Structure,* Berkeley, CA: University of California Press, pp. 22–43.

WOLCOTT, H. F. (1988) ' "Problem finding" in qualitative research', in TRUEBA, H. T. and DELGADO-GAITAN, C. (Eds) *School and Society: Learning Content through Culture,* New York: Praeger, pp. 11–35.

WOLCOTT, H. F. (1989) *Class Notes,* University of Oregon, Eugene, OR, April 13.

WOLCOTT, H. F. (1990) 'On seeking – and rejecting – validity in qualitative research', in EISNER, E. and PESHKIN, A. (Eds) *Qualitative Inquiry in Education: The Continuing Debate,* New York: Teachers College Press, pp. 121–52.

WOLCOTT, H. F. (1991) 'Propriospect and the acquisition of culture', *Anthropology and Education Quarterly,* **22**, pp. 251–73.

WOOD, D. R. (1992) 'Teaching narratives: A source for faculty development and evaluation', *Harvard Educational Review,* **62** (4), pp. 535–50.

ZEICHNER, K. M. and LISTON, D. (1985) 'Varieties of discourse in supervisory conferences', *Teaching and Teacher Education,* **1** (2), pp. 155–74.

ZEICHNER, K., LISTON, D., MAHLIOS, M. and GOMEZ, M. (1988) 'The structure and goals of a student teaching program and the character and quality of supervisory discourse', *Teaching and Teacher Education,* **4** (4), pp. 349–62.

ZEICHNER, K. and TABACHNICK, B. (1981) 'Are the effects of university teacher education "washed out" by school experience?' *Journal of Teacher Education,* **32** (3), pp. 7–11.

ZEICHNER, K. and TABACHNICK, B. (1985) 'The development of teacher perspectives: Social strategies and institutional control in the socialization of beginning teachers', *Journal of Education for Teaching,* **11** (1), pp. 1–25.

Index